Inside the
Rehearsal Room

Inside the Rehearsal Room

Process, Collaboration and Decision-Making

Robert Marsden

methuen | drama

LONDON · NEW YORK · OXFORD · NEW DELHI · SYDNEY

METHUEN DRAMA
Bloomsbury Publishing Plc
50 Bedford Square, London, WC1B 3DP, UK
1385 Broadway, New York, NY 10018, USA
29 Earlsfort Terrace, Dublin 2, Ireland

BLOOMSBURY, METHUEN DRAMA and the Methuen Drama logo are trademarks of
Bloomsbury Publishing Plc

First published in Great Britain 2022

Cover design: Ben Anslow
Cover images: Open Red Door (© BamBamImages / Getty Images); Iridescent
background in white, blue and orange (© Flavio Coelho / Getty Images)

A catalogue record for this book is available from the British Library.

A catalog record for this book is available from the Library of Congress.

ISBN: HB: 978-1-3501-0365-8
PB: 978-1-3501-0366-5
ePDF: 978-1-3501-0368-9
eBook: 978-1-3501-0367-2

Typeset by Newgen KnowledgeWorks Pvt. Ltd., Chennai, India
Printed and bound in Great Britain

To find out more about our authors and books visit www.bloomsbury.com
and sign up for our newsletters.

For Lydia, Harry and Emily

Contents

Preface

As I write, in the autumn of 2020, I am in self-isolation, having just tested positive for Covid-19. I have not set foot inside a rehearsal room for nearly a year. It's hard to articulate how viscerally I miss the creative crucible of the rehearsal room.

Having also taught acting and directing online for several months, I also miss the humanity of the theatre-making process. Whilst we can creatively explore theatre-making through virtual means, many examples of which have enabled surprising and inspiring innovation through expediency, not being able to share the same space has made me yearn for the sheer spirit and collective energy of face-to-face work.

It has therefore been a huge privilege to be able to write about the process, even though the events of 2020 and 2021 have meant that many of the world's theatre-makers have had a struggle, if not a battle, to survive, let alone create. There are many past examples of how theatre-makers across the UK (and further afield, of course) have 'proved astonishingly resilient [at] re-inventing [themselves]' (Coveney 2017: 10). To take one example, this from the long history of ecclesiastical attempts to suppress performance: in 1244 Robert Grosseteste, Bishop of Lincoln, banned his priests from taking part in parish plays. Nevertheless, these stories still needed to be told. They needed to be heard by an illiterate population.

What happened? Theatre survived.

Trade guilds began to perform Bible stories outside the churches on pageant wagons, with amateur players from the laity taking on parts such as Satan, which priests felt uncomfortable playing, even had they been allowed to. The compromise ultimately worked to the benefit of the church, the very institution that had attempted to proscribe theatre, by rendering the words of its creed more visual, more immediate and more readily comprehensible for those unable to read, or unwilling to engage with the less animated sermons of the clergy. Theatre-makers, audiences, even the church itself, benefited from this adaptability, ingenuity and perseverance.

The Puritans forcibly closed both public and private theatres in 1642 and this is perhaps the most well-known closure of the theatrical industry in England, from which a path to recovery had to be found. By 1649, the Puritans had 'gutted and demolished' (Styan 1996: 237) most theatre buildings. Others were repurposed; the Cockpit, for example, was turned into a school for the duration of the Interregnum of 1642–60. That theatre nevertheless continued to stage 'illegal performances and was raided by soldiers in 1649' (Law 1999: 106). Although the building was returned to use as a theatre, with the introduction of patent theatre licences in the Restoration, it was ultimately forced to close permanently in 1665.

What happened? Theatre survived.

Without necessarily flouting the law as brazenly as the Cockpit, many actors and playwrights nonetheless continued to create work that circumvented proscription during the Interregnum, with the theatrical form shifting to remain within the law. Plays were reimagined as private musical interludes, operas and masques. William Davenant created a theatre within his home and produced *The Siege of Rhodes* between 1656 and 1658, which naturally played to a Royalist crowd. When the reinstatement of Charles II signalled the return of the monarchy in 1660, new forms of permanent theatre buildings were created. The Duke's Theatre, a proscenium arch building with a scenic stage and a downstage playing area, was one very different from the type of 'wooden O' which had housed the Jacobean dramas. The design of the Duke's was patterned, rather extraordinarily, on the tennis courts in Lincoln's Inn Fields. This was because, in 1661, indoor tennis courts had, with typical invention born of necessity, already been converted into public theatres. The need that people had for the ritual of a story, shared and told breathing the same air, had not abated during the Interregnum. With no playhouses, new spaces were created and others adapted for theatrical purposes.

Even as late as 1737, the Licencing Act was the state's way of controlling theatre-making, giving it the opportunity to consent to the performance of some plays and veto others; an attempt, initially, to prevent satire aimed at Robert Walpole, first prime minister of Great Britain. Variations of this act were not abolished until the Theatres Act of 1968. Throughout more than two centuries when the iterations of the act held sway, theatre-makers invented ingenious ways to circumvent both censorship and censure, innovating, reimagining and reinterpreting.

Fast forward to 2020 and the global pandemic engendered by Covid-19. The UK government at first suggested (then subsequently ordered) the closure of all theatres when the virulence of the pandemic became evident. When finally allowed to reopen, the industry did not immediately bounce back. Insurance companies would not insure against the future lockdowns that occurred and logistics, especially when dealing with productions on a large scale, became intensely complicated.

What happened? Theatre survived.

Some building-based production companies moved their work online. Others moved outside: for example, both the Barn in Cirencester, which produced BarnFest, and The Watermill Theatre in Newbury created socially distanced seasons of work. Producer David Pugh opined via Twitter, on 16 July 2020: 'I am a theatre producer so I should produce theatre and so I am' (Pugh 2020). His subsequent production of *Educating Rita* performed at the open-air Minack Theatre in Cornwall, replacing a planned UK tour of indoor venues.[1] With the 2020/21 pantomime season under threat, Lyngo Theatre created *Play@Home: The Gift of Winter*, enabling families to rehearse and present a Christmas story at home, making props and costumes, and rehearsing the script themselves.[2] Interactive pantos made their way into our homes via the internet.

'Pop-up' and 'take-away' theatre was brought by actors to people's gardens, through initiatives such as Bard in the Yard and Revels in Hand theatre.[3] Companies isolated their actors and found ways through, from distancing

---

[1]   https://www.minack.com/whats-on/willy-russells-educating-rita.
[2]   https://www.youtube.com/watch?v=_aeSkWhNO6M&feature=youtu.be.
[3]   https://www.telegraph.co.uk/theatre/what-to-see/dramatic-delivery-strange-delights-takeaway-theatre/.

performers in the blocking stages (where impulse could not always be followed) to the ways in which props were handled.

Theatre practice has continually altered, and rehearsals have changed accordingly throughout the ages.

As you move through the following pages, you may have to creatively imagine how some of the thinking could be adapted to any current situations. The ideas, philosophies, ethical considerations and methodologies that thread through this text can be applied to many types of text -based rehearsal processes.

Theatre-makers adapt.

Stories are still told.

The ways in which this happens continue to change.

Acknowledgements

M any people and organizations have allowed me to pursue this work. I am profoundly grateful to the following:

Artistic Director Kate Wasserberg and all at Stockroom (previously Out of Joint) and Sheffield Theatres for enabling me to observe rehearsals for *Close Quarters*.

Simon Sladen and the archivists at the Victoria and Albert Museum, London.

The Society for Theatre Research (STR), for support in the funding of my research.

Dr Astrid Herhoffer and Professor David Hawkins, Deans at Staffordshire University, for providing time and financial support.

Dr Kelly Jones for motivating, encouraging, and always supporting

Richard Cheshire for lending me his ears and encouragement.

Alex Scott Fairley, proofreader supreme, for his extraordinary care, good humour and patience.

The supervisors of my PhD, from which much of the critical frame of this text emerged, Professor Ross Prior and Professor Paul Johnson.

All the professional and student companies with whom I have worked who have informed, directly and indirectly, the work on this page.

Editor Anna Brewer for her patience, care, compassion and critical eye.

And finally, my mum Carol and dad Michael, for taking me to the theatre as a child and getting me hooked on it.

A note on referencing in the text

D ue to their prominence, and to aid the flow of the text, direct quotations from the personal interviews I undertook with the practitioners are not referenced formally in the body of the text. Details of the interviews can be found under the name of the relevant interviewee in the references section. All secondary source material is referenced conventionally.

1

Prologue

There is a paradox of sorts within the very title of this text, *Inside the Rehearsal Room*. In all likelihood, you are not inside of one as you read this; nor am I as I write. How am I to lead you into the very creative engine of the theatre-making process through the written word? How can this form hope to capture the 'mystery' (Alfreds 2010: 27) of the 'chaotic business of rehearsals' (Crawford 2015: 195)? Critic David Jays states, 'The rehearsal room is a mysterious space: a crucible, sealed off to the public, from which a production will eventually emerge' (2011). *Inside the Rehearsal Room* demystifies some of the processes of rehearsals and celebrates different methodologies whilst recognizing and promoting difference.

For director Katie Mitchell, rehearsals are 'ninety-seven per cent hard graft'. If so, can we deconstruct the graft of rehearsals and reveal the art and craft within? Although 'much thought has gone into the deepening of the craft of acting in Western theatre over the past century, how much of that thought has affected the craft of rehearsal? Not nearly enough' (Christie 2015: 168). Academic Paul Christie forcefully acknowledges that rehearsals have been overlooked by practitioners and academics alike. Nevertheless, the rehearsal process is an essential part of theatre-making and so the collaborative nature of the rehearsal room process is at the heart of this book, which primarily examines the interplay between directors and actors on the rehearsal room floor. This book concentrates explicitly on the rehearsal of text-based theatre, drawing from professional practice and theoretically contextualizing this, bringing together references from the extant literature in line with professional options, reflections and ideas. In doing so, I seek to answer several questions. How are rehearsals organized and structured presently? Should this be challenged? What conditions must be in place for rehearsal room breakthroughs to be made? How does the playwright directly (or indirectly) inform production and rehearsal choices? Finally, how do pre-rehearsal decisions influence the work in rehearsals? It is worth stating here that my personal field, and my ethnographic research, sits within text-based theatre; readers may therefore be disappointed by the lack of coverage this text affords to immersive, site-specific or other forms of performance practice. It is unfortunately beyond the scope of this book to include these fields, but I encourage readers to map the philosophies and methods contained within onto their own personal areas of interest.

I also examine the importance of all collaborators who impact upon text-based rehearsal room decisions, including movement, intimacy, voice and fight directors, scenographers and others who are at the heart of creating the world of the play, and their voices are woven into the text.

The structure of the book

Following on from this Prologue, Chapter 2 sets out a potted history of the rehearsal, from ritual, via the early modern period, to the present day, as well as setting up the role of the current artistic director. Chapter 3 examines how pre-rehearsal collaborative decisions ultimately affect the rehearsal process. Chapters 4–6 highlight the early, middle and late stages of the rehearsal process, leading readers through varying rehearsal methodologies and encompassing a variety of genres and rehearsal styles. Each of the chapters examine the interconnectivity between all component parts and how the cumulative effect of weeks in rehearsal influences a final production. Chapter 7 charts the trajectory of the piece after the rehearsal room has been left behind. Chapter 8 comprises a collage of industry voices, discussing how rehearsal rooms may operate in the twenty-first century and how emerging theatre-makers can embrace and facilitate change. Chapter 9 provides a short coda, positing conclusions and looking at the experiences of theatre-makers in the wake of the Covid-19 pandemic. *Inside the Rehearsal Room* will also examine the notion of rehearsal breakthroughs in depth through Chapters 4 to 6, advancing an original framework I have developed, which directors and actors can utilize, to promote the conditions in which a breakthrough may take place.

Running through *Inside the Rehearsal Room* is an examination of the ethics of rehearsing. The spirit of openness, playfulness and exploration must be set within safe and consensual boundaries. Current considerations of ethics, inclusive practices and lived experiences, including how we cast and rehearse, as well as power dynamics between directors and actors, are considered.

The structure of each chapter

Each chapter includes the following:

1. Central ideas and concepts, outlining key ideas.

2. Exercises and questions in the boxes, often taken from my own practice as an educator and director, which are contextualized. In describing an exercise, its legacy is explained, as well as how this can impact a rehearsal process. This is a conscious effort to counter the 'somewhat surprising fact that notwithstanding a century or so of scholarly concern with theatrical performance, relatively little has been written about the rehearsal practices from which . . . performances emerge' (McAuley 2012: 3).

3. Interviews. Most voices are woven into the fabric of each chapter, but some are included in their entirety between main chapters, as they cross between many subject areas. Joint interviews with RC-Annie, and with Rufus Norris and Katrina Lindsay, are included in their entirety, due to these interviews being in dialogue form. Through interviews with these leading practitioners, *Inside the Rehearsal Room* aims to capture and communicate the energy, spirit and dynamism of that elusive environment, from a variety of theatre-making viewpoints.

The interviewees featured throughout come from diverse backgrounds who are involved in many aspects of the theatre-making process. Sir Alan Ayckbourn is one of the world's most performed playwrights. Nicky Bligh is a casting director and a member of the Casting Directors' Guild. Stephen Boden is a commercial theatre producer working across the UK, producing pantomime and theatre for young audiences. Rachel Bown-Williams and Ruth Cooper-Brown run RC-Annie, which is one of Britain's leading fight directing companies. Brian Conley is an experienced performer. Paule Constable is a Tony Award-winning lighting designer. Jess Curtis is a freelance theatre designer. Philip Dart is a director, working extensively at Vienna's English Theatre. Kirstie Davis was formerly Artistic Director of Forest Forge and is now freelance. Yarit Dor is a freelance intimacy, movement and fight director. Adrienne Ferguson is a Canadian director working in Austria. Gareth Fry is a sound designer who has worked across numerous genres and scales of production, from Complicité to *Harry Potter and the Cursed Child*. Tamara Harvey is Artistic Director of Theatr Clywd. Theresa Heskins is Artistic Director of the New Vic Theatre, Staffordshire. Max Jones is a designer, who has worked for organizations ranging from the RSC to Theatr Clywd. Wyn Jones has been an actor, director and actor trainer. Lucy Kerbel is Artistic Director of Tonic Theatre. Katrina Lindsay is a designer and an associate of the National Theatre, London. Tom Littler is a freelance director who also runs Jermyn Street Theatre, London. Ian Manborde is Diversity Officer for Equity. Chris Martin is an actor, director and writer. Gay McAuley is one of the world's leading exponents of rehearsal room studies. Stephen Mear CBE is one of musical theatre's most sought-after choreographers and the recipient of an Olivier Award. Katie Mitchell is an international theatre director. Rufus Norris is Artistic Director of the National Theatre, London. Ken Rea is Professor of Theatre at the Guildhall School of Music and Drama. Jenny Sealey is Artistic Director of Graeae Theatre, making work with D/deaf and disabled artists. Tiffany Stern is a leading British scholar of rehearsal practices. Michelle Terry is current Artistic Director of Shakespeare's Globe, London. Ivo van Hove is Artistic Director of the Internationaal Theater Amsterdam. Rachel Vogler is the director of Houselights, a company dedicated to consent and ethical practices in performance. Kate Wasserberg is current Artistic Director of Stockroom (formerly Out of Joint). Roy Alexander Weise is joint artistic director of the Royal Exchange Theatre in Manchester. Matt Wilde directs in UK drama schools and is an associate artist of LAMDA. Finally, Matthew Xia is the Artistic Director of the Actors Touring Company.

Rehearsal studies as a field

In 2001 Dale Lorraine Wright argued that 'theatre rehearsal needs to be discussed, [as] literature on theatre rehearsal is limited and sketchy at best' (2001: 24). Rehearsal studies, as an emerging academic field, also includes what is known as 'genetic studies', drawn from French theatre scholarship, which grew out of the literary movement and concerns itself with the study of all documents of a performance and creative process. Ethnographic rehearsal room accounts, pioneered by Gay McAuley in the 1970s, allow for researchers to directly observe rehearsals to capture and then make sense of the theatre-making process. In 2018 I undertook an ethnographic observation of Kate Bowen's *Close Quarters*, a co-production between Out of Joint and Sheffield Theatres, which explores the lives of three pioneering female squaddies, and I will draw on aspects of that observation throughout.

Academic Josette Féral, of the Université du Québec, opens *The Genetics of Performance* with a series of questions relating to rehearsal room breakthroughs: 'What led the director and the actors to this transformation? . . . What discussions led to these choices?' (2008: 224). I take 'transformation' to mean an 'aha' discovery moment in a rehearsal process, discussed in depth in Chapters 4–6; the moment Avra Sidiropoulou believes directors pursue, since they must be 'especially sensitive to . . . epiphanies' (2019: 7) and their importance cannot be taken for granted.

Féral's studies of the assistant director's notes from productions (which are equivalent to the British deputy stage manager's 'book') include practical accounts of moments, the notation of the actor's blocking and a record of decision-making. Féral questions whether they are 'reliable memories, created to last, or are they fleeting points of reference inscribed in the immediacy of the moment?' (2008: 228), as rehearsal notes and books are made primarily for the simple purpose of the practical running of the production. Féral states that the creative (rehearsal) process can be on a par with the 'analytical rigour of theatre' (1997: 1) and argues that critics rely too heavily on analysing the end result, whilst ignoring the 'process which gave it meaning' (1997: 5).

Rehearsal studies is maturing as a field and as it defines itself, other fields are included in its grasp, including philosophy, sociology, musicology, scenography, phenomenology and performance studies, as well as theatre studies. Whilst it is evident that 'there is a pressing need to develop solid methodologies that can enhance the genetic study of the performing arts' (De Laet, Cassiers and van den Dries 2015), the exponents and contributors to the field are aware of it as a growing, shifting and developing area without too many fixed boundaries.

Pre-rehearsal decisions impact dramatically on rehearsal room practices and is the subject of Chapter 3. Researchers Timmy De Laet, Luk van den Dries and Edith Cassiers have studied in detail the notebooks of directors across a range of rehearsal practices, from those of Saxe-Meiningen's court theatre, to those of Belgian director Jan Fabre, stating 'director's notebooks are tangible documents in which annotative strategies are visualized and become perceptible' (2015: 51). These have yielded up insights into the meaning-making processes directors undertake in their pre-rehearsal period. The study of these notebooks relates to the final production itself, forging links between the director's idea and the eventual execution of the play. De Laet, Cassiers and van den Dries argue that the German *Regiebuch* (direction book) is the 'materialised outcome of the emancipation of the director, whose function only emerged when the privileged status of the dramatic author began to erode' (2015: 45). The annotation of a notebook or text is, therefore, 'a starting point for genuine creation, whereby not only directors but also performers adopt and appropriate material according to the specific needs of performance [and] function as an impetus for the work that goes on in the studio and vice versa, constituting a continuous feedback loop that eventually leads to the staged performance' (ibid.: 51).

Rehearsal origins and definitions

Rehearsals have taken place since the 'formalization' of storytelling in Egypt, though these early forms were markedly different from rehearsals as we might understand them today. Formal rehearsals did not begin in England until the early modern period, notably in tandem with the professionalization of theatre in London in the 1560s, and the arrival of permanent playhouses.[1] It is not

---

[1]   This line of argument is pursued in Stern's seminal work of 2000.

helpful to impose modern thinking and terminology surrounding rehearsals on the period prior to this, since not until the rise of the professional director in the nineteenth century was there a rehearsal period as we might recognize. When the term 'rehearsal' first came into usage explicitly in a theatrical context is difficult to ascertain, although the *Oxford English Dictionary* notes its use in 1825 in Thomas Sharp's *A Dissertation on the Pageants or Dramatic Mysteries Anciently Performed at Coventry*. Sharp draws on a note from 1490, where the Smith family list their outgoings in preparing their play cycle: 'this is the expens of the furste reherse of our players in ester weke' (1989: XIII 529). Tiffany Stern posits that 'rehearsal' as a term in the early modern theatre derived from the verb 'to recite', borrowed from the schoolroom, where 'children learnt to rehearse, repeat or say over their lessons' (2000: 24) and from the noun applied to a passage repeated from a previous sermon in church. Stern's scholarship returns to two early glosses of the 1580s; here, the verb 'to rehearse' does indeed equate with 'to recite' (similar to the notion of the rehearsal being a repetition) but can also mean 'to declare'. The philosophy of simple repetition, in preparation for a performance of sorts, does seem nevertheless thereby to have been transposed into the rehearsals of early modern drama.[2] Stern is at pains to indicate that the major usage of the term 'rehearsal' during the Renaissance period was that of a 'practice and approval of text' (2000: 26), frequently in front of the town's mayor. Since the removal in the UK in 1968 of the need to submit all new plays to the Lord Chamberlain's Office for approval, we have thankfully dispensed with this stage.

Throughout this book, rehearsals are viewed through the lens of Western contemporary text-based, character-driven theatre practice. In the UK, for example, rehearsals usually constitute the three to four week process that evolved following the demise of fortnightly repertory in the 1970s, discussed in Chapter 2. Yet it should be remembered that this is merely one model; there are many rehearsal room cultures worldwide and it is impossible within the scope of this text to explore these. For those wishing to do so, *Theatre Histories*,

---

[2] There is no need to repeat the excellent scholarship of Stern in this book, as her published work comprehensively documents British rehearsal practices and processes of the sixteenth to eighteenth centuries, asserting that the forms of rehearsal during that period were very different to those of contemporary Western text-based theatre practice.

by Bruce McConachie, Tobin Nellhaus, Carol Fisher Sorgenfrei and Tamara Underiner, is highly recommended as it contextualizes theatre-making across the globe.

The formalization of a directorial figure throughout the nineteenth century onwards was seminal in shaping both the practice and the analysis of rehearsal processes. Peter Brook in his ground-breaking text *The Empty Space*, affirms that 'a director learns that the growth of rehearsals is a developing process; he sees that there is a right time for everything, and his art is the art of recognising these moments' (2008: 118) and that, in rehearsal, 'form and content have to be examined sometimes together, sometimes separately' (ibid.: 138). In the writing of theatre history, it has often been the (white male) director who has primarily defined rehearsals and the transmission of what happens within those spaces, and it may be unsurprising that with the rise of the study of theatre within universities in the UK, an increase in academic texts on acting and directing surfaced from the 1960s.

Contemporary definitions of 'rehearsal'

Brook states:

> The French word *répétion* is already the kiss of death for anything that wishes to be fresh each time. But it is worse in English. A rehearsal. Do we ever pause to listen to this awesome word? Crouched in the middle, between the 're' and the 'l', is the hearse, the wagon that carries the lifeless body to the grave.
>
> (2019)

But let us leave the French notion of repetition and the 'death wagon' of England for a moment and move to Russia, for less literal etymologies, which embrace more optimistic definitions of this word. For Constantin Stanislavski, rehearsals were concerned with 'ploughing and sowing ... and then gather[ing] the fruit' (2008: 139). The origin of this lies in an agricultural term from the thirteenth century, and as Gay McAuley informed me, 'the word "rehearsal" relates to ... the agricultural implement known in French as a *herse* (harrow) which was dragged over the ground to rake the soil, but the *herse* from the thirteenth century is also the frame that they put candles on, in ritual practices and services.' We can therefore imagine the process as one of nurturing and respect through ritual, rather than the reductive approach of repetition. Similar to Brook, Russian director Lev Dodin does not like the Russian word for 'rehearsal', *repetitsiya*, which comes from the French *répétition* and which 'implies repeating something learnt, internalised and remembered' (Innes and Shevtsova 2009: 44), even though American director Anne Bogart posits that 'it can be argued that the art of rehearsal is the art of repetition' (2001: 45). Nevertheless, playwright and director George Bernard Shaw called, in 1949, for a stop to repetition: 'a director who says, "We must go over and over this again until we get it right" is not directing: he is schoolmastering . . . repetitions on the spot do not improve, they deteriorate every time' (West 1958: 283). McAuley states that

> the German word is *Probe* (literally, 'trial' or 'test'), and the French is *répétition* (repetition), but rehearsal is all of those things: the trying out and the finding and then finding ways to repeat, and to repeat safely. What you may do in rehearsal can be dangerous, so you have to find ways emotionally and physically to protect yourself, so you can do it night after night.

Simon McBurney of Complicité sees the raking over as 'prepar[ing] the ground in order to plant the new growth . . . for repeating is not, as is sometimes thought, the enemy of originality and inspiration. It is its source' (Schmitz 2010: 9). Dodin's preference is for the Russian term *proby*, a probing and investigation of the text, where exploration is foregrounded over the discovery of something that is definite. Academic Jen Harvie concurs with this, supporting the creation notion, whereby rehearsals are not 'for repetition of learned delivery but the *creation* of a performance' (Harvie and Lavender 2010: 1; emphasis in original). German-born American practitioner Uta Hagen similarly expressed a preference for 'German *die Probe*, which sounds like what a rehearsal ought to be: the probe! I want to probe, to test, to try, to adventure' (Harvie and Lavender 2008: 190). Anne Bogart recalls that 'in Japanese, *keiko* translates to practice' (2001: 45). Artistic director of Leeds

Playhouse, James Brining, stated in his column for *The Stage* newspaper that 'every rehearsal [is] an enquiry, not just into the questions posed by the show we [are] working on, but into the process of theatre-making itself' (2018), clearly articulating the additional need for exploration and interrogation into the ways in which a production is created.

Stern, to add nuance to the definition, describes the different types of rehearsal that can be undertaken as 'private rehearsal, partial rehearsal, group rehearsal, dress rehearsal and technical rehearsal' (2000: 6), with reference to the early modern processes. She continues by stating that the partial rehearsal (where actors are split-called, to rehearse only the sections they are involved in) is where most rehearsal room breakthrough moments are potentially made. Australian practitioner Terence Crawford's definition of a 'sub-rehearsal' is also useful and defined as a 'moment that occurs outside the specific organised schedule of the rehearsal, outside the direct interrogatory gaze of the director, or beyond or beneath the understood agenda of a rehearsal moment' (2015: 187). Examining sub-rehearsals may open up how we think about defining and running a rehearsal period and we will return to this concept later.

Documenting the process

How have researchers, practitioners and academics captured rehearsal processes? McAuley uses the categories of 'insider vs outsider accounts' (2006: 11) detailed below, and I offer a third category: the 'outsider-outsider' account. Offered below is a mere glimpse into the wealth of accounts readily available.

Insider accounts

Theatre Quarterly journal ran a series of 'Production Casebooks' from 1971 to 1976 in an early attempt to formally document rehearsals. They include play synopses, cast lists, diary accounts, ground plans, photographs and critical reactions, mainly foregrounding directors, but were an attempt to expose the mechanics of theatre-making. More in-depth insider accounts include the seminal texts *Letters to George* by Max Stafford-Clark (2008), written as he progresses through the rehearsal for George Farquhar's *The Recruiting Officer* and *Peter Hall's Diaries* (2000) capturing his years at the National Theatre. Actor Antony Sher's diaries have been a major contribution to insider accounts. *Year of the Fat Knight* deliciously details his playing Falstaff for the RSC. In his entry of 28 February 2014, he describes a choice between playing a line ironically or realistically. Justifying how the line could be played both ways, Sher states that 'I'm choosing this second way. A good find' (2015: 137), giving us a glimpse of his thought processes.

Information about rehearsals can be found within company production files housed in archives. In particular, the archives of notable directors Peter Brook and Josie Rourke are retained by the Victoria and Albert Museum in London, as are those of companies including the Royal Court, Sphinx, Talawa, Young Vic, Monstrous Regiment, Cheek by Jowl and Paines Plough. Staffordshire University holds the Peter Cheeseman archives from his time as director of the New Victoria Theatre, Staffordshire, where he pioneered the musical documentary form and Leeds University Library holds the archives of director William Gaskill, who founded Joint Stock and was Artistic Director of the Royal Court. These production files, when examined, illustrate how some rehearsal choices are made from an insider's perspective. When examining Rourke's rehearsal script for the 2006 production of Hall's play *The Long and the Short and the Tall*, annotated prior to rehearsals, we see that the ground plan[3] is vital for her. She has broken down the script into Stanislavskian bits[4] with titles, with the script to one side of the page and her notes to the other. Sometimes, the notes relate to actioning such as 'to patronise', but there are also words and events that she feels are important, which are circled and underlined, and so we glimpse the specific foundations that hold up her work.

Gillian Hanna's archived script is a rich source of information from an actor's perspective. During her rehearsals as Beatrice in the 1992 Royal

---

[3] The ground plan is a bird's-eye view of the layout of the staging arrangements, indicating entrances, exits, furniture and other scenographic properties to scale.

[4] 'Bits' is the Stanislavskian term used to describe the chunks of the text worked on in rehearsal, decided upon by the actors and creatives either in rehearsal, or by the director, pre-rehearsal.

Exchange production of *A View from the Bridge*, Hanna writes notes from the runs, vocal sessions and other ideas in her script, rather than using a separate notebook. Her annotated script allows an examination of what was salient to Hanna, giving us a glimpse into the spirit and energy of her working processes. She often records the results of her subtextual code cracking; she writes, for example: 'Why are you mad these days? Why don't you think about what's making you this way?' (1992) in relation to the line 'You're the one who is mad.' A common preoccupation is her concern not only for what she is doing, but how other characters are affecting her, as well as explicitly writing down the immediate circumstances prior to a scene. She also poses vital questions in her script margins, creating imagined circumstances to make sense of her world. In the play Eddie, Beatrice's husband, has developed sexual feelings for Beatrice's niece, Catherine, even though she is engaged to Rodolpho. By the second act, Rodolpho has been reported by Eddie for being an illegal immigrant, following Eddie's attack on Rodolpho in front of Catherine. Beatrice's next conversation is as follows:

> **Beatrice** What you done to him in front of her; you know what I'm talkin' about. She goes about shakin' all the time, she can't go to sleep! That's what you call responsible for her?
>
> (Act 2: 62)

Hanna's notes reveal her strategy. They run: 'C did not tell B about Eddie kissing *her*? Or did she. YES!' (1992; Hanna's emphasis) and: 'She can't *say* what he actually *did*' (ibid.; Hanna's emphases). A few lines later in the margin she writes: 'Can't think about anything to do with sex because of the kiss' (ibid.) and 'papers over the cracks' (ibid.).

Outsider accounts

McAuley argues that there are few outsider accounts where there is a documented observation of a rehearsal due the fact that 'directors fear the disruptive impact an outsider can have on the chemistry that is occurring in the room' (2012: 7). David Selbourne's *The Making of 'A Midsummer Night's*

Dream' is an early contemporary outsider diary account of Brook's seminal 1970 production, yet Selbourne often succumbs to an obsession with Brook as director rather than with the production. McAuley's 2012 text *Not Magic But Work* details an overall ethnographic account of Neil Armfield's 2007 production of *Toy Symphony* by Michael Gow, produced by Company B, Sydney, Australia and journalist Jonathan Croall's *The National Theatre at Work* series includes several useful observational accounts of rehearsals at the National Theatre, London of, amongst others, *Hamlet*, in 2000 and Mark Ravenhill's *Mother Clap's Molly House*, in 2001.

Outsider-outsider accounts

A third category of 'outsider-outsider accounts' describes rehearsal narratives when a journalist or researcher does not even enter the rehearsal room. Interviews with directors in texts such as Maria Delgado and Dan Rebellato's *Contemporary European Theatre Directors* document how rehearsals are a 'voyage of discovery' (2010: 156) for Cheek by Jowl, for example. Duška Radosavljević's interviews in *The Contemporary Ensemble* demystify a range of rehearsal methods in relation to ensemble companies from Michael Boyd and his RSC ensemble processes of 2002 to 2012, through to those of Elizabeth LeCompte and her New York company The Wooster Group. Wendy Lesser's 1997 text *A Director Calls* examines the work of Stephen Daldry, using its title to capitalise on his iconoclastic production of J. B. Priestley's *An Inspector Calls* for the National Theatre in 1993. Lesser makes a priori links to how Daldry and his designer Ian MacNeil created the visual landscape of the production, whereby she links Priestley's stage direction of 'dispens[ing] with an ordinary realistic set' (1997: 1) to how 'Daldry and MacNeil unlock the whole play. For by placing the Birlings and their *dinner* guest inside the comfy house on stilts ... Daldry has freed the play to generate all the various meanings it is capable of conveying' (ibid.: 19). A director can never 'free' a play to generate all possible meanings, but Lesser's salient point stands: when breakthroughs are made, these are not always in the rehearsal room.

What happens in a rehearsal?

Anne Bogart states that, in a rehearsal, 'an actor searches for shapes that can be repeated. Actors and directors together are constructing a framework that will allow for endlessly new currents of vital life-force, emotional vicissitudes and connection with other actors ... Paradoxically it is the restrictions, the precision, the exactitude, that allows for the possibility of freedom' (2001: 46). For practitioner and academic Bella Merlin, 'collectively we want to work out how to tell the story. Individually [as actors] we want to build our particular characters' (2016a: 147). Director Thomas Ostermeier states that the goal of his rehearsals is to 'transform language into action' (2016: 147) whilst, for Simon McBurney, it is not about having ideas, but rather about 'finding how to transmit them' (Schmitz 2010: 115). All of the above practitioners affirm that there is an end point to the rehearsal work, which, through repetition and moving the language from page to stage via the actor's embodied knowledge, is eventually shared with an audience. In *Different Every Night*, director Mike Alfreds demystifies rehearsals and the 'complex relationship between a group of people struggling to create something three dimensional' (2010: 27) and rehearsals, according to Di Trevis, are there 'to discover how to do the play' (Manfull 1999: 106).

Bella Merlin's *Acting: The Basics* recounts director Max Stafford-Clark's description of the rehearsal room 'as either a magical world like a second childhood or a prison camp' (2010: 93), before articulating that rehearsals are '(1) to collectively map out the territory of the fictional world; (2) to tell the writer's story as clearly as possible; and (3) to create characters who seem plausible within the dramatic style of the piece' (ibid.: 93). Alfreds states categorically that 'the purpose of [a] rehearsal process is to immerse the actors so thoroughly in the world of the play that they'll have the complete confidence and ability to play freshly, with freedom and spontaneity, at every performance, living in the moment, in a continuous creative flow, able to adapt to – and absorb – change, variation and discovery' (2007: 141).

Gay McAuley defines the overall construction of a production as

the creative process ... there's the casting, the directorial 'hunch' as Peter Brook says, which is already taking place when the director is choosing their designers. This is all creative preparation prior to rehearsal ... The relationship between the actor and the costume designer is also interesting to pursue as many conversations happen around rehearsals in costume fittings ... to do with character. So, the creative process is longer, more diffuse and occurs in multiple places and the rehearsal is when the actors come together.

The impact of the director on the rehearsal process

The director is the 'tone-setter' of rehearsals that use a director-led model. Whilst contemporary practices continue to flatten out the hierarchy between the actor and the director, the director remains the final arbitrator in the collective decision-making process and leads on the type of rehearsal methodology (how the piece is rehearsed overall) and methods (the precise techniques and exercises are employed to do this). Directors are at the top of this hierarchical creative chain and shape the form, concept and rules of the production. In relation to directorial pre-planning, Mitchell ensures that 'for me, most of the discovery process [sits] outside the rehearsal and involves director-led solitary textual analysis and work on concept. The rehearsal process itself then occurs inside this predetermined framework.' A director's presence is a formidable one in rehearsal studies literature, as it is the 'director [who is the] lynchpin of the whole enterprise. In a good rehearsal process it is the director who stimulates, facilitates and elicits the creativity of a large number of different artists and then somehow draws all these inputs together and shapes them into a coherent work of art' (McAuley 2012: 230). Many practitioners describe the director's relationship to the actor as 'one of the most influential and personal you can have' (Merlin 2010: 94). Interactions between the actors and the director focus on how 'rehearsal attains (and does not attain) its goals' (Baker-White 1999: 26), and Brook, who outlines a potentially ideal rehearsal situation in *The Empty Space*, sees rehearsals as 'a dialogue and a dance between director and player' (2008: 138) and as the tone-setter, and the director as integral to the creation of a healthy, safe and creative rehearsal process.

Ownership of work within the acting process has also undergone a paradigm shift in British theatre, as theatre-making has moved towards an ensemble philosophy, shifting from a 'director's theatre' towards actors' agency of their process, with 'a single body [comprising of] interdependent differences' (Britton 2013: 13). These differences do interrelate, however, with an actor often needing a directorial outside eye, which can confirm whether the company is still 'breathing as one' (ibid.: 11) within the frames (or core idea) of the production: this concept is set out in Chapter 3. This seismic shift has some of its origins in Stanislavski's later period of 'active analysis', developed from 1916 onwards and made more concrete during his last years of working life from 1935 to 1938. Active analysis is where actors may make 'discoveries of a profound kind' (Christie 2015: 158) through études, improvising scenes and examining key events, all with the actor in the space, often using their own words initially and moving towards the playwright's words as opposed to the round-table[5] mental reconnaissance activity of Stanislavski's early process. Even if directors do not use active analysis explicitly, then its philosophy has certainly infiltrated rehearsal rooms, as actors move towards having 'creative agency' (McAuley 2012: 4), such as through Mike Alfreds' process, or in Michelle Terry's way of working, which places the play and the text at the heart of the rehearsal room. This is not always the case in certain auteur-led theatre practices, where the production concept is at the heart of the room with a directorial signature evidenced. Walter Meierjohann testifies that 'the main difference is that the role of the director in Germany is much more the role of the auteur. The actors look at you and expect you to do something radical with the text . . . Young directors in Germany don't care who's written it – they just want to do something with it' (Swain 2011: 27).

Rehearsal process polarities

Here I wish to establish five key polarities through which many of the rehearsal ideas contained within Chapters 4–6 can be filtered. These are deliberately provocative and in reality, more mercurial in nature.

---

5   Literally sitting 'around a table' and analysing the play.

Polarity 1: Impulse versus technique

What is the balance in rehearsal between freedom and structure? Actor trainer Wyn Jones is 'fascinated by the relationship between impulse and technique and what other people call fire and ice. If you have too much of one it kills the other'. As Ivo van Hove states:

> If you think you can start preparing a week before rehearsals and go with impulses alone, you aren't aware of all the options. I think in theatre you have to go deeper than impulse. As a director, though, you need to be open, as actors bring a lot to the process. Sometimes, something you've been thinking about for ages is confirmed in rehearsals.

Working on instinct as an actor or knowing when to follow a directorial hunch is technique in itself. Yet, there is a balance between working on impulse, in the moment, following a hunch through somatically encoded knowledge and when technique explicitly kicks in, or is necessitated by the director or the text. An instinctive decision may take the director or actor so far in rehearsals and technique is then utilized to scaffold the instinctive decisions made. The text will look at the interconnectivity between explicitly using methods and technique and natural organic impulses and as Leon Rubin states, 'in rehearsal, it is both instinct and knowledge that work together' (2021: 94).

Polarity 2: Auteur directorial concepts versus the 'invisible' director

An auteur director, a concept drawn from the world of film of the 1950s, has a strong visual concept and directorial vision. Often, as van Hove states about his own work, this is still very much rooted in the text. Tom Cornford notes that the auteur concept is the 'idea that the director should be considered the primary author of the film' (Fowler 2019: 75) and this can be extended into theatre. Charles Marowitz famously moved away from the auteur approach and tipped his directorial process into one where he would be guided by the impulses of actors in the rehearsal room. Marvin Carlson's notion of 'ghosting' is useful here, whereby 'the present experience is always ghosted by previous experiences and associations' (2006: 2) and where an audience encounters something similar, but 'now in a somewhat different context' (ibid.: 7). Auteur directors are often ghosted by their past productions and the expectations of audiences are palpable. This is in direct opposition to Kate Wasserberg of Stockroom, who thinks of the director as invisible in their service of the text. Echoing Elizabeth LeCompte of The Wooster Group, who sees herself as a ' "director in a group" rather than "director of a group" ' (Radosavljević 2013: 19), Wasserberg wishes to make herself 'essentially invisible' (2018: 194) through her directorial approach. This is not to say that her footprint isn't present on the rehearsal process, or that she has not fundamentally constructed the rehearsal frames but rather she is not ghosted by a 'Wasserbergian' aesthetic: scenographic ideas are born of the text itself, not overlaid. Tiffany Stern warns a concept may be commercially needed and where sometimes the 'director's concept is re-authoring the play . . . there's a battle between the playwright and the director. A director might now not be praised without a concept.' We will explore both sides of this polarity and celebrate and champion their differences.

Polarity 3: Cerebral versus somatic myth-busting

The belief in a duality of cerebral versus somatic (primarily physical) rehearsal work, which was formerly held, has now been debunked, as our understanding of neuroscience gathers apace. Dualism was upheld, whereby cerebral methods such as actioning, where actors begin by selecting a transitive verb to 'action' each thought, were set against somatic processes, such as exploring text through Rudolf Laban's physical techniques. Actually, all rehearsal techniques are psychophysical. At its simplest, what is thought affects the body (actioning is pointless if it remains as academic activity) and any bodily movement affects thoughts and feelings. Think of this polarity as being on a continuum, whereby some rehearsal methods begin cerebrally, and others begin somatically but essentially there 'is no dualism . . . they have not been separated in the first place' (Whyman 2016: 161). Each one is simply a tool by means of which the actor and director can unlock a moment in rehearsal. Dick McCaw's excellent work *Rethinking the Actor's Body: Dialogues with Neuroscience* draws upon current neurophysiology, setting out the move away from dualism, which is a 'seductively simple way of understanding the operation of the human body with its separation between a mind/self and a body'

(2020: 4). All acting is about embodying the words on the page and this text supports the debunking of this division.

Polarity 4: Character versus self (dual consciousness)

To what extent are those words, when embodied, the actor themselves, or how much is a 'character' created? How much should be the self and how much the other? How does merging self with the character's situation needs to happen and does the genre in which you are working shift this? Jean Benedetti, in *Stanislavski and the Actor*, talks about the 'Real I' versus the 'Dramatic I', in relation to creating a role, and Bella Merlin's 'Third Being' in her book *Konstantin Stanislavsky* is the result of merging the character's traits with the self. *Inside the Rehearsal Room* examines the contested notion of 'character' and to what extent it is created, or whether this is simply a natural merging as the actor encounters the given circumstances of the play.

Polarity 5: To plan versus not to plan

The final polarity relates to pre-planning. How far should the schedule be planned in advance? How much of the blocking or events should be decided prior to rehearsal? How much does this depend on the genre or the material conditions in which you are making? *Inside the Rehearsal Room* takes Ivo van Hove's 'backpack' of preparation and finds that, sometimes, the backpack needs to be opened up, tipped out and the contents used. At other times, though, the backpack can simply stay at the door of the room, with the knowledge that it is there, if required. Slavishly pushing through with a predetermined set of rehearsal exercises can often be counterproductive: 'the biggest error with young directors is to work with exercises that are not necessary for the work in hand' (Rubin 2021: 59). Adaptability in the moment is vital for directors as well as actors.

The genres

All the above polarities are affected by the text's genre and style. Directors may have common approaches when approaching a rehearsal, but the genre and text that they work with naturally change the type of methodologies employed. The key genres that affect rehearsal structures returned to in this text include the musical, comedy and farce, psychological realism, classical and verse drama, Restoration comedy, British pantomime and theatre for young audiences, amongst others. Certainly not exhaustive (and any attempt to classify plays into genres is hardly failproof), this goes some way to highlighting key differences in rehearsal approaches.

Exercise: Exploring influences on aesthetics

Theresa Heskins: At school, we were all taken to *Evita*. I remember clearly the moment Elaine Paige sang that song. The whole ensemble was on stage looking up to her on the balcony. They reached out to her, and all froze. My memory of the song was that they were in this freeze. That blew me away. That theatricality was so exciting and I'd never seen anything like that ... I love theatre where it's rich in theatricality. That *Evita* moment, when I look back on it now, was about loving the ensemble and not the star actor. For me, that's very political and about the democratization of theatre in how an audience relates to it and how a cast works.

Heskins works primarily using a theatrical aesthetic, with large actor-based ensembles, often weaving together musicianship and aerial work. Think back to when you became interested in theatre, acting, drama or storytelling:

- Was there a production that influenced you?
- What it is your overwhelming memory of it?
- Can you trace your aesthetic to here?

Exercise: Why choose theatre as your storytelling medium?

Making good theatre is difficult, especially when coupled with budgetary constraints and time pressures. Working out why you would want to set foot in the exposed and exposing territory of a rehearsal room should be at the forefront of being able to articulate practice. Theatre's 'liveness' is at its heart and, as Alan Ayckbourn remarked of the increase in live streaming during the Covid-19 lockdown, 'you might as well be watching television

... It has to be a moment when I always say to an audience who come on a specific night, this performance is purely for YOU.'

   With this in mind:

- Read the quotations below from Tamara Harvey and Kate Wasserberg.
- Does anything resonate with you?
- Sum up why you want to tell stories in a theatrical medium.

Tamara Harvey: I passionately believe in the ability of theatre to change lives at best. At least it should open up conversations and enable people to ask questions and to see the world from different points of view. I feel we go to theatre to feel we aren't alone. We go to theatre to feel that people share our viewpoints; but we can also come to understand other viewpoints. That understanding feels more and more important in a world which is becoming increasingly one where we don't really listen to each other.

Kate Wasserberg: I am entirely narrative-driven as a human being; I only consume narrative in my spare time. It's to do with putting order, sense and harmony on a world that I find traumatic and brutal. I make art because I need to and, as it's theatre, I need to make that art in and for real time. I need to craft that in real time with a real audience who are present, as it's about a core belief in uniting people through, to counter my feeling of the world's divisiveness and the concept of humans as ultimately hostile.

2

Rehearsals: Historical overview, current challenges and future opportunities

Africa, Asia and Egypt: Storytelling and ritual

Nobody truly knows exactly how, when, or where formalized theatre began. What we do know is that storytelling and the enactment of ritual have been at the heart of the human experience across the world cultures. With the rise of language since around 200,000 BCE, the need for humans to make sense of the world through story and metaphor has dominated. Sharrell D. Luckett and Tia M. Shaffer articulate 'long before the Greeks, wall painting and drawings in African caves suggest that humans participated in spiritual rituals that were theatrical in nature' (2017: 1). Similarly, Ronald Harwood in his observations on the Balinese Barong dance, ultimately a story of good triumphing over evil, notes that ritual requires repetition and therefore rehearsal. The teacher of that particular ritual is known as the *dah-lang*, a parallel for the modern theatre director, overseeing the practice required for the impersonation and embodiment of the Barong itself, the leader of the spirit world and the hosts of good.

Someone had to therefore lead the ritual, whether priest, shaman or teacher. We can surmise that such leaders would have had to instruct their participants, due to the highly coded nature of the work, for the ceremonies to take place in a structured, ordered form. In Africa, 'the shamans (actors)

dressed in religious clothing (costumes) and enacted rituals (scripts) to
their tribal members (audience)' (Luckett and Shaffer 2017: 1). The ancient
Egyptian festivals of the gods were rehearsed using music and dance, and the
archaeological evidence on the reliefs of tombs suggests that there was a leader
for these processions (carrying a baton) who would ensure that the dancers
and musicians were kept in order. As Daniel Meyer-Dinkgräfe argues, 'these
performers have to be highly skilled and trained, especially if minute details
are to be followed precisely' (2001: 5) and thus needed to be rehearsed.

Ancient Greece

It was Ancient Greeks who took a step towards professionalization of theatre,
from the fifth century BCE onwards. Actors began to be paid; the rise of
literary skill initiated by the emergence of the Greek alphabet in approximately
1200 BCE ensured that playwrights were producing plays; there were initial
temporary theatre spaces (and permanent stone structures in Athens by 330
BCE) and with this the seeds of rehearsal were watered further.

Although we know about some Greek plays, we know comparatively little
about how they were rehearsed. We can, however, make certain suppositions
based on the structure of the five-day religious drama festivals, pottery artwork
and the plays themselves. Thespis[1] has become a legendary figure and evidence
suggests that the professionalization of the actor occurred with acting prizes
and with payment from the state; scholar J. Michael Walton argues that this
was theatre as an early commercial enterprise.

Initially, the style was for one actor with a chorus, who corporately
added a visual narrative to support the storyteller. Aeschylus appears to
have introduced a second actor to this set-up, with Sophocles later adding a
third. Thus, dialogue was created, characters engaged with one another and
multirole work was introduced. The chorus numbered up to fifty and whilst
the plays themselves reveal little evidence that suggests choric speaking, there
was much singularity of voice in the chorus, with a few speakers and the rest of
the chorus undertaking most of the dance and movement required.

---

[1] Supposedly the first actor (hence the term 'thespian'), in 530 BCE.

Playwrights staged their own works, as well as writing the music and, initially, acting in the pieces. Another figure, whom we might now recognize as an early commercial producer, evolved from these pragmatics. Since ancient Greece was composed of city states, several leading citizens would finance elements of the state's proceedings, including religious and dramatic festivals. The *choregos*, or sponsor, would pay for costumes, masks, musicians and the choreographer, as well as financing the chorus and a chorus leader, who would train for up to a year prior to the competition. A magistrate would draw lots to choose the playwright and lead actor, and the playwright would secure his second and third actors, all of whom were paid by the state, as was the dramatist. Whilst there was a professionalization of acting, it has been assumed that the actors were illiterate, so rehearsals would have likely begun with the playwright reading out their words for the actors to memorize by rote. In many ways, ancient Greece witnesses the birth of commercial and subsidized sectors working together.

Rehearsals would have had to integrate the actors with the chorus, as well as make sense of entrances, especially given that spaces could measure up to fifty metres from the *periaktoi* (the revolving panels depicting scenery) to the centre of the performance area. Decisions would also need to be made about when to use the upper levels of the space and the *ekkyklema* (a wheeled truck, which could enter from upstage centre) and evidence suggests the use of props in the plays, from pots to letters to military equipment, all of which needed coordination with the playwright acting as a directorial figure.

Ancient Rome

It is important not to see Roman theatre as a linear development of Greek theatre. With Athens in decline in the first century CE, its theatrical heritage had grown roots into what would eventually become the Roman theatre, which germinated and took root until the sixth century, when all of the theatres closed as the empire collapsed. The theatrical mechanics of production were drawn from the Greek processes. With stock characters drawn from the masked, improvised farces known as the *fabulae atellanae*, actors were able to rehearse themselves in a way similar to that used by pantomime today in the UK. Just as an actor in British pantomime often plays a stock role, so too Roman actors understood their type and thus a form of self-rehearsal would have been undertaken. As Jean Benedetti argues, many Romans spoke Greek, and so would have been well versed in Aristotle's *Poetics*, as well as the more contemporary *De Oratore* ('On the Orator') of Cicero, where we find the antecedents of psychophysical acting, with emphasis placed on the body's role in the delivery of speech and verse. Similarly, Quintilian's *Institutio Oratoria* ('The Institutes of Oratory'), partially intended for the young, meant that gestural language and notions of voice and delivery of words were taught to all. Actors would have this embodied knowledge as a starting point and we see female actors take to the stage in mime drama, although they were not allowed in the masked plays.

Rehearsal would have required music to be practiced, such as in the plays of Plautus. Actors would have been strong improvisers, in terms of the actor–audience dynamic, with prologues being riffed, according to the energy of the audience (and it is worth noting that the word 'audience' derives from Latin *audire*, 'to listen'). Meyer-Dinkgräfe (2001) emphasizes the importance of the managers of the acting companies, who staged the plays for the games created for the public holidays. An embryonic profit-share theatre was born, as the five to six actors (now shorn of the earlier chorus) shared a fee. Some actors were slaves, and this fee would potentially allow for emancipation from slavery from the managers. Yet these managers were not 'producers' in a contemporary sense. They were often the *dominus gregis* (literally, the 'master of the pack'): actors were seen as herds of animals, reflecting their low status in society. This 'master . . . hired the actors and arranged rehearsals' (Taylor 1999: 61) supported by the *choragus* who, like our stage managers today, sourced properties, costumes and masks (and whose name clearly harks back to the *choregos* of ancient Greek theatre).

The collapse of the Roman Empire meant the end of a formalized Western theatre tradition. Drama, although its apparatus was dismantled after 312 CE following Emperor Constantine's conversion to Christianity which saw actors excommunicated, did not disappear. In Western cultures, the travelling players continued to present work, alongside minstrels, who offered entertainment at local religious festivals and carnivals. Yet from the sixth to the tenth centuries, until the early Middle Ages, formal theatre and therefore the rehearsal of plays had all but disappeared.

The medieval period

Whilst the first extant reference to a formal rehearsal comes from the 1490s as introduced in Chapter 1, this is not to say that conscious rehearsals for the medieval biblical plays of Britain and mainland Europe had not taken place long before. It is all too easy to lump the British theatre of the Middle Ages into one homogenous era (it spans some six centuries), and there is a tendency to concentrate on British theatre prior to the Renaissance in some extant texts, ignoring European influences.

A baton appears in the hand of the *maître de jeu* (literally the 'master of the game') or the 'pageant master' in an illustration by Jean Fouquet in the early French prayer book, *Livre d'heures d'Étienne Chevalier*, which dates from around 1452. We can surmise that this was the early director of fifteenth-century France, marshalling performers in their parts and bringing in choirs on cue. In Britain, we know with certainty that the Latin Bible was 'performed' in church ceremonies from the eleventh century onwards, fulfilling the need to express Christ's stories and morality. As Ronald Harwood explains, drama was now required by the Church to personify and '[re]express its mysteries' (1984: 78). Mary Marshall argues that the very nature of the Catholic Church expresses an embodied theatricality with a 'symbolic use of place and space and movement within the church' (Taylor and Nelson 1972: 36) during the liturgical plays, including angels singing high in the roof and a throne in an aisle to the side of the nave for Herod. The twelfth century saw biblical plays spoken in the English vernacular and with the introduction of the Feast of Corpus Christi from 1264 onwards, processions spilled out from the church buildings and into the streets. The Church had moved outside, and these processions formed the prototype for a style of theatre associated with the mystery plays.

Yet, there was a moral problem to overcome. Costumed priests and choirboys took the parts of the biblical characters in the Middle Ages, but how could they perform Herod, for example? To do so would be flirting with mortal sin in taking on such a role. As the rise in church drama gathered apace in the late Middle Ages (from 1300 onwards), different ways of rehearsing and presenting these stories were needed. Guilds of artisans and merchants took charge of creating the stories by the late Middle Ages, with each trade concentrating on a story apiece. The work of the guilds was reflected in the stories they told, with Noah and the Flood being presented by the Shipwrights' Guild, for example.

There were enormous demands on the actors, who repeated their performances up to sixteen times a day if the pageant-wagon system of 'stopping off and repeating the piece' is to be assumed. There were repeat performances even with static productions, with hundreds of actors and creatives working on the piece. In the York Cycles there were 'twenty-four Christs' (Happé 1984: 65), with huge choirs providing the singing with priests copying the 'parts' for the actors, and nobles supplying specialist costumes from their own wardrobe.

Given the lack of psychological realism (with potentially twenty-two actors playing God across the different wagons) and with the devils and supernatural characters wearing masks, the directorial role was mainly a logistical one. Actors may have repeated bold and gesturally coded characterization from previous years. 'Character [was] always subordinate to narrative' (Beadle and Fletcher 2008: 34) and there was no need to create motivated performances over the course of many weeks. The short rehearsal time would have seen actors being instructed where to play: on the flat general playing space, the platea, or the locus-specific environs, such as Hellmouth, as well as interpreting stage directions. A prominent member of each Guild, instructed and given licence by the local councils, acted as pageant master in organizing logistics, especially with the rise of theatrical machinery and effects such as fire to be marshalled. They would also have to employ the (mostly male) actors; these would often have to supply their own costumes and would rehearse in the rooms of private houses. Evidence suggests that Coventry went so far as to employ a professional director on a twelve-year contract to oversee their play cycle (and a twelve-year contract to a director today would be a welcome novelty). Glynne Wickham outlines a series of rehearsals, from the first blocking rehearsal to a second and

SOUTHWARK PLAYHOUSE

24 FEB - 26 MAR

THE WOODS

BY DAVID MAMET

"Mamet's language has never been so precise, pure, and affecting."
The New York Times

THE WOODS

Nick and Ruth are spending the weekend at a remote cabin in the woods. Their sweet escape from the city descends into a night of stories and fights, pushing their relationship to breaking point. As the sun rises, their need for one another is palpable but will a final reconciliation be threatened by the violent core simmering beneath?

David Mamet's extraordinary 1977 'battle of the sexes' play gets its 1st UK revival after 25 years.

Francesca Carpanini (Ruth) has appeared on Broadway in All My Sons with Annette Benning and Tracy Letts and The Little Foxes with Laura Linney and Cynthia Nixon, and Shakespeare in the Park's The Tempest.

Sam Frenchum (Nick) can soon be seen in Bridgerton season two (Netflix) and has appeared in Valued Friends (Rose Theatre), The Outsider (Print Room) and Loot (Park Theatre).

"Carpanini is delightful and shows uncommon natural assurance." Ben Brantley, The New York Times for The Tempest

"Frenchum is an actor of extraordinary intelligence and magnetism." Rachel Halliburton, The Arts Desk for The Outsider

Director Russell Bolam
Set/Costume Designer Anthony Lamble
Lighting Designer Bethany Gupwell
Sound Consultant Ali Taie
Fight/Intimacy Coordinator Haruka Kuroda
Accent Coach Nina Zendejas
Producer/Casting Director Danielle Tarento

Cast Francesca Carpanini
Sam Frenchum

3 WAYS TO BOOK

PHONE
020 7407 0234
Mon – Fri 10am – 6pm

ONLINE
southwarkplayhouse.co.uk

IN PERSON
Mon-Sat from midday

TIMES

24 FEB - 26 MAR 2022
Mon - Sat 7.30pm
Matinees Tues & Sat 3pm

TICKETS

£22 / £18 concessions
£14 preview performances

VENUE

SOUTHWARK PLAYHOUSE
77–85 Newington Causeway
London SE1 6BD

f SouthwarkPlayhouse
🐦 swkplay
📷 swkplay

third 'checking' of blocking and whether lines were learnt, through to a dress rehearsal, which introduced costumes, and a general rehearsal (in situ) for the benefactors and management committees (1974: 83). There is also evidence of ' "property-players" who are director, stage manager and producer rolled into one' (Beadle and Fletcher 2008: 226) co-ordinating logistics.

Whilst in the late Middle Ages the stories were enacted by amateur players (townsfolk not working as actors at other times of the year), they were nevertheless paid, obliged to work for two weeks to rehearse and to perform for a period between three days and a week, with their remuneration dependent on role. 'God' was paid three to six shillings; the 'Souls', however, a meagre one shilling and eightpence. Players were also all provided with victuals during rehearsals since these would often take place between first light and the start of work. There were variants, with some actors working around their regular jobs and others working full-time on the production. Fines were imposed on the amateur players for dereliction of duty and to ensure, with limited rehearsal and a reliance on repeating the performances of previous years, that actors could rehearse quickly and efficiently, a call for 'able players', as was issued in 1476, meant that they would be to begin rehearsals with a minimum of ado; actors were also asked to learn their lines prior to the rehearsal period.

As Protestant Renaissance England began to proscribe the Catholic practices of the Middle Ages, the play cycles began to be banned across England from the late 1500s. Street theatre did persist with strolling players continuing to work in the halls and yards of houses and inns. With this, in time, came the rise of secular drama.

The Elizabethan and Jacobean periods

Tiffany Stern argues that the professionalization of theatre in England began with the construction of the first permanent playhouse in London, The Red Lion, in 1567. Rehearsals became structured and much of the terminology and philosophies underpinning current rehearsal practices can be traced to this point. Actors would 'study' their parts (the term 'understudy' is a remnant of this period), and the 'part' was literally his portion of the overall physical script with his 'role' coming about because said part was rolled up and handed to him. Dramatists were now professionals, paid for their services, and actors were no longer seen as 'rogues and vagabonds' under the Vagabond Acts of the 1500s, *if* they belonged to a company under royal patronage.

With scant evidence available, we can nevertheless begin to build a picture of the ways in which the plays were rehearsed. Excellent academic work by Stern and Patrick Tucker has paved the way, coupled with original practice traditions at Shakespeare's Globe Theatre, London. Scholarship oscillates between twenty and seventy plays being performed in repertory, with six-day weeks programmed, so that a different play was performed each afternoon. The very construction of the plays themselves allowed them to be performed with little rehearsal and most fascinating for me, the playwright almost directs the actors through the very structure and shaping of the plays and their textual layout. We can get a glimpse of how plays were rehearsed through *A Midsummer Night's Dream*, with the mechanicals having several days before performing their play, as well as through Hamlet's advice to the players of 'The Mousetrap'. Yet, we must not assume a literal mapping here, as Shakespeare the dramatist would have shaped reality for comedic or tragic effect, with story taking precedence over verisimilitude. There are clues, however: the individual parts being given out by Quince, or Hamlet instructing the Player King in the art of gestural language, which had its roots in the gestural books that appeared after the rise of the printing press in Europe from the 1440s onward. The use of classical rhetorical rehearsal devices, advised by Hamlet, has its roots in the teaching of classically patterned rhetoric in education of the time. The overall structure of the rehearsal period would have, most likely, been as follows:

1. The playwrights read their play out to the company.

2. The actors received their 'parts'. These included their lines, with between one and three words as 'cues'.

3. Actors memorized their 'part'. They had to hand their parts back so that other actors could learn them, or so that lines could be refreshed later. Woe betides them if a part went missing, since it might fall into the hands of the unscrupulous, who might copy or sell the plays, given

the lack of a concept of intellectual copyright in the early modern period.

4. Any group rehearsal was mainly logistical, with entrances and exits marked, costumes allocated and actors made aware of whom their character was addressing. This rehearsal took place in the morning, prior to the afternoon's performance. A fine was issued for those who did not attend.

5. Any music, jigs and fights were rehearsed, but separately from the text rehearsals.

6. In performance, the actors responded in the moment, after hearing their cue. Actors followed a backstage 'plot', detailing the order of scenes, entrances, exits and key logistical issues.

Rehearsal was primarily the responsibility of the actors, who would undertake private study and arrive at the group rehearsal with a performance fleshed out. With no formal director, the prompt and the Master of the Revels would oversee logistics. Research by Laura Ginters and Tim Fitzpatrick has also noted that the clear stage markers even direct the actors in where to pause between scenes, depending on the scene context, exploring how final rhyming couplets and those between scenes can create pauses that might 'serve to mark the point of fictional segmentation' (2019: 53), allowing for changes of time and location to be signalled to an audience.

With the Puritan closure of the Playhouses in 1642, it was not until 1660 that the theatre in England was officially reborn. Yet, the rehearsal practices picked up where they had left off.

Exercise: Original practices of early modern drama

Actors were attuned to look for several clues that the playwright embedded in their texts, such as the following:

1. Verse to prose, whereby an actor sees a shift in emotion or an acting clue for a change of tactic.
2. A shared line between characters unlocks how the situations of the characters are enmeshed.

3. The physical layout on the page and/or counting the beats are the means by which the playwright has given clues for pauses or other stage business in the gaps.
4. The length of line versus the length of thought, where a regular iambic pentameter beat may suggest a character aiming to control their emotions whereas irregular cadence and/or more beats in a line unlock potential clues for states of mind, emotional being or stress levels.

In the below extract from Shakespeare's *Timon of Athens,* spot the textual clues as discussed above, which can help the actor to rehearse without the aid of a director. Timon of Athens is bankrupt. A servant of Timon has arrived to ask for money from Sempronius (who has been given money and gifts by Timon in the past). Sempronius, however, is not going to give away any of his wealth.

3.3 *Enter Timon's third Servant with Sempronius, another of Timon's friends*

> **Sempronius**   Must he needs trouble me in't? Humh! 'Bove all others?
> He might have tried Lord Lucius, or Lucullus;
> And now Ventidius is wealthy too,
> Whom he redeem'd from prison. All these
> Owes their estates unto him.
> **3 Servant**   My lord,
> They have all been touch'd and found base metal,
> For they have all denied him.
> **Sempronius**   How? Have they denied him?
> Has Ventidius and Lucullus denied him?
> And does he send to me? Three? Humh?
> It shows but little love or judgment in him.
> Must I be his last refuge? His friends, like physicians,
> Thrive, give him over; must I take th' cure upon me?
> H'as much disgrac'd me in't; I'm angry at him,
> That might have known my place: I see no sense for't,
> But his occasions might have wooed me first:
> For, in my conscience, I was the first man
> That e'er received gift from him.
> And does he think so backwardly of me now,
> That I'll requite it last? No:
> So it may prove an argument of laughter

To th' rest, and 'mongst lords I be thought a fool.
I'd rather than the worth of thrice the sum,
H'ad sent to me first, but for my mind's sake;
I'd such a courage to do him good. But now return,
And with their faint reply this answer join:
Who bates mine honour shall not know my coin.

Exit

3 Servant   Excellent: your lordship's a goodly villain. The devil knew
not what he did when he made man politic; he crossed himself by't: and
I cannot think but in the end, the villainies of man will set him clear.
How fairly this lord strives to appear foul! Takes virtuous copies to be
wicked, like those that under hot ardent zeal would set whole realms on
fire: of such a nature is his politic love.
This was my lord's best hope; now all are fled
Save only the gods. Now his friends are dead,
Doors that were ne'er acquainted with their wards
Many a bounteous year must be employ'd
Now to guard sure their master.
And this is all a liberal course allows:
Who cannot keep his wealth must keep his house.

Exit

(3.2)

The Restoration

In *The Rehearsal* (1671) by George Villiers, Duke of Buckingham, three actors
meet for a group rehearsal to perform a play:

First Player   Have you the part perfect?

Second Player   Yes, I have it without book; but I don't understand how it
is to be spoken.

Third Player   And mine is such a one, as I can't guess for my life what
humour I'm to be in; whether angry, melancholy, merry, or in love. I don't
know what to make on't.

(1.2 ll.1–6)

Having learnt their parts, the actors need to ask the author about the potential meaning and appropriate humours.[2] *The Rehearsal* can provide clues as to the spirit of rehearsal, as when the playhouses were reopened following the Interregnum theatrical traditions had shifted. Charles II, the new king, had spent his exile absorbing and embodying the culture and theatre of the French Court, under the reign of Louis XIV, the Sun King. Theatres reopened with royal patronage and actresses on the stage followed the French model. Moreover, the court now kept a firm rein on the theatres, as per the Académie Française, who controlled the language of plays on the French stage. Theatres needed product and that began with extant works, although often rewritten, informed by the neoclassical models of the continent including decorum. With the printing press came a reintroduction of classical forms including those of Aristotle, which heavily influenced the playwriting form. The adapted indoor tennis courts (informed by the French designs) produced an intense intimacy between player and audiences, with entrance doors opening straight on to the apron stage (with a forestage playing space, or platea, and a scenic stage upstage). The period from 1660 to the early 1700s brought a new wave of ideas, energy and stories with the production of Restoration tragedies and comedies by both male and female playwrights alike, including Aphra Behn, Mary Pix, William Wycherley and William Congreve. In an annual season of plays, we know that there were over fifty produced and a number of those were new works: actors had to retain a substantial amount of material.

Yet the rehearsal methodology picked up, for the most part, where it had left off in 1642, with the playwright reading out the play and the prompter writing out the parts, which were taken home and learnt prior to the group rehearsal, of which there could have been between one and three. After the third 'benefit' night, if the play proved popular, it would most likely have remained in the repertoire. Even with rewrites, actors would have learnt these in private. Cue systems remained in place with the actors learning the last few words of a previous part. Similar to the early modern period, actors were cast according to 'type': fops, rakes, wits, gentlemen, gentlewomen, breeches roles, servants,

---

[2]   The ancient Greek physician Galen used 'humours' (chemical systems in the body) to explain different temperaments.

whores and lovers; and actors would have known their appropriate gestural languages of fans, snuff boxes, canes, greetings, bows and masks. This coded world was passed down from actor to actor, from the Parisian etiquette books and through some early drama schools, termed 'nurseries'. Robert D. Hume argues that the type of actor that a part went to can give us a clue as to how it may have been intended to be performed by the playwright:

> Mr Sullen in Farquhar's *The Beaux' Stratagem* is now cast as a booby. Was this true in 1707? Far from it. The part was not given to one of the company's clowns (Jubilee Dicky Norris or Bullock) but rather to John Verbruggen, a heavyweight tragic actor who played Iago against Betterton's Othello. For Verbruggen to take the part makes the abuse of Mrs Sullen frightening, upsetting and unpleasant and lends weight to the seriousness of the presentation of marital discord in the play.

> (2007: 20)

Actors would also have echoed the ambulatory habits of the gentry and their evening promenades through London's St. James's Park in their stage positions, allowing the blocking to be influenced by social conventions. The architectural placement of the scenic doors, arriving straight on to the stage space, furthermore allowed for asides and soliloquizing to be immediate and direct.

The Georgian period

The rise of the actor-manager, following on from Thomas Betterton in the Restoration period, enhanced the nascent 'star' system. This sat alongside the rise of the printed word and the dominance of texts on acting, which often called for new approaches. Through all of this, there was an increased conscious professionalization of the theatre-making process in the eighteenth century, which aligned with the Age of Enlightenment, and the growth of modernity. The period also saw the Licensing Act of 1737 come into force, whereby two main theatres were licenced, and all plays had to be approved by the office of the Lord Chamberlain. It also ushered more sentimental and romantic dramas, in line with European shifts. Along with this came scenic realism and David Garrick's removal of the apron stage. His friendship with the painter Hogarth has been discussed by Peter Thompson in *Essays on the Eighteenth-Century Stage*, in relation to their similar observation of human behaviour, prior to the creation of their respective characters and paintings.

Rehearsals saw playwrights reading their texts out loud, prior to private study, group rehearsals and performances. We know from research by George Rowell and Anthony Jackson that in the 1860s the cue scripts and 'sides' rehearsal method remained in operation. Tiffany Stern acknowledges that actor-managers, including Garrick, layered in interpretation and suggested revisions during the reading. With the rise of the actor-manager came more group rehearsals (although actors still only received their own lines and cues, known as 'lengths'), spread between the private rehearsals. This also became a space in which the managers and leading actors (if they attended) could instruct the younger actors, since the hierarchy of actors remained, as did adherence to stock types. Codified mannerisms of the melodramatic and pantomimic genres were built out of necessity as without a royal patent, theatres could only present non-spoken drama overall. Rehearsals would normally last for four hours a day (although Edmund Kean would rehearse all day) and actors had to produce their own costumes with leading actors 'training' apprentices privately in the art of the gestural language and the correct scansion of lines to aide delivery. Garrick led several 'summer schools' prior to the theatre season opening in the autumn, whilst Germany developed an academy for actors. A recent study of Johann Wolfgang von Goethe's theatre in Weimar outlines how the rehearsal was structured, stressing the importance of the actor's private study, since 'rehearsal in early nineteenth-century Weimar consisted of a "reading rehearsal" (*Leseprobe*, 1–3), blocking rehearsals (*Setzprobe*), theatre rehearsals (1–2) and a dress rehearsal (*Generalprobe*). All in all, a new play might have 4–6 rehearsals' (Ginters and Fitzpatrick 2019: 60).

An increased preoccupation with how characters looked and sounded continued through this period, with evidence of actors holding positions and gestures until the audience applauded their efforts. Below is a selection of some of the texts on theatre and acting across Europe that proliferated from 1710 onwards:

1710	*The Rules of Oratory Applied to Acting* by Charles Gildon
1734–50	*The Prompter* by Aaron Hill (a theatrical journal)
1746	*Essay on Acting* by Aaron Hill
1747	*Le Comédien* (*The Actor*) by Pierre Rémond de Sainte-Albine
1755	*Reflections upon Theatrical Expressions in Tragedy* by Roger Pickering
1761	*The Art of Speaking* by James Burgh
1762	*Course of Lectures on Elocution* by Thomas Sheridan
1773	*Paradoxe sur le comédien* (*Paradox of the Actor*) by Denis Diderot (published in 1830)
1781	*Elements of Elocution* by John Walker
1803	*Regeln für Schauspieler* (*Rules for Actors*) by Goethe

Many of these texts explored how emotion was linked to gesture, in line with scientific advancements and studies in emotion and behaviour, coupled with the numerous pamphlets that were issued on gestural language. Diderot's famous text is another fulcrum in the development of acting. In suggesting that the actor must be in control of their emotions and utilize imagination and observation to achieve this, he foreshadows Russian practitioner Nikolai Demidov's warning against a 'motor-storm' (Malaev-Babel and Lasinka 2016: 55) of neurosis a century and a half later. Yet, as Michael Cordner argues, we need to ensure that we do not transpose our own ideas of truth and naturalism on to actors such as Garrick, even though commentators at the time were keen to highlight these points. Garrick's truth was relative to the truth that preceded it, concentrating on rapid transitions between emotional expressions as the emotions shifted on each thought.

Naturalism, directors and scenographic advances

Rehearsing a play in the way that the West might recognize today had its roots in the Georgian period and grew from the mid-nineteenth century onwards, intertwined with three other movements. These were the rise of the figure of the director (in its broadest sense here, including the British actor-manager system of Henry Irving and his like), naturalism and the increased use of spectacle. This intermingling created the conditions for contemporary rehearsal processes to emerge.

In Germany, the Duke of Saxe-Meiningen sought a new way of working through his ensemble company from the 1860s onwards. Travelling throughout Europe saw other actor-managers adopting many of his core tenets, including the following:

1. An ensemble system
2. Pictorial realism of the mise en scène
3. A detailed building of character and backstory, even for the supernumeraries.

As an early auteur director, the Duke had complete control as demonstrated in his *Regiebuch* and was an *Intendant* (the equivalent of an artistic director) of the theatre in Germany, then divided into smaller dukedoms: 'In contrast to the English-speaking theatre's focus on stars, in the form of the actor-manager, the *Intendant* system encouraged ensemble acting. And unity of expression on the stage, as well as ensemble work, was epitomised by [Saxe-Meiningen's] players' (Innes and Shevtsova 2009: 38). André Antoine was one of those that witnessed the Duke's company in Brussels in 1888 and built upon the ensemble company's sense of verisimilitude, bringing an artistic coherence to a production, unifying the outer world of the production values with the inner world of rehearsals and building characters that were naturalistically motivated. In Russia, Constantin Stanislavski's notion of 'experiencing' the role, as opposed to merely representing a role, aimed to serve the developing realistic plays of Pushkin, Gogol and Chekhov. Rehearsing for longer than simply four sessions was vital for Stanislavski as he worked towards a 'system' of acting where experiencing became the central tenet. Vasili Toporkov, writing on Stanislavski's rehearsal methods at the Moscow Art Theatre, reflects on the definition of experiencing, connected with 'genuine human behaviour ... which hook[s] an audience and influence[s] their hearts and minds' (Toporkov and Benedetti 2008: 115). To achieve this required rehearsals and immersion in the world of the production and a collective response to the play. Stanislavski was directly influenced by Saxe-Meiningen's company, whom he observed performing in Moscow in 1890, attending eight of the company's performances. However, initially in his directing he created an entire 'score' for his whole production and his rehearsals, giving less creative agency to his actors during his earlier periods. Stanislavski was initially more interested in Meiningen's pictorial realism and directorial tricks, rather than the ensemble nature of working with actors. As his practice evolved, he gave more agency and creative freedom to his actors in order that they 'arouse their own psychological and physical resources' (Thomas 2016: 4). Throughout his later career, from 1928 onwards, Stanislavski developed several experiential rehearsal techniques, including the 'Method of Physical Action', morphing into 'active analysis'. The stage had therefore been set, as it were, for rehearsals to be built around an individual director's working methodology. For Stanislavski's active analysis, for example, to be used as a formal rehearsal methodology, a directorial figure must lead a company through this process of working since it depends on a specific rehearsal methodology, as opposed to actors bringing their individualized processes to the table.

Early directors in Europe rebelled against previous systems, which were often patriarchal, controlling and hierarchical, with actor-managers creating their own rehearsal processes. Henry Irving famously rehearsed over eight to ten weeks with intensive four-hour rehearsals every day and Herbert Beerbohm Tree rehearsed Shakespeare's *Henry VIII* at Her Majesty's Theatre in 1897 over two months.[3] Photographic realist box sets coupled with the increase of stage electricity and lighting, scenic devices and other elements of the mise en scène meant that a unifying figure had to coordinate this work. In the UK, exponents such as Edward Gordon Craig, whilst not working with naturalism, highlighted the importance of the scenic picture as narrative, downplaying the importance of the actor. Swiss designer Adolphe Appia simultaneously bought the notion of light to the heart of the production whereas British actor-managers would take the reins at scenic rehearsals (equivalent to technical rehearsals), and Henry Irving would prepare his own lighting plot. The style of plays altered during this period with the advent of naturalism in 1881; Émile Zola's *Naturalism in the Theatre* championed a move away from romantic, sentimental drama to naturalism, as had happened in the development of the novel. Zola became

---

[3] See Michael R. Booth's *Victorian Spectacular Theatre 1850–1910* (1981).

an advisor for André Antoine's Théâtre Libre and supported Antoine's idea that a unification of all the different elements of the production was essential. Similarly, the rise of psychological realism in Russia meant that Diderot's long-sought-after fourth wall became commonplace, with plays continuing their move behind the proscenium arch that framed the stage. Norwegian dramatist Henrik Ibsen created naturalistic productions where characters were influenced by their environment as well as by past events, such as in *A Doll's House* (1879) and *Ghosts* (1881). Dan Rebellato eloquently articulates that naturalists wanted to

> not just represent the world, but . . . understand the world, and they thought that in order to understand the world and the way people behave, you have to understand the environments in which they live, because they believed our behaviour was the product of not just biological but also sociological causes. What that means is that, on stage, the set is one of the key ways in which the environment of the characters expresses itself. The more realistic you are about that, the more precise and accurate you can be about the effects it will have on individuals.

(Fowler 2019: 41)

In England in 1900, Harley Granville Barker founded the Stage Society, the precursor to London's Royal Court, positioning the dramatist centre stage and with every role in a play being given the same attention throughout rehearsals. George Bernard Shaw suggested in *The Art of Rehearsal* that this period should mainly be about 'stage business' (West 1958: 155), whereby actors would be taught the blocking and gestural language predetermined by their director. He also stated in 1921 that 'no strangers should be present . . . rehearsals are absolutely and sacredly confidential. The publication of gossip about rehearsals . . . is the blackest breach of stage etiquette' (ibid.: 159). Furthermore, he called for an understanding of prior conventions (such as a knowledge of Greek theatre and its methods of production) by directors and actors attempting to mount a production from that period.

Yet, if there was a movement across Europe towards longer rehearsal periods, with an emphasis on experience of and immersion in the world of the play, this was not happening in the UK.[4] In a move against the London-centric theatre-making of the Edwardian period, whereby stars joined the strolling players across the country to 'give' their performances often with no rehearsal with the wider company, a repertory movement was born from a need for regionality and a locality having an ownership of a theatre company and building. Prior to television, repertory companies would provide several stories per week. Jens-Morten Hanssen recently reminded us that the term 'repertory' has lost its etymological meaning; according to Patrice Pavis, for instance, ' "repertory" is a body of plays performed by a theatre in the course of a season . . . [where actors can] develop, rehearse and refine a role over time' (cited in Hanssen 2020: 143–4). Sometimes actors played twice in one evening, where a company would present the same piece at 6.00 pm and 8.00 pm. This moved to weekly repertory (with one play rehearsed in the day and the actors performing another in the evening), then to fortnightly repertory with a two-week rehearsal period. Following the increase in home television sets, the regional repertory system diminished from over one hundred repertory companies in 1952, to fifty-five in 1954 according to George Rowell and Anthony Jackson in *The Repertory Movement: A History of Regional Theatre in Britain*.

Interview: Chris Martin on repertory

Chris Martin began his career in 1963 in very different times in weekly, then later fortnightly, repertory.

Chris Martin: Basically, the longer you have to rehearse, the more detail you can perfect. I did 120 plays in weekly rep before going into fortnightly rep. We did some heavy plays by Shakespeare, Bernard Shaw, Brecht, Restoration and somehow you did it. It was pretty standard where I worked: Swansea Grand, Hastings Pier, Barrow-in-Furness, amongst others from the age of eighteen to twenty-one, when I arrived at the Victoria Theatre, Stoke-on-Trent where I stayed until I was twenty-eight.

---

[4] A major exception to this was the British pantomime, which, in the late 1800s, might often be rehearsed for as long as three months, since the pantomime (as today) was required by the theatre to be successful. Augustus Harris at Drury Lane had 650 people to marshal: a time-consuming undertaking.

In weekly repertory, every play opened on a Monday night and finished on Saturday night. A rehearsal would start on a Tuesday morning at 10.00 a.m. and finished at 5.30 p.m., as you'd be performing in the evening. On this morning, a director would try in three hours to read and sort out all the moves for the play, which they'd done in advance. All the problems were sorted, and the French's Acting Editions helped with all the moves: 'move down left, move down right, she goes to the cabinet, drinks, smiles, cries'. For plays without stage directions, the director worked this out and gave them to you. At lunchtime on Tuesday, we learnt the first act for the following morning. Afternoons, you rarely rehearsed. Wednesday morning, you knew the lines and worked act one; Wednesday afternoon, you learnt act two; Thursday morning, you blocked and worked act two; Thursday afternoon, learnt act three (most plays were in a three-act structure), and Friday morning, worked act three. Sometimes you'd work Friday afternoon, but Saturday morning, you'd run the whole play. On the Saturday night (I was an acting ASM at the age of nineteen), we changed the sets over to be ready on Monday morning. Sunday, you slept; we were knackered! On Monday morning, you put the costume on that had been lined up ready and you had a morning to do a rough technical of the whole play, top-to-tail, per cue. Forget pausing to work out your motivation; your motivation was to do it as fast as you could, in order! In the afternoon, there was a dress rehearsal and on the Monday night you put the show on. You were told on the Saturday night what the part was for the following week. Sometimes you wouldn't know what the play was. You learnt the last three words of somebody's speech as there was no real rehearsal. With one rehearsal an act, you had to be ready and really listen.

Don't forget too, you wouldn't really get paid for rehearsals: that came in later with Arts Council money and local council grants. Even when I was at the National Theatre in the early 1970s, we were paid less for rehearsal weeks.

When we went to fortnightly rep, it took me ages to work out how to use the extra time. Now we rehearsed morning and afternoon often and with double the amount of rehearsal time; we opened on Tuesday. We called it 'two-plus-two'. But in fortnightly rep, you could find subtlety and could explore it a little bit more. It felt like a luxury, suddenly. Also, we started to explore fashions in theatre in fortnightly rep. When I first started a lot of acting was quite representational. But when I think back to Swansea Grand in weekly rep, with over a thousand seats, I felt like I went on stage and shouted all my lines. But we'd explore techniques more in fortnightly rep. I remember doing a whole session on timing in farce, then verse in Shakespeare, then this chap from Russia, Stanislavski, was introduced . . .

A major part of the changing climate of those theatre-making practices which have an effect on decisions made in the rehearsal room has been the influence of feminism and feminist performance. As Kim Solga argues, can we call the current era a 'post-feminist age' (2015) when women in the arts are paid 10 per cent less than men in the UK[5] and 31 per cent of artistic directors are female,[6] even in the wake of the #MeToo movement? Michelle Terry, current artistic director of Shakespeare's Globe, describes explicitly how she is taking the lead in breaking down patriarchal rehearsal structures. Similarly, since the mid-1980s, social activism and scholarship around minority sexualities has affected theatre-making. From bringing stories that embrace a spectrum of sexualities to the stage, to the formation of numerous LGBTQ+ theatre collectives, our ways of telling stories (not to mention the stories themselves) have undergone a shift.

Over the past few years, the global Black Lives Matter movement has also been a catalyst in dramatically accelerating the necessary changes required of representation in theatre, both in terms of casting decisions and 'colour-conscious' (as opposed to 'colour-blind') casting and in relation to a more diverse body of artistic leadership in arts organizations. In the UK, one condition of the Covid Arts Council England Cultural Recovery Fund was to demonstrate that equality, diversity and inclusion were at the heart of an organization, in order for it to be successful in receiving a grant, ensuring that diversity is threaded through the workforce, governing bodies and programming. The climate has been changing and must continue to do so, at a more rapid pace.

Current rehearsal movements

The rehearsal period for the actor primarily concerns the process of merging self with the words on the page (to create a character, or a 'third being') and of becoming immersed in the world of the play, responding to its given

---

[5] https://www.artsprofessional.co.uk/news/exclusive-gender-gap-dominates-latest-arts-pay-figures.

[6] https://www.theguardian.com/stage/2020/jan/27/sexism-gender-divide-ingrained-uk-theatre-study-claims.

circumstances.[7] How this comes about, supported by a director, is contingent on the genre and style of the piece, as much as it is on servicing the needs of the play. The following two practitioners place particular emphasis on changing how rehearsals operate.

Ivo van Hove is now one of the world's most sought-after directors, following many years of working steadily in his native Belgium. Let us return to Carlson's notion of ghosting as for van Hove, there is an expectation placed on his work by audiences due to his aesthetic, since 'the innovation and imagination of the director's new interpretation requires that a significant part of the audience be aware of the interpretive tradition that is being both carried on and challenged' (Carlson 2006: 100). Van Hove stops at describing himself as an *auteur* director however, as he has given 'total fidelity to every text I ever did' (2019: 12). He has, furthermore, been able to carve out the way he would like to make theatre and therefore rehearse, given his position as Artistic Director of Internationaal Theater Amsterdam. The methodologies he employs include the following:

1. Taking several years to prepare a play, through dramaturgical and scenographic working groups.
2. Short working days, with an intense three to four hours of work and time for actors to prepare beforehand and consolidate afterwards.
3. Scenographic elements are created in the rehearsal room, which harks back to the Duke of Saxe-Meiningen, who had all production elements in rehearsal.
4. A strong understanding that an external physical action can create an internal feeling or emotional justification.

Michelle Terry is the current director of Shakespeare's Globe in London; although she carries the title of artistic director, she remains an actor within the company, whilst determining the choices for each season. Two key processes include the following:

---

[7] 'Given circumstances' are the indisputable facts that can be used to build a role and support an understanding of the world which the characters live within.

1. 'Anti-literal' casting, whereby any actor can play any role in the classical canon, regardless of gender or race, for example.

2. Creative-friendly rehearsal rooms, which build on from parent/ carer friendly rehearsals. Terry considers how rehearsals need to be creative spaces for actors and directors:

The idea that an actor can only be creative with a director in the room is quite a paternal way of thinking and [such] an infantilised way of thinking about their creativity that you have to think: what is the enormous amount of work being done outside of the room? This could be quantifiable, such as line-learning, or something unquantifiable about what your unconscious is doing to assimilate the information, interrogate the play, prepare yourself for performance. The idea you must be in a room to get that work done suddenly became a bit of dishonest gesture. Then you look at mental health, and you think, we are in London; it takes people at least an hour to get to work, you're asking people to travel at the busiest time of the day and then be creative on cue and be inspiring on cue. You start to unpick systems that are just not creative-friendly.

3. Collective storytelling means that no casting is done prior to the first day of rehearsal and the play becomes the centre of the rehearsal room. All are co-collaborators of the process, flattening out the hierarchy between actor and director in the traditional theatre-making process.

Whilst there has been a flattening of rehearsal room structures this doesn't, as Heskins states, 'mean it's a democracy, where everyone gets a say on everything, but where everyone is valued'. New systems recognize the director as the person who still makes the final decision, even if the solving of the problem is more collegiate.

A summary of Chapter 2

It is a truism so obvious as to be cliché that theatre is a multifaceted art form. This is partly due to its collaborative nature: a script is merely a blueprint, a given production is merely one iteration of that blueprint and one with a limited lifecycle. This is also partly due to the sheer age of theatre which lie deep in the visceral human need for storytelling and ritual that underpins forms as diverse as Egyptian drama, Japanese *noh* theatre and Balinese Barong dance. A notion returned to is uniqueness: every production is unique; every genre has its own 'rules' and the approach of every practitioner is unique especially in terms of how they approach rehearsals. The key is finding your own approach, informed by the approaches of those who have gone before, and being prepared to temper and adapt those as part of the collaborative process. Though naturalism remains one of the dominant forms in Western theatre, perhaps it is best to regard this as part of the long continuum of the art form rather than as an independent phenomenon, just as the rehearsal room is one moment in the continuum of the life of the production. Whilst the actor in the rehearsal period aims to merge and immerse, the director must steer, guide, order and structure. Past rehearsal structures should be analysed within their social, cultural and historical contexts, yet Tiffany Stern's notion that there is a 'tendency to conflate modern and past theatrical practice' (2000:3) across rehearsal studies warns us not to use previous rehearsal methodologies and transpose them onto contemporary theatre-making.

Interview: Stephen Boden on the producer as collaborator

Stephen Boden has produced commercial theatre pantomimes throughout the UK for several decades. He runs Imagine Theatre, based in Coventry, with his wife Sarah Boden. The interview below is given in full since it covers a wide range of topics.

How did you end up working in theatre?

It was a journey from a very young age: loving the art form and very quickly getting an energy from the audience. Panto only works with an audience connection, you are sensitive to what the audience is feeling and you take that back into musicals and plays also. I joined youth groups and got a sense that there was more to theatre and the arts than just being on stage. I realized I could always do theatre regardless of my degree, so I trained to be a teacher, using design and technology with secondary pupils, with drama alongside.

I got my theatre fix doing university shows and crewing at the Belgrade Theatre in Coventry. I struck up a relationship with Iain Lauchlan, who was doing the pantomimes there. He was looking for a company manager on tour. I loved the business side: working out how to make money, but also, I worked out how not to lose money, which is a great grounding as a producer.

And there weren't MA courses in producing then?

No, the only way you became a producer then was to have deep pockets or [if] you knew someone who was doing it. Being in the Midlands, there wasn't that level of opportunity.

Has working across all those departments, the 'nuts and bolts' as it were, helped to set you up to produce?

Like all careers, you learn far more on the job. The opportunity to work from the grassroots gives you a sense of how all departments communicate. Every department has to talk about the project and every decision made affects someone else in the process. I enjoy trying to facilitate that at any level.

There are many misconceptions about the role of the producer. How do you see your role?

The first side is having a vision for a project. The art form is something that I enjoy and want to deliver. Secondly, it's about bringing together groups of people who you think can support that vision. It's not necessarily about finding the most highly skilled practitioner; it's about finding people who you know can work together. I have the ability to think: 'I like your work ethos, you're open and a good communicator and you understand the art form and work well with similar people.' We work at Imagine with choreographers, MDs, lighting, sound and set designers, prop makers, set builders. It's about bringing all those people together and allowing them to share ownership in the project and have autonomy, whilst creating a framework for that to commercially operate in. That's the hardest bit, as I'm responsible for livelihoods. There has to be a strong business sense underpinning the operation.

So, it's the two core pillars of the creative side working in tandem with the business side?

One hundred per cent. The hard bit about that is that commercially you are looking at the bottom line of what the show is to earn. It would be folly to embark on over-ambitious elements, from cast size to special effects.

How do you pick the 'right' people?

Openness is so vital, as well as an understanding of their particular area. If we are looking for a designer, they might need to be an illustrator, [with] an illustrative understanding of the artform, rather than the architectural understanding of the physical elements. When looking at directors, I look for those who understand performance, pulling people together, bringing directorial, choreographic and musical elements together, able to facilitate a production in a relatively short period, which is pertinent to pantomime.

What do you expect from your directors and actors collaborating in the rehearsal room?

No two directors or actors are ever the same. If you are employing them to create for you, then there has to be a degree of freedom for interpretation, even if it's not to my taste. My job as a producer is to ensure we have a happy company, the product is strong and meets the remit of the theatre and their audiences. I want my directors and groups of performers to work from the text, offer constructive alterations within the framework we have to deliver, whilst giving autonomy to be creative, within the boundaries set out in the advance production meetings. As a producer, you want a team of people who can think tangentially through a production's options. We try to keep creative teams together where possible and key performers, as it allows a director to go into a rehearsal knowing the traits of the performers, pull out the strengths of that and concentrate on other areas of the production which require more focus.

What other elements or conditions should be in place for a successful rehearsal period?

Having the actors present! We want to create an atmosphere where rehearsals are open and fun, sometimes actors or company members take this too literally and feel they have the autonomy to jump in and out! The rehearsal period is also about building up stamina for the run. Having a suitable rehearsal space is also very important. As you are in rehearsal for under two weeks, you need several spaces to work in. Rehearsals should be about getting everybody confident with the flow and the mechanics of the production, but leave time for the comedy routines and choreographic routines. A slosh scene can be done in isolation from the rest.

How does your relationship with the director shift and change from pre-rehearsal through rehearsals, tech, previews and during the run itself?

During pre-production, you are charging a battery up: pumping enough information into the director without restricting their autonomy to create. Within a commercial environment there may be more caveats a director has to operate within. After decanting that information, the director needs minimal interference on all parts. We then support them to get answers to problems, so they don't feel they are in the field on their own. Then I will reconnect with a director in a producer's run. I'm not looking for polished performances, but whether the story arc is clear and if the music choices are working, and that there is the right balance of comedy and if the running time is what is expected. I don't insist on changes unless there's something fundamentally wrong. The director is in the room and the performers have to deliver on the first night. I need to respect the director to make the right call in those situations, so we all reach the opening performance with a safe and happy company and a strong show. In previews and dresses, I'm working with the director to check whether it looks smart. Have we brought all the disparate elements together? Are they in balance? Is the theatre coping with the scale of the show? Is it safe? Actors are often exhausted by that point and might not compute lots of new information. I'm looking for a motivational director to give enthusiasm and support for actors and all those involved with the delivery of that show. I'm looking for the director to then problem-solve and deliver on amendments that may need to take place, or if any tricky elements technically can be re-rehearsed. As a producer, I am here to support them and their relationship with their artists.

So, the producer can help the director to fill in gaps? There may be directors who have never done a slosh scene, for example.

Yes; directors don't train in pantomime often. There is no checklist to ensure the director has all the skills you need; nor should there be, as the producer's role is to support the director within those areas where they may need more skills. We should share that knowledge and create an environment where we can. Essentially, directing and producing is about people management and communication.

3

(Pre)rehearsal early decisions

Sound designer Gareth Fry states that 'the pre-rehearsal period is an often-overlooked, yet utterly critical part of the process'. This chapter asserts how the (pre)rehearsal period can be used

1. for the director and designer to create worlds and frames;

2. for a creative interpretation of a play; and

3. for deciding upon types of rehearsal philosophies, methodologies and strategies.

Many directors consciously think about how they can shift the theatre-making process towards one that is more conducive to creativity. Working out how a rehearsal room will operate as a director or what to bring to rehearsals as an actor are vital.

Choosing a piece to direct

There are two scenarios:

1. You pick the piece. It's new to you and you want to do it; or it's a piece that you have known for a while, which won't leave you alone. It's grown older with you, continually tapping you on the shoulder requesting: 'Direct me!' You have something to say with the play, or you want to forefront some of its qualities in a way others have not.

2. The play is chosen for you by the artistic director or producer. If it speaks to you, then that's a bonus. If not, you need to find a way in. If you really cannot find a connection with the piece, is taking the job morally right?

Regardless of this scenario, ask, 'Why this play? Why now? How might it speak to and resonate with us?' I chose to direct *Measure for Measure* against the backdrop of the #MeToo movement, for example. For Ivo van Hove,

> preparation starts at least one to two years before I actually do it. The decision of the title is the most crucial decision a director has to make. He or she has to be two hundred per cent convinced that he or she really wants to do this. That's why to decide long before is a good thing, as you have to consider and reconsider and be really sure that you'll be interested in this material in a year or so, that the material has a personal and societal urgency. It makes me think much more deeply and helps me make the right decisions. So, the decision-making is crucial.

Much debate accompanies a production when a director picks a 'contentious play'. This is typically a classical piece, such as *The Taming of the Shrew*, with its implicit and explicit misogyny, gaslighting and domestic emotional violence. Questions arise as to how and why we should tell a certain tale for a contemporary audience. For the Globe's Michelle Terry,

> contention is a subjective viewpoint and I think that part of the point of theatre is to invite debate and discussion, but it's not able to hold the ethical or moral high ground and shouldn't be held responsible [for] that. Shakespeare and most playwrights hold multiple truths. They are trying to ask questions of our time, but not necessarily be held accountable for the solutions of our time. When we did the history plays, I was often asked: 'What does Shakespeare want to tell us about Brexit?' And I say: 'Nothing. Because he wasn't alive [then]'.

Terry believes that the production should stand for itself and resonate subjectively with a particular audience member; otherwise 'it's slightly too much pressure on a playwright and abdicates responsibility from ourselves to reflect and ask what our ethical response [is]'. With a classical play, you can't assume the playwright is racist, anti-Semitic or misogynistic. If you do, it means that we don't have to interrogate our own racism and misogyny; we can't demand our theatre do that work for us. Theatre and plays can provoke the questions and pose the problems. We still have to do the work to find solutions. There's something much more dynamic and less infantilising from these plays that say: 'On your imaginary forces work' and: 'What do you think?'. Theatre can provide options, but we can't say one is better or worse: they are just alternatives. You decide how you want to take the plays and live in the world. I think of Sarah Kane's *Cleansed*. That's not an offer of the world [as] she wants it to be, but an offer of the way the world could be.

Interpretation over analysis

'Analysis' is the term often used to describe the early work on the play prior to rehearsal. I prefer to adopt the notion of 'interpretation', popularized by Anne Fliotsos, Professor of Theatre at Purdue University and author of *Interpreting the Play Script: Contemplation and Analysis*, as practitioners can see that a mere shift of word can create a shift in thinking, as she encourages us to 'find more questions than solutions' (2012: 153). Rather than a positivist approach of looking for a certain truth, Fliotsos encourages us to connect fundamentally with a personal 'perception of the script, including the reader's emotional responses, visceral responses, metaphorical interpretation, and an individual sense of meaning rooted in personal experience. In essence, the question [when] interpreting a script shifts from "How do you work on the play?" (i.e., the analysis of a text) to "How does the play work on you?"' (ibid.: 153–4). In attempting to approach every play as a new text and to not be trapped by notions of ghosting, possibility generation is promoted. By asking how the play resonates, the actor or director is free to connect to the story in a way that is individually meaningful and discover a personal 'lure'.

The interpretive choices pave the way to create both the frames of the production and the world which the characters will inhabit. The frames are a set of conventions that govern and bound the choices made within a rehearsal process including the acting style required (pantomime, for instance, requires a different style from Pinter), the conventions worked within and rehearsal methodologies employed and are often decided upon prior to the rehearsal period. The world of the play is the environment which the characters perceive and therefore operate and respond to. This can consist of both the world of the playwright's words, as well as the world created by the director and designer through the mise en scène.

Creating directorial frames

Peter Boenisch reframes the process of directing from 'what it is that "the director does" or what they should do, to what directing does and may do' (2015: 5). Directors create a frame to act as a benchmark for when directing, against which measures can be made of the relative truth of the actor, moment to moment. I am not advocating a scientific approach in rehearsals but wish to create edges in order to bound a rehearsal process, which is often messy and (rightly) chaotic, no matter how structured the rehearsal methodology might be. Actor trainer Ken Rea's rehearsal process is 'a series of controlled failures that gradually reveal to you the best way of telling the story' (2015: 178). Yet failure still must be measured against a benchmark implicitly or explicitly. Phillip Zarrilli relates the creation of framing conventions to the idea that the director brings a 'logic [to] the production as a whole' (Daboo, Loukes and Zarrilli 2013: 13) and this production logic is part of the frame in which a cohesive world is created.

Workshop and R&D periods

James Macdonald creates a frame with his actors via a pre-rehearsal workshop period which concentrates 'on practical problem-solving and design. A lot of the basic production ideas [are] generated at that time' (2008: 142). Macdonald believes that it is difficult to create the rules and frames within the main body of rehearsals due to the short rehearsal period within the UK system,[1] so these

---

[1] Lyn Gardner states that 'British theatre has become so much more interesting since mainstream rehearsal periods changed around the 1980s from the two or three weeks that was a legacy of the repertory model. But those who are just starting out – and essentially inventing the future of British theatre – remain the most squeezed, and it is hard to be inventive under so much pressure' (2019: 7).

must be decided upon prior to rehearsals. If for director Gwenda Hughes, 'rehearsals are a process of experiment and exploration' (2011: 16) then the need to discover the 'rules of the [production]' (Macdonald 2008: 142) prior to rehearsals is paramount as, for Wendy Lesser, the 'director's role [is as] the primary interpreter of a play' (1997: 4). Like Macdonald, Katie Mitchell also undertakes a workshop period, as 'workshops are about exploring ideas' (2009: 103). For Mitchell, the workshops are the 'starting point for rehearsals' (2009: 103) and are the space in which to 'create a maximum environment to discover ... and [think] how I will take that discovery into practical exercises I can set the actors'. Lyn Gardner, writing in *The Stage*, warns against turning a workshop period into product-in-miniature, as you 'discover very little when you are in a rush. Even the sharing culture of funded R&D weeks can be problematic when you know that on Friday afternoon venue bookers, producers and artistic directors – the people who are crucial to the future life of your show – will be in the room' (2019).

For Mitchell, the workshop period is where 'emphasis is on the discovery of ideas or starting points for working on a production; to discover, whereas in a rehearsal process *for* a production, you have to use your time delivering a product the audience to see and there is less time for exploration and discovery.' This relates to the moving from content to form over a rehearsal process, yet Mitchell places discovery over content generation in the workshop period, whilst the rehearsal period is where the form is moulded as there is 'a deadline of a production an audience will pay to watch and delivering that product on time and in budget is a big responsibility for the director.'

Catherine Alexander, documenting her time on Complicité's *The Elephant Vanishes* (2003), sees the workshop period as 'extensive provisional "sketching" ... [which] feels like an archaeological excavation and is nearly always slow and painstaking' (Harvie and Lavender 2010: 63). This sketching builds the frames for the main rehearsal period. Director Hugh Morrison is governed by the contrasting needs of different playwrights and genres, '[from] Shaw's logic, linear thinking and cause and effect to the non-events and metaphor and intuitions of Beckett' (1984: 104). Conventions and frames must also be clear within a genre, as the concept of discovering a 'truth' is relative. If there is a short rehearsal period, then pre-rehearsal decisions around the frames that bound choices can allow for a more productive rehearsal period, as actors have a roadmap and ultimately this offers freedom. Frames contain the rehearsal room choices and enable theatre-makers to undertake Terence Crawford's notion of horizontal projection, 'regularly look[ing] to the artistic horizon to seemingly set their coordinates for onward journeying' (2015: 191).

Code cracking

Finding clues to settle on a production frame is a form of 'code cracking' (Stern 2000: 9) for directors, as pre-rehearsal work on a text 'decode[s] its performativity' (Sidiropoulou 2019: 86); building from Stanislavski, this suggests that like a riddle, 'works have to be decoded' (Stanislavski 2008: 99). James Thomas calls this the 'internal plausibility' (2016: 18), whereby all genres and styles must live within their own rules and logic and where '[it] needs time and care to crack the code' (Cole 1992: p.11). Rose Whyman, Senior Lecturer in Drama and Theatre Arts at the University of Birmingham, discusses the problems that arose when Stanislavski directed the 1907 symbolist play *The Drama of Life* with an internalized psychological technique. As the acting style was not congruent with the genre's codes, the 'actors became . . . fearful of what was required of them, too focused internally and there was no justification for the absence of gesture' (2011: 29). For Katie Mitchell, her code cracking relates to pre-deciding the concept and then events of a scene, which are the 'deeper structures that run beneath the surface of the words' (2009: 8) and which are key moments in the play that affect all of the characters, without which the scene(s) would not be able to move forward in the way that they do. This comes from a deep investigation of the text prior to rehearsals, allowing Mitchell to own and be 'in charge' (ibid.: 6) of the play. She describes the realization that events are a key directorial concept as

> an epiphany. It was great to discover that you can analyse a play text by
> looking for the changes or events effecting all characters in a scene. The
> change happened and then alters the characters' intentions and behaviours

until the next change occurs, and so on. The defining shifts in the action are legible in the way the events change what everyone is doing or playing. Consequently, I begun to understand plays in performance as being about watching these changes happen, and this helped me analyse play texts more precisely and stage the scene in a more dynamic way.

Decisions on events rest in Mitchell's pre-rehearsal period, which she describes as 'director-led solitary preparation, [where] sixty to seventy per cent of the events can be analysed before a rehearsal begins, sometimes a higher proportion, so there's less discovery of events in the rehearsal room'. Deciding during the pre-rehearsal period means that rehearsals become the home of

working out how to perform [the events], not how to discover them. Of course, the actors' insights do alter some of my event analysis (normally resulting in a change to about 10% of the pre-prepared event structure), but I'm less interested in collective discovery in a rehearsal room and more interested in a process that ensures the audience get high quality work with an enactment of top-notch analysis. If the director goes into rehearsals with an unprepared script, they are reliant on the discoveries they or the actors make, and this way of rehearsing strikes me as somewhat precarious, over-reliant on in-the-moment chance discoveries. If those chance discoveries are not made, there is no fall-back position, and the production could end up reflecting the somewhat chaotic and uneven discovery (or non-discovery) procedure where one moment is solved by a great discovery and the next moment is unclear because there was no strong discovery.

This enables a company to begin shaping and creating the form immediately, as opposed to waiting for discoveries to occur. Mitchell's logic is that you may only then have 'forty per cent of good discoveries and sixty per cent of the time, you've discovered nothing and the live performance is only forty per cent dynamic'.

Daniel Johnson also suggests that meaning is embodied within the text, and that the company is searching for *aletheia* (an 'un-hiddenness' in the concept of revealing a meaning). Each production (and genre) has its own inner logic that needs to be revealed. Jonathan Croall highlights this in relation to Sean

Mathias's production of the pantomime *Aladdin*, produced by London's Old Vic in 2004:

> Sean talks of the difficulties actors have in switching to pantomime mode. 'If they get too psychological about it, if there's too much character exploration, the whole fabric dissolves. . . . You have to do something very sculptured and clear, in bold colours, and then find out what works and what doesn't. It's no good doing it as if it were a straight play'.
>
> (2014: 115)

The director and designer locate the world of the play

To create the frames, code cracking needs to locate the world of the play to reveal its meaning. Robert Knopf states that the 'director's primary responsibility is for the "big picture" of the production' (2017: 5) and the focus must be on keeping 'all collaborators on track to this goal, the core action' (ibid.) or, for Ivo van Hove, the 'core idea' (Bennett and Massai 2018: 9). This core idea relates to the world of the play, as in rehearsals 'the actor's understanding of action with the playwright's concept of action [functions] as an overall engine for the production . . . which therefore also includes the designer's notion of stage action' (Knopf 2017: 5). The relative truth that the actors need to portray within the frames is linked to the needs and demands of both the play and the world.

'Just as an animal's behaviour is a response to their given environment, so an actor's response is a response to the world of the play (this is an expanded version of Stanislavsky's given circumstances)' (McCaw 2020: 51). Therefore, the design is the form for the world of the production and how actors interrelate with their world is essential. Directors understand that designers, as Max Jones states, are 'looking to provoke feeling and manipulate experience'. Jones sees himself

> as a performer; I put a performance on that is in tune with the play and the venue. Firstly, it must serve up a space in which the play can exist, within the truth of that play. And secondly, you are finding a poetry and emotionally underscoring moments. When I'm initially breaking down a play, I'm

thinking about it in a way that a composer might: where are the peaks and crescendos? In a way, you might manipulate feeling in the sense music does. I think of my work sculpturally in that way, trying to find physical shapes, moments of high drama or transcendence that you take the audience on a journey with.

There are numerous ways to create a world. When directing *Cymbeline* at Shakespeare's Globe in 2001, Mike Alfreds worked with the whole company to create their environment. Most creatives, however, bound by commercial production restraints and extant systems, are forced to pre-decide the world prior to rehearsals. Directors should work together with as many creatives as possible to build the world, regardless of whether the design concept must be signed off prior to rehearsals, or during the process. Max Jones argues passionately that

> what I am trying to do within the design community is make a stand for what a designer's role is, in terms of a conceptual ownership over a production. . . . [It's] a two-way partnership with the director that's becoming increasingly important. . . . There isn't a situation when a director comes in with an idea for a design for a show, or at least that's not happened in my career for a long time. The hierarchy has shifted. . . . Creative teams are becoming increasingly recognised as artists in their own right.

Exercise: Unlocking the clues to locate a world (developed with Richard Cheshire)

The questions and prompts below allow a director to unearth textual clues. These findings are used to create a potential world. This should ideally be done in collaboration with designers and dramaturgs, if working within a larger team, and can also be explored with actors as a collective exercise.

1. Locate the given circumstances. These are the undisputed and categorical facts:
    i. Where is the play set? What is the geography, location, or climate?
    ii. When is the play set? What is the date, year, season, and time of day?
    iii. What are the specific religious, economic, political, social, and cultural facts?
    iv. Are there any other undisputed facts?

2. Concepts and ideas:
   i.   What does the title of the play suggest?
   ii. How does the action of the play reveal key ideas?
   iii. How does the play resonate with current world views? Peter Brook notes that an author whose work is still told, means that the play can be re-examined and the story remains alive.
   iv. Why do you want to tell this story now? Why should it be told? What are your instinctive responses and gut reactions? Why tell it in the theatrical medium, as opposed to a recorded or digital one?
3. Original practices:
   i.   How might the architecture of the original playhouse, for which the production was written, affect directorial or acting choices?
   ii. If appropriate, are there any other ideas from the original practices that can aid understanding of the play and rehearsal choices?
4. Bits and events:
   i.   Identify the play's 'bits'.
   ii. Title the bits. Josie Rourke labels her bits creatively, foregrounding an interpretation. In her script for *The Long and the Short and the Tall* bits were called 'a proposal overheard' (2006a) or 'the first plot laid' (ibid.), to give two examples.
   iii. Identify the key events.
   iv. Are there any events that occur before those of the play, or before scenes, or between them, that are significant and must be honoured?
5. Characters:
   i.   Consider any core motivation for each character.
   ii. What are their wants and needs?
   iii. What might be their moral, religious, cultural, political, or social stances?
   iv. Write a list of character qualities from their actions and behaviour in the play. Find contradictions.
6. Scenic images:
   i.   Draw and/or create an image for each scene.
   ii. Create a small installation of each scene using objects.
7. Practicalities:
   i.   What are the practical problems needed to be solved?
   ii. How can these problems become narrative opportunities?
8. Write a sentence about what the play is about. Not the plot, but your 'core idea'.

Polarity: Auteur directorial concepts versus the 'invisible' director

There is always some form of directorial concept. The 'small c' concept is where the directorial aesthetic may not be as overt, yet there is still a set of choices made and relates to the concept of the 'invisible hand' for Artistic Director of Stockroom Kate Wasserberg, for whom 'the director is essentially invisible. What I and the company have in common is that moments of visual innovation have come necessarily from the text. It's not about me demonstrating my skill or putting something on top of the play. The production grows up and out through the play.' Choices are often finalized by the director of the company. The concept may also relate to the rehearsal methodologies undertaken unique to that director, such as choosing to rehearse using active analysis, or creating a specific rehearsal methodology such as that of Mike Alfreds, which, although giving agency to the acting company, is shaped by a process.

The 'big C' concept relates to the director as auteur, with a vision and a visual aesthetic which becomes a signature. At this extreme polarity, the actor can become a tool in the building of this world.

Between these polarities come nuances and intricacies. Ivo van Hove, like many other directors, articulates that his production choices are born out of the text. However, there is a specific, consistent aesthetic that is created which is evident to many of those examining his oeuvre, much of which has involved long-term collaboration with partner and scenographer Jan Versweyveld. Wherever you work on this continuum, an aesthetic is still born. Van Hove's two working groups is well documented, not least in Bennett and Massai's text *Ivo van Hove: From Shakespeare to Bowie*, published in 2018. I invited van Hove to discuss further his preparation, in terms of interpreting a play prior to rehearsals, and why it is important to him to have an extensive road map of preparation:

> [For] each team, different journeys start. One is the visual dramaturgy: how can we tell the story, tell the characters' stories, give them a life visually? So, the visual dramaturgy is about how to tell the story through meaningful images; that is deeper than just decorating the text. Theatre is a language

of words, but it's also a language of bodies, of spaces, of movements. For me, it's equally important. The visual team creates a document for complicated productions, such as *Network* or *Kings of War*, where the composer writes his notes, as does the video designer, the set designer and sometimes the costume designer. Separately, I've started my dramaturgical sessions thinking: 'What does the play really mean today?' It's the journey to try to understand the text, questioning every line, every character and look at the choices to make. There's never one choice about one moment in the play. If I say, 'I love you' [I] can have ten different intentions. You shouldn't fix and contain, but see the possibilities of the text. This gives a clear intention of what you want with the text, which has to be clear at the start of rehearsal. Rehearsals are like a journey. A director has to say: 'We start in London and go to Edinburgh', but if the whole company ends up in Bristol, then there's a problem. If a director cannot be clear at the beginning of rehearsal what the intentions are content-wise with the text, you're lost.

The directors and designers collaborate

Theresa Heskins states that she aims to work with collaborators with a similar aesthetic to her own and

> to find people who love the same things as I do: who make the work for the audience, plus a love of plot, story and a physicality that is ensemble and complicity driven. This, with an awareness of us making a piece of theatre and that the audience know that they are in a theatre – I'm not interested in creating an illusion of reality for the audience. I'm interested in co-creativity and the collaborators must understand that the audience must play their part in the creative process.

Mike Alfreds, in his approach to the classics, hopes that 'the audience will collaborate in an act of shared imagination by which we suggest what's there and the audience sees what isn't there at all' (Bessell 2001: 3). This resonates with my contention that the final collaborator in any live theatre-making process is the audience who become a character in a classical play, as actors make them a confidant in asides and soliloquies and in pantomime the audience are complicit in the action, often bringing about the denouement of the piece.

Although Heskins has her regular design collaborators, there are key issues that they need to agree on before working together, as

> a beautiful design is a wonderful thing, but if it doesn't accommodate action and is a series of pictures, that won't appeal to me. A dynamic of the space is more important. Costumes that don't allow actors to move but look beautiful don't work for me either. Actors need to be enabled and the relationship between the actor, the space and the audience is the essential thing.

Above all, Heskins sees herself as an enabler, seeing her job as one of 'making everyone else able to do their job very well'. Designer Jessica Curtis and director Kirstie Davis work together whenever they can, since their first collaboration at Watford Palace Theatre on Martin McDonagh's *The Beauty Queen of Leenane* in 2006. Davis notes that site visits play a key part in stimulating a world: 'I went to Leenane and all I could see was mud. I also hate naturalistic sets so the thought of setting the play in a cottage with literal walls would be problematic. Jess made the most beautiful set, with bits of a house on a mud mountain.' Curtis elaborates how, in the production, 'everyone and everything was sunk in it. Since then, everything we do comes from a trigger that's designer friendly. Those triggers are very clear emotionally and atmospherically, as opposed to solid geography. That was bold as an initial offer, looking back and thinking about it.' Davis relates this to the eventual creation of a world which the actors can inhabit spatially, yet at the same time creates a metaphor for the play. Davis states:

> All I saw was mud and mountains, and the next thing I have that in all its glory and more, as everything became symbolic and metaphoric, creating the claustrophobia that I witnessed in Leenane. I find clutter difficult; I like minimalism and like to concentrate on the actors in the space. Actors are the most important thing and we both share that actor-centric philosophy.

Both collaborators are keen to point out that their shared aesthetic starts with the real world, then building on that to create a poetic parallel, whereby, as Davis notes, 'we are often looking for the epic and the personal. The world that the characters inhabit is much bigger than is often shown in the play.' Curtis adds that 'if you're trying to conjure an atmospheric landscape then it's about perspective and scale against your own environment. You can tell so much from something very simple.'

Davis and Curtis work in environments where often they must decide on their designs prior to rehearsals, for the theatres to execute those designs. Gareth Fry notes that 'this also involves key conversations with the producer and production manager to get these into place. The time/money/quality triangle of resources has to be worked with there. The construction of the set often begins before rehearsals begin.' At the ideas stage for designer Max Jones, 'budgets also become a later collaborator, but the initial seeds of the idea don't have a price tag on them'.

So, how to move from ideas to final design? For Curtis, 'to come up with poetic decisions we start in real places, to get the essence of that. All decisions come from talking about the script; that becomes the arbitrator, and we can see those things in the bones of the play.' Davis and Curtis then 'come together and consider those elements. When we meet, we then have a good understanding of the whole play. But initially Kirstie talks in broad terms, then I come back with a mood board, often with colours and textures,' which moves them into the model box stage, where the practicalities are also solved, rather than being left to rehearsal stages. A unique element of their collaboration is that, as Davis notes, they 'always storyboard after the model box. The storyboarding is just before I go into rehearsals.' Intrigued by this, I asked why whether it imposes constrains on decisions, but Curtis explains that this stage allows her to spot any omissions, for 'any gaps to be identified' to 'test the ideas for each scene', without locking those in. Whilst not using the term 'storyboarding', Max Jones thinks of this as, 'alongside the director, plotting the production. I don't like to say the architecture of the show, as architecture suggests bricks and mortar, but it's more in a philosophical sense as you are creating the architecture of the staging, which everyone else responds to.'

Jones begins with his three key collaborators being 'the play, the space and the director, with the director being the primary collaborator. Obviously, the actors become a fourth collaborator later, but at the earlier conceptual stages it's those three key elements.' The first layer of the collaboration is a design conversation after the first read of the play; the first visit to the venue and then 'the first tea or coffee with the director in terms of shared ideas or approaches'. Jones also likes to work with certain directors repeatedly, including Philip Breen and Kate Wasserberg. He discussed how he worked on *Close Quarters*, collaborating with Wasserberg, whom he has

> worked with a number of times, including five years at Theatr Clwyd. We start with a conversation and a shared response to the piece, both sourcing between us where the strength of the piece lies, where the drama is and what we want to emphasise or underscore. We don't start with production answers or images at that point but start with conversations. I can do that over weeks and months before putting pen to paper, finding a shared way of getting under the skin of the work and letting ideas incubate. A longer lead-up time can allow for that fermentation process to take place with a show ticking at the back on your mind; even if you're working on something else, you're still mulling over the show. It really does incubate and by checking in with the director, you see whether either of you have had any further thoughts. But it is that two-way dialogue that is the root of the collaborative process.

For Jones, a major collaborator is the space. Although he is keen to point out that his work is not an installation, it is certainly congruent with the architecture of any space. Personally, when directing *The Wind in the Willows* with designer Mila Sanders at the Birmingham Old Rep in 2016, we worked with the tall vertical lines of the auditorium, which then spilt onto the stage with vertical lines of forest as well as the tall oak panels of Toad Hall. Jones describes what happens when he enters a venue:

> I'm allowing my senses to open for a feeling: I walk in, sit down in the nearest seat I can find for ten minutes and look around. You're tuning into the feel of the space and the potent aspects of theatre architecture. My designs have always had a manipulative quality: to manipulate the venue a little bit and allow the space and the design to intertwine, as opposed to [being] some-thing that is put in. I'm therefore looking at ways of piggybacking onto the venue and incorporating what it has and absorbing that into the world of the performance.

Sound designer Gareth Fry's key collaborators are the

director and writer [for a new play] in the pre-rehearsal and rehearsal stages. If the writer is present for rehearsals, they are often super-useful to discuss themes and concepts with, to talk about their intentions versus their implementation. In the latter case, some of the decisions they made in the writing process are key decisions relating to the themes and plot. Others might be more arbitrary. If we're looking at a scene that is set in a specific location, and perhaps trying to convey a sense of that location is proving difficult to do whilst simultaneously telling other story arcs, we can ask the writer whether the fact that scene is set in a café is a decision [made] because it had to be [set] somewhere, or whether they have a partic-ular reason that [makes it] important. If the former is the case, we can relax trying to do 'café' and perhaps focus on the emotional arc in that scene. During this time, I'm often working with the director and other creative team members to develop our concept for the show and ensure we start rehearsals with clear ideas of what we want to achieve, and the resources in place to do so. The entire creative team needs to have a strong sense of what the final production will be like by the first day of rehearsals, so that we hit the ground running.

Castings: Breakdowns, collaborators and auditions

Harold Clurman's adage of 'cast good actors – and you'll all be good directors' (1972: 64) holds much truth as the actors ultimately become the primary collaborators during a run with the audience. Tamara Harvey was the director of *Home, I'm Darling*, a co-production between the National Theatre and Theatr Clwyd in 2018 and notes that, from the outset, when reading a play, she is

thinking about casting and some projects are led from that from the get-go. In *Home, I'm Darling*, [the writer] Laura Wade and I were setting out to create a play for Katherine Parkinson built around the person. In relation to ethni-cally diverse casting, I think the Equity 'Manifesto for Casting' is fantastic. I hope that I've been working in an ethnically diverse way for a long time, though I'm aware too of how far we have to go. When I was doing *Pride and Prejudice* at Sheffield Crucible [in 2015], we tried to ensure we were diverse in our casting in terms of ethnicity and that became the thing that everyone talked about, in a slightly exhausting way. I hated that it was the only thing people were talking about, as [did] the actors. Michele Austin, playing Mrs Bennett, got frustrated that everyone was talking about the colour of her skin.

Matthew Xia discusses his 2019 inaugural production for the Actors Touring Company, *Amsterdam*, when considering casting. He asks:

Who is going to leave their fingerprints on this piece of work? Let's take Maya Arad Yasur's *Amsterdam*, a play about foreignness in Europe. Otherness, alienation and, of course, the Holocaust sit across it in a massive way. So, it was really crucial for me that everyone in the room cared about those things in their core. I made sure that with people at auditions we talked about the piece, that I was getting enough "Ping! Ping! Ping!" off the pinball machine that is them, and they were connecting to this idea. By the time we went into the rehearsal room, there were people there who identified as LGBTQ+, as traveller, disabled, Jewish, Black, African. Many of the people who would have been viewed by the Nazi regime as undesirables.

A director, working with their casting director, will initially create a casting breakdown, detailing requirements for the role, including any specialist skills required. Tonic Theatre's Lucy Kerbel challenges the industry to rethink these breakdowns, specifically from a gender perspective:

We've been creating a toolkit for UK Theatre as a series of provocations, to try to get a wider variety of people into auditions and therefore on stage. The provocations are for directors in terms of questions about who that character might be. Instead of thinking: 'Police officer, who is he?' let's not jump straight to a white guy who is a policeman. It's not just about gender or race, but what are the qualities of the character that they possess? What is their physicality?

This is particularly pertinent when casting the classics. Echoing Carlson, Kerbel suggests that we need to shift expectations about who Juliet is, for example. When thinking about who the actress is that can play Juliet, if there are pictures that come into my mind, who or what is that based on? Is that replication that has been handed down, or historical baggage that I have accumulated, or is it from the text and the production we want to put on? That form of slowing down thinking may benefit the production, as a phenomenal actor who may have never entered into the audition room would have been overlooked.

The lived experience of the actor needs to be embraced from casting stages. Equity, the British trade union for creative workers for example, has recently been working with organizations representing trans performers to publish a set of guidelines aimed at empowering directors and casting directors in casting more diversely, as well as also seeking to ensure that appropriate language is used and that the right questions are asked of LGBTQ+ performers; trans performers need to be approached for trans roles, so that lived experience brings real depth and understanding. Casting trans performers in cis roles ensures that there is 'invisible' diversity at the heart of the company: both with the company of actors and for the production company. Authentic casting is also part of Ian Manborde's remit at Equity balanced against a need for stretch and flex as

> people should be able to portray diverse roles, other than their own identity and characteristics. With D/deaf and disabled actors, there's too little work and there should be fairness of roles. But on top of that, there aren't enough roles for D/deaf and disabled performers, and these are the highest percentage of our members out of work. This is a political issue for us, but it catalysed a discussion to move away from stereotypical casting. The reverse of this coin was that there wasn't even stereotypical casting, as a disabled actor wasn't cast in the role in the first place. Our work is also often around the type of imagination that is used in casting.

Returning to classical texts, opening up the casting process is important for director Simon Godwin. Writing for *The Stage*, he states that

> it's a natural rebalancing of the canon: our world is half men and half women, so if Shakespeare's world is going to be our world, there has to

be a rebalance. It has to feel as if these are no longer dramas about men, performed by men – that they're dramas that are fighting for their relevance, performed by and for a balanced group of men and women.

(2018)

Kerbel describes how, when she directed Shakespeare, often 'agents would submit clients that they thought would look like Juliet. We are now seeing a much more thoughtful engagement in casting approaches.' Nevertheless, she is keen to point out that 'it's not happening everywhere. There remains a way to go. Change happens gradually.'

Michelle Terry applies the term 'anti-literal casting' to ensure there is a rebalancing of casting for classical roles. At the Globe she can

liberate and illuminate this canon. There is something [in their] very nature, some plays more than others, that [are] anti-literal. *A Midsummer Night's Dream* is by its very essence anti-literal as, as far as I know, I'm not aware of any fairies, pucks, gods or goddesses walking on the earth. So, through the prism of the protean art form, [Shakespeare] is asking us to question our own ability to be mercurial and fluid. We all have the capacity to be envious, jealous, ambitious, cruel, loving, kind. Shakespeare frames most of his plays metatheatrically and he never apologizes for the art form or tries to disguise theatre as anything other than theatre. Part of the function of anti-literal casting is a purely theatrical gesture. Theatre has been appropriated by realism and naturalism, so we are attempting to liberate a different type of theatre again.

Terry's call to think differently about casting is echoed by Jenny Sealey, Artistic Director of Graeae Theatre. When founded in 1980 by Nabil Shaban and Richard Tomlinson, one of the initial aims of the company was to shatter myths and misconceptions about disability. Describing themselves as 'led by D/deaf and disabled people pioneering a new inclusive dramatic language' (Graeae 2020), their work enables theatre stories to be told through integrated casting and with disabled and D/deaf actors as integral storytellers. Referring to the company's 2017 co-production of *The House of Bernarda Alba* with Manchester Royal Exchange, Sealey notes that the moment she casts a play is where [it's] all thrown into the air. Kathryn Hunter as the matriarch had two deaf daughters, the eldest and youngest; I just cast the best actors for the job. It so happened they were both deaf, so I then thought: 'Does Bernarda sign?' I decided that she's fluent, but only choses when to sign, and the power that comes with that. It was a glorious finding.

Narrative possibilities were thus generated. Essentially, Sealey 'needs good actors in a good play', alongside the artistic mission of weaving access into every production, as 'if the two actors hadn't been deaf in *Bernarda Alba*, it would have been a different production. It's precarious as a director, as the casting can always take the play in another direction. There is always a spontaneity. It's exciting.'

Alongside the need for the industry to embrace non-literal approaches to casting and what that may unlock, it is essential in the wake of the #MeToo movement, which aims to combat sexual harassment and abuse and to expose sex crimes committed by those in positions of power, that the casting breakdown articulates, alongside other requirements such as ability to play musical instruments, singing and stage fighting, what intimacy may be required of the actor. Sometimes a play may contain no scripted intimacy, but a production of it may choose to include intimate scenes. Intimacy director Yarit Dor works with directors, to

help to advise on ways to consider how to offer more of a safe space in auditions; what to ask actors, how to clarify for actors what the intimacy or simulated actions might include. Performers can then truly consider what whether they wish to engage in the show and know what's expected of them. [It's the] same for the agents; they need to know exactly what is written down; what the current position of the director in relation to the intimacy scenes [is]; what body parts may be on show; what the audience configuration [is] and if there is simulated sex then what kind of action will their client be expected to perform. All of this then gets communicated to an agent, so the performer knows all of this before they sign the contract. All of this is clear, transparent and clarified.

Dor insists that directors shouldn't be constrained in terms of making all the decisions in advance and that at a basic level they can communicate what they are thinking of doing; it doesn't have to be chiselled in stone. There can be room for new ideas in the rehearsal room – that is the nature of ensemble or company after all. Not all directors can give info so detailed in advance, they need the shared brainstorming process with the actors. It is however super important to state that the character may need to perform kissing, physical touch, making out/groping, nudity and/or simulated sex (plus whether any of it is non-consensual) and that this will be discussed with them so boundaries and how it is rehearsed and performed is clear and agreed by all parties. That helps to highlight the collaborative nature and that the production team is fully aware and sensitive to how intimacy should involve the actor from start to finish.

The other alternative would be, unannounced, to ask the actor to undertake this in rehearsals, which may result in them retreating to a place of fear rather than safely exploring the intimacy scenes as required of both the play and the production concept.

Directors and actors collaborate intensely in the rehearsal room and, I argue, need to share a theatre-making philosophy and overall methodology, ethos and values, if not actual methods. Heskins will

> look for the same with actors as with creative teams. For me, it's about the space between the performers and then the space between them and the audience, plus an awareness of that space. My cast should all the time be thinking about: 'How can I make what you're doing fun and make an offer you can find joy in, so the audience can find joy in that?' Those actors are wonderful. They also need to have an awareness of their body in space and their physicality; like the Liverpool football team, where [the] person who has the ball knows where all the others are at any one time, without even turning around. I love actors who know where their other team members are, they know where each other are, they've got each other's back and they know where to pass the ball.

As Heskins works with an ensemble visual storytelling approach, it's important that her actors can work within that frame and the audition becomes the core event in discovering that alignment. Heskins, however, does not undertake workshop auditions as for her there's something I find about workshop-based auditions that becomes a little bit of a competition that makes me feel uncomfortable. [Participants] feel they have to fight someone else for a job, and how is that collaboration? It feels to me it's a contradiction in terms to come into a room and collaborate with people who might get the job instead of [you]. So, I do a conventional twenty minutes: three minutes chatting, then a bit of time on the text and then I ask them if they have questions at the end. Some people are amazed by that, but I feel it's right that they should interview me as well. And if there is something in the piece that's rigorous and complicated physically and another creative's work might suffer by having a cast that doesn't have the right skills then I will workshop then, like a fight, or ballroom dancing workshop. And then the actor also knows what's required of them.

Member of the Casting Directors' Guild, Nicky Bligh, gives an example of how an actor got a job at a casting, 'because he had done his research on the show and knew from the scene he was asked to prepare, who he was talking to, the backstory and as a result he knew how to pitch the comedy. There was an assuredness to the performance, without me filling in the blanks for him.' Although she states that 'how actors prepare for a casting is their own responsibility and what suits one will not suit another', her main advice is that an actor needs to be

as prepared as possible. Some people say: 'Don't learn it', so you're flexible for direction and some people prefer to learn it. Every actor has their own method. Actors shouldn't be afraid to ask questions and say in the room: 'I'm sorry; this didn't make sense to me. Can I check this?' or 'I've got two different ways to do this part: what would you prefer?' Actors should take ownership of their own audition. We are looking forward to what they bring to the role; what thoughts and creative ideas they may have. We may think that a role has to be performed or thought about in a certain way but actually it could be done differently, and we really enjoy seeing what the actor brings to the room.

Ian Manborde highlights the need to combat inappropriateness in the casting process: 'sometimes there have been inappropriate questions asked; from the Equity Women's Committee, there are problems with questions around age, pregnancy and maternity. All of which have reduced as a result of introducing the *Manifesto for Casting*.

Exercise: Questions and provocations for the director approaching the casting process

1. Which of the methods in Tonic Theatre's 'Theatre Casting Toolkit'[2] can be useful to you when planning the overall casting process, including prompts to ensure diversity, how the space could be used and other legal considerations?
2. Have you consulted Equity's Inclusive Casting Policy[3] when writing the breakdown? This challenges you to think of the actor's personal characteristics as incidental only to the role.
3. How are you going to structure the audition process to ensure there is enough time to ascertain skills or to discuss the play? Is there time to find out about each other and processes of working?
4. Is there enough time for co-collaborators to undertake their work?
5. How are you going to create an environment in which actors can give their best work?
6. Have you used the Equity Casting Questions sheet[4] to explore the dos and don'ts of appropriate questioning? For example, you can discuss playing age, but not actual age.
7. Have you used Equity's LGBT+ Guide[5] that supports the industry on approaching casting and auditions in relation to supporting trans performers?
8. Do you need to articulate the ways in which you will be rehearsing? Tamara Harvey notes that, 'for *Orpheus Descending*, there's a particular way I want to do it so I'm having those conversations in the audition room, as if the actors aren't up for it, then it isn't going to work'.

Combatting the traditional casting process

Michelle Terry is aiming to work differently in regard to casting. At the beginning of her rehearsal period, she has 'a very intersectional company and I have no

---

[2] https://www.theatrecastingtoolkit.org/tools/.

[3] https://www.equity.org.uk/getting-involved/campaigns/play-fair/equity-inclusive-casting-policy/.

[4] https://www.equity.org.uk/media/3286/equity_casting-questions.pdf.

[5] https://www.equity.org.uk/media/3465/equity_lgbt-casting-guide.pdf.

idea who will play what'. As artistic director, she chooses the season, but she does not direct; rather, she remains an actor. For Terry, 'how casting happens is important', and she states that this cannot be based simply on whether

> you have done the most or have the most experience. Alongside questions of equality, we also need to be looking at equitability. There are so many barriers to access when it comes to theatre and particularly to Shakespeare. We're not all starting from the same place. So how do you look at new systems, structures, ways of working that enable and empower more people to enter the rehearsal. And then once people are there, how do you continue to create safe and brave spaces for diverse minds, hearts, bodies, ways of working. Where do you put the centre of the room? The famous person? The director? Or the play? So [I am looking at] how we put the play back at the centre of the room, which means that the casting has to be [done] differently. With the Ensemble work, we are casting people who are up for the process as much as the play. . . . Where does your nature meet the alchemy of this play, at this time, with these people? How can you bring all of you to the play without cancelling out, or appropriating yourself to fit preconceived ideas about the plays? That's hard with Shakespeare because we have over four hundred years of preconceived ideas and judgements! That's where the work on decolonising the plays and the rehearsal room begins, shifting the power imbalance. For example, as the artistic director there is a power that comes with that role, and a natural assumption is that I will play Katherina [in *The Taming of the Shrew*] for example. But I will almost certainly not. My nature in the room with the alchemy with the rest of the company may well lead us and the play somewhere entirely different. So, how do we continue to diversify the room, the imaginations contributing to the room, and put the needs of the play at the centre of the work, continuously asking: why this play, why now, why this theatre and why this group of people? That's the alchemy of the hive mind that continues to ensure Shakespeare remains authentic and necessary.

As with all his work, Matthew Xia begins by asking the central question, 'how does the work reflect the world back at itself?' When directing *Into the Woods* for Manchester Royal Exchange in 2015, Xia describes how it struck him that we're setting this on the outskirts of Manchester, somewhere like Alderley Edge, that has a lot of folk history and magic in and around it. Here's Little Red Riding Hood. She's anyone. She's a young woman who wanders into the woods and gets lost. And she is on the edge of a sexual awakening, because I think if we look back into the psychology of the fairy tales, there's a lot of that going on, strangers in the woods: amorous, vicious men, who want to devour you in a number of different ways. 'Be careful, as you walk through the woods!' says mother. So, who is she? All she needs to be is to be able to play a certain age and have a technical ability to hit this note that Sondheim has written in the middle of this song.

Once those conclusions are reached, Xia then invites into the casting process 'everyone who is within that, and is interesting; I'm not sitting there with a chart, going: "Have we got four East Asians, two Asians, two Jamaicans, and a Nigerian?" I'm just going: "What does the world look like?" I want the end result to look like the world.' When asked to expand how he achieves this practically, Xia points out that it is an ongoing process. If, along the way, the makeup of the cast is culturally 'heavy, in a particular place, I address that, as we move through the process, and by going to the protagonist quite quickly and making a radical – and it doesn't feel radical to me, but the world might think it is – intervention into the casting'. Meeting criticism of these casting choices from certain quarters, Xia states that

I will always achieve excellence because I will only bring excellent people into the room. I'll bring five hundred, Black, excellent people into the room. I never use the phrases 'colour-blind' and 'gender-blind' because I'm not asking you to imagine that they don't have colour, that you can't see their gender. Nor am I asking you to take their colour or gender to be what is assumed to be default, which is white and male: I want you to see all of it. I want you to be aware that they are an actor in a space – pretending. What some people do is to think: 'this character was written as this. Therefore, it must be this, forever'. Which again, just feels bizarre. It feels like they've not understood the liveness of the form of the work.

To create a culture of casting conscious of colour is the way in which, as Justin Emeka puts it, theatre-makers 'invite the audience to recognise the character as a Black person within the world of the play and incorporate this dynamic into their understanding of the story' (Luckett and Shaffer 2017: 94). Actors, at auditions, should be able to own their lived experience. When casting a character who has traditionally been played by a white male, there is an inherent danger of 'whitening' the part by ignoring colour and not having explicit conversations at auditions and in rehearsals. To do so, 'forces people of colour to function in an environment where their culture must be left outside of the rehearsal room' (ibid.: 103–4).

Actor preparation pre-rehearsal

Antony Sher's notion in his 2018 memoir *The Year of the Mad King: The Lear Diaries*, that rehearsals begin for the actor long before the physical encounter with the rehearsal room and the director, is useful to shift thinking about *when* rehearsals start. Gary Sloan exclaims: 'Hold on. Adjustment. There isn't *any* time spent with script that is *outside* of rehearsal! [An actor's] time with the script is the *heart* of . . . rehearsal' (2012: 17; Sloan's emphases), suggesting that there is no separation between the sub-rehearsal and the formal rehearsal.

Sub-rehearsals begin with

> the actor's first private read through of their text which should be under-
> taken with [a] level of anticipation and excitement. . . . [We should] enjoy
> a first encounter with the text, story and character: the character we are
> about to inhabit, the character whose energies we will allow to penetrate
> our incarnate selves. (Harrison 2019: 3)

Every piece of information informs an actor's impression of the text they will embody. This also includes details from the casting director and the breakdown, knowledge of the playing style, production frames or the world.

In relation to the polarity of 'to plan versus not to plan', one issue that remains contentious is that of line learning. One thing is certain: if a rehearsal process requires you not to learn the lines, then you must not. Several experiential rehearsal methodologies, including Stanislavski's active analysis, invite you into the words of the text through structured improvisational techniques, which would not work were you to know the lines. Knowing what rehearsal strategies are being embraced is necessary. Some actors like to be word-perfect (whilst assigning lines neutrally) to be able to be present with their fellow actors and not have their heads in a script, especially true for comedies, pantomimes and working with puppetry. Some prefer to be familiar only with the text on day one and consolidate in the evenings. This also depends on you, your working style, home responsibilities and memory. However, most directors require for you to be 'off book' by the middle of a rehearsal period, regardless of whether this is a week, a month, or three months, in order that the company can connect and experience.

Exercise: An actor's first encounter with the play (developed with Richard Cheshire)

1. Locate the given circumstances for your character: the undisputed, categorical facts:
   i. What does the playwright say about you? In the introduction to the published play, stage directions or past interviews. If working with a playwright, ask them directly.
   ii. What do other characters say about you and why?
   iii. What do you say about yourself?
2. Build some imagined circumstances:
   i. What are your character's qualities or characteristics they display? Find all the contradictions and explore what events may trigger a shift from, for example, great compassion to great jealousy.
   ii. Create a small installation from objects that your character would possess, or ones which relate to their world. Add in music choices.
   iii. What are any potential inner (e.g. guilt or self-doubt) or outer (e.g. another character, war, or poverty) obstacles?
   iv. What might be your core motivation?
   v. How does the play or role relate to your lived experience?
3. Concepts and ideas.
   i. Is the character's name a clue to an acting choice?
   ii. Think of your character functionally. Why are they there? What do they do? If you removed them from the play, what would be missed?

iii. How does the character's world view, opinions and values differ or align to yours?

iv. Find out the directorial frames, or the world within which you will be operating; how might this potentially affect your choices? How might the genre of the play affect any preparation?

4. Events.

   i. Identify key events in your scenes. How might they change you?

   ii. Are there any events that occur before the span of the play, or between scenes, which are significant? Do some imaginative daydreaming about what these might be.

The director's overall rehearsal philosophy and methodology

One part of the director's pre-production thinking concerns how the rehearsal period will be structured. Theresa Heskins wants actors to be

> able to live the rest of their lives and not be completely dedicated to the show. There may be a Saturday to see family, or [the chance to] drop their kids at school on a Monday, or go to the doctors, then come to us. I don't like the idea that actors are at our beck and call and, at 6.00 pm the day before, they jump to it, learning lines around the edge of the call. Planning is so important. I've also learnt that if I want a particular choreographer or fight director and I've planned it six months before, I'll get the right collaborators in the room.

Tamara Harvey is keen to move away from the traditional 10.00 am to 6.00 pm structure and is 'scheduling in advance, with a shorter day and a shorter break where possible. At auditions, I'll [ask] actors about their caring responsibilities and life pressures. In the audition room they sit forward in response to that – it's still unusual to be asked.' Harvey is keen to ensure, however, that there is inbuilt flexibility. The polarity of 'to plan versus not to plan' must oscillate for her, as she makes sure that

> the actors know it might change, due to costume fittings, outside auditions, and all those other things. But I say: 'Here's the schedule for the whole

rehearsal process and we are grown-ups, so if it has to change, we talk about that'. So that does something to everyone's agency in the room. It's also about everyone's right to have a life, to make that life equal to, if not more important than, the work we are doing.

Outsiders have the impression that Heskins's work is improvised, but this isn't the case, as

the piece is so rigorously planned. The only thing I haven't planned before rehearsal is the solution. I plan the journey we will go on to find the solution. Instead of sitting down approaching it [in terms of] how I'll direct a scene, I'll think about when I'll direct it. I then think about the how. Will a dense scene need a lot of table work, or is it simple? Or is it seemingly simple and the choreography underneath it will be complex?

It takes a bold director to disrupt the traditional structure of how to work, particularly if freelancing for a company with historical working conditions. I encourage graduates creating their own companies not to appropriate the rehearsal structures of others but create new ways of working. As the 'tone setter' of a rehearsal room, the director has the responsibility of establishing these and building creative-friendly environments.

Rehearsal structures and methods are chosen specifically to unlock further meanings within the frames established. In relation to the genre, overall rehearsal structures will shift accordingly. I direct pantomime out of sequence, beginning with complex musical numbers and slapstick routines in the first few days, allowing maximum time for embodiment. Opera often begins with music rehearsals, as does actor-musicianship, with the learning of scores. Actors in comedy and farce voice their frustrations at directors who sit around the table for too long: I roughly staged a production of Brandon Thomas's *Charley's Aunt* within the first four days of rehearsals in order to time entrances, exits, gags and physical slapstick. For pieces that employ psychological realism there may be specific skills, such as military training, that need to be undertaken and scheduled. Each genre, play and production will suggest its own process.

Exercise: Choosing rehearsal methodologies and structures

Overall structure:

- Consider how you would like to structure your working week. Do you want to work for an intense four-hour period each day, allowing time for actors to prepare beforehand and to consolidate afterwards?
- How will you structure rehearsals to allow time for actors to embrace sub-rehearsal work?
- How do the specific caring and parental responsibilities of your company affect structuring?
- When might you put in stumble-throughs, stagger-throughs and run-throughs (of short sections, acts and the entire piece), to achieve flow?
- When do you want your actors to be finally 'off book'? This, along with other expectations, needs to be communicated to your company.

Methodologies:

- Take a play you want to direct. How might the genre of the piece influence decisions?
- Do you want to rehearse out of sequence? Or will the cumulative effect of the narrative be important to follow?
- Which collaborators do you want in the room and for how long? Musical directors, arrangers, choreographers, vocal or accent coaches, movement directors, fight directors, intimacy directors, designers or other specialists (such as academics or military experts) will all need to be scheduled. What budgetary implications will this have?
- Do you have an overall rehearsal methodology? This is the overarching strategy or philosophy you are using.
- Could you base your rehearsal methods (i.e. rehearsal exercises) around practitioners? You might direct using Michael Chekhov's psycho-physical work. Know whose shoulders you are standing upon.

A summary of Chapter 3

The maxim would have it that all beginnings are difficult; this may be even more so in cases where it is difficult to pinpoint where the beginning is. Before setting foot in the rehearsal room itself there is often much work to be undertaken, and many decisions to be made, by all collaborators, particularly the director. This is especially true where economic constraints proscribe the actual amount of time allowed in the physical rehearsal toom itself. This, again, links to the notion of the director steering and guiding the production: those interviewed tend towards the 'invisible hand', rather than overtly embracing the concept of the auteur director, even in the case of directors recognized by a distinct aesthetic, or an especial high concept that carries across productions. Artistic and aesthetic considerations must be balanced with practical ones, such as how the working day in the rehearsal room is structured. Again, the keystones here are both collaboration and uniqueness, in terms of locating and defining the world, both through practicalities identified by collaborators from other disciplines and the demands of the genre, whose codes must be cracked and interpreted. The complexities of auditions and casting have been interrogated: the majority of those interviewed have indicated the need for addressing traditional models, to promote a more inclusive, less limiting approach which seeks to widen narrative possibilities just as it seeks to diversify the company to reflect the world in which we live and embrace the lived experiences of individuals. Safety is also a keystone concept here for many interviewees: balancing the demands of the piece with the vision of the director and the paramount well-being of the performers. The specific preparation undertaken by actors prior to entering the rehearsal room is, as has been seen, as various and unique to the individual as the preparation undertaken by directors and other creatives. Following the next interview, Chapter 4 moves us into the rehearsal room proper, where each collaborator brings with them a personal backpack of pre-rehearsal preparation.

Interview: Rufus Norris and Katrina Lindsay on their collaborative process

Rufus Norris is Artistic Director of the National Theatre. I met with him and one of his major collaborators, designer Katrina Lindsay, in the summer of 2019 on London's South Bank. This interview is given more or less in full due to the natural dialogue between the two.

Katrina, you talk about creating a 'world' and Rufus, you've spoken about not being a 'visionary' and that you embrace the collaborative nature of rehearsals. Could you talk me through how your pre-rehearsal work operates?

Katrina Lindsay: Usually it's to do with the story you're about to tell, and the ideas contained within the script. Rufus and I then meet and chat about that. A lot of it is about emotional journeys. . . . There has to be some heart, or an emotional drive behind it. If it's not there, we try to find it as we need to give that to the audience. Following that, we'll be timetabling the process to meet the design deadlines often many months ahead. Rufus is always sketching as we are talking, and I do that more privately. I tend to write notes and then I'll be by myself when I draw.

Rufus Norris: The challenge is [going] from content to form. The content is what is underneath the story and at the heart of it. Sometimes the content is not necessarily what the writer has written, but what is underneath that. . . . When you get stuck is [when] you have a great idea, [but] it's not what the heart of the piece is. We both draw, as it's a visual medium, it's not an intellectual medium; we are summoning up a total experience and trying to think of the people and objects in space.

Katrina Lindsay: Yes, it's the moment you are capturing, and drawing makes you think about a moment as animated, rather than intellectualizing it. When you draw it, you conjure up in your imagination what the moment might be on stage. That's not necessarily the scenery, it could be about two people talking, or where they come in from. It helps you establish the rhythm of the piece.

Rufus Norris: Katrina normally brings a lot of visual imagery, which relates to the feeling of something, as part of the atmosphere or capturing a moment. We've done over thirty-five shows together and one of my flaws is that I try to endgame it, thinking, 'it's this' and Katrina says: 'I don't know', until we've been through every bit. What the show is emerges after we've gone through that. I always resist that, but Katrina's always right. Once you've done that, the ideas that emerge are tested against the real structure of whatever the content is.

So, the sketches could be pragmatic, or about people, or entrances and exits? Is it also expressionistic, from the text, or from other visuals?

Katrina Lindsay:	They start as stick people, but then I add mood also. I am always trying to find out what the atmosphere, the feeling and the tone of the piece is. Until I understand that, I can't make the design very solid. I need to have those things. I am always looking for the feeling that we are trying to give to an audience, and what the tone is. These are hard things to answer, before you bring everything together. When Rufus says he's not a visual director, that's not true; he's saying he doesn't have a big concept. It's not: 'This is my big idea.'

Is it more of a case of collaborative decision to come up with the concept?

Rufus Norris:	There's never a big concept.
Katrina Lindsay:	But there's always a moment when you say something and that's what you're interested in and why you want to do this piece.

And you're attuned to that moment?

Katrina Lindsay:	I do ask Rufus 'why?' quite a lot. 'Why do you want to do this?'
Rufus Norris:	One of the real values of working with someone you know very well is that you don't bullshit. I don't feel we ever get lazy or take shortcuts. Every show requires a different process. When we started working together in 1992, we put in many years where the only thing we got out of it was the value of the work being good or not. We were skint for a long time. However fancy we think we might be now, with Katrina in Australia doing *Harry Potter* and me running this building, we still find the time to have proper conversations and Skype calls. The intent for us is always to make the work as meaningful as possible.

Have those core principles you started out with been kept, despite the scale changing? What has kept you together?

Rufus Norris:	Honesty. The work we like is theatrical, but not in a showy way. Some of the work we've done, such as

	London Road, has been quite contained and not flashy. . . . Our latest piece is *Small Island*. . . . There's no way you can throw scenery at that to solve the challenges of the stage directions. You have to keep the pace going in the piece. Katrina and I also have quite a low boredom threshold, so we both like dynamism.
Katrina Lindsay:	Even when we had no money, we always tried to be theatrical with everything we tried to tell. I remember during an early workshop with Rufus thinking: 'This is what I've been waiting for; someone who understands how to play'. Playing and discovery is key to the work that we do. We share the sense of play, excavation and discovery.
Rufus Norris:	If you're exploring, it's useful to have two heads; one saying: 'Let's do this', and one to sit back and see it. I might be focusing on one area, and Katrina may say: 'What's much more interesting is what's happening over there'. . . . It's a new perspective. You can stand back and see it differently.
Katrina Lindsay:	I still worry, as sometimes I want to solve something in the model box, but Rufus wants to do it on its feet and then in that process it makes sense to me. You put yourself both in the arena and then step back and watch it also.

Does that happen both in pre-rehearsal work and on the rehearsal room floor?

Katrina Lindsay:	It's mainly in the rehearsal period or workshops before.
Rufus Norris:	And then in the theatre with an audience. Almost every show we've done has been in a flexible space, like the studio we started in, or the Dorfman or the Young Vic, or indeed the Olivier. We've done half a dozen shows in there and that's a nightmare of a space, as you often have to remake things again. With *Small Island* there have been quite major changes about the scenography, thinking what works, what doesn't, then saying sorry and rework. One of the pressures we've had over the last few years is a lack of time together, so you come in with a plan. Changing a plan later is easier than starting a plan when the clock is ticking.

As you know each other so well, does a look or a gesture allow you to cut through the bullshit and not waste time?

Rufus Norris: We can be a couple of old curmudgeons at times, but there's an inherent trust, to do with a shared mutual respect and aesthetic and a belief in what theatre is about from an emotional perspective, rather than an intellectual one.

Returning to theatricality and a shared aesthetic, when I look at the theatricality of your work, it's always absolutely anchored to the text. It never feels imposed.

Rufus Norris: That comes from the content. For me, you can read the play, and know it takes place in a marketplace and a house and a police cell. You could say: 'Let's design the marketplace, the house and the police cell.' There are various literal environments, but [you need to think] about the whole cosmology. That's what the play is about. . . . You [need to] get underneath where [the writer] is writing from, to dig in and understand what they're talking about. When you get in there, you realize that everything has a spirit. A building has a spirit, a table has an energy. Then you start to think about that and realize a table can be animate and then you make an actor a table. If you look at [it from] a British perspective, you think a table cannot be animate, but [from] the Nigerian one, it has a spirit. There was a text that Katrina found, a piece of West African cosmology that unlocked it for me. Two people had gone over to Africa and were studying different belief systems through ceremony. They spoke to a priest and asked what he thought of the West [viewing it all as] hocus pocus, but the priest said: 'You cannot explain sight to a blind person.' . . . On one research trip to Nigeria we were coming back from a slave port and we had an hour's journey, which became six hours. It was incredibly frustrating, crawling through the heat in the traffic jams. I was getting increasingly distressed, as our plan to visit a market at the end of the day wasn't going to happen and I wanted to use every minute that we had. Katrina said: 'Look around you',

	and as it got dark, you realized that there were no street lights, [but a] sense of dark blackness beyond the human construct. There is just eternity. That really unlocked the design of it.
Katrina Lindsay:	For me, theatricality is about engaging the imagination of an audience. We know we are starting a journey and we are going to take them, through their imagination, into whatever we are going to do with the play. We use these tools to get into somebody's imagination. That's what theatre does more than anything else. We both understand and share that; it excites us and makes us like kids again. . . I'm on this journey where things surprise me.
Rufus Norris:	It's very childlike in an unashamed way. I'm not embarrassed about that. It's great.
Katrina Lindsay:	If it's great, you've been in this experience and theatre can do that, rather than other mediums.

How important is it that a production concept creates a world which engages with contemporary theatregoers?

Rufus Norris:	When I read something for the first time, I'm asking: 'Do I feel that it's got something to say?' That doesn't mean it has to be about Trump or Brexit. But it needs to resonate. The classics resonate; that's why they are classics. *London Road* is about community and really about the state of the nation in another way. With *Small Island*, when that was programmed, the Windrush scandal hadn't happened, Brexit hadn't happened. Now it feels massively prescient. [But even] before that, we both felt an extraordinariness about it.
Katrina Lindsay:	Instinctively it's tied into why we are doing this, why [we are] interested in this play.
Rufus Norris:	In a simple way, you ask: 'Why do it?' . . . Finding a personal and emotional way into the play makes it a direct route. And then: 'Why do it in theatre as opposed to another medium?' Finding out [what] celebration of theatricality this piece, in this medium, can allow. I don't ask those explicitly but instinctively, [but] they are good to fall back on if you get stuck a lot.

Rufus, you've commented in the past of the 'primacy of the writer'.
Could you expand on what you mean by this?

Rufus Norris: The idea of a director is a fairly recent one. ... You need some words and someone to speak them, really. Everything we do around that can elevate and celebrate that, but when I've seen work [that features] a strong conceptual imposition on a play [and that concept] doesn't feel born of the play, I find it very difficult to emotionally engage with it. I might find it fascinating visually, and that's where some people might find their way in. [You need] a character with a dilemma and a challenge, a human, where we can step into their shoes and think: 'How are they getting around that?' or 'Blimey, there's a truth in their story I recognize'. But if there's no dilemma, there's no story. So, it's about stating the obvious: the writer is the creative source but it doesn't mean you can't bring more to the production. You can have a complex story with no words. Someone wants something and takes action to achieve it, which results in consequences or dilemmas; that goes back to the Greeks, obviously.

Katrina Lindsay: Is the writer always in control of that?

Rufus Norris: Normally they are. Our roles are interventionalist [in terms of] the storytelling and we can enhance and find stuff that's not there. The kernel is always in the story, though.

Katrina Lindsay: We come from a culture where the writer has been 'the thing' in this country, that is seen as the creative source in theatre but I don't think it's now the writing, the text, that is the only 'thing'. Like Rufus says you can have and tell, a complex story without words. I don't believe the starting source is explored enough. Other mediums contribute in a really strong way, and yet they're not seen as a driving force or as the starting point in the telling of a story. If someone wants something and takes action to achieve it – can this only be explored through writing and words? The exploration between dramaturgy, scenography and other forms is barely discussed, yet we centrally rely on this all the time when making theatre. This has not been explored yet much in our world of theatre because we come from a culture, historically, where the work or the story has been born out of the text (a play) and therefore the writer. A story can be told through visuals, sound, action as much as through words. Therefore the 'author' of a work could be a person whose language is one of visuals or sound as much as one of words, which doesn't automatically mean the work will be conceptual if it is not born out of text/writing. Is the dilemma only conveyed in the writing, in the words? I think in theatre, which is ultimately storytelling, it is how any of these components are put together that tells the story, conveys the dilemma. Is theatre a form that is just about plays? I don't think so. I would say it is storytelling and so it doesn't just have to be the words or the writer that is the primary author or starting source of any given story/piece of theatre. Words and writing are good and useful in stories, but they are tools as much as any other medium in the piece. I think for me it is the difference between writing and what it is to be an author/creator of a story. I don't feel it is always the writer that has to be the creative source of a story. The primacy is that of the story itself which doesn't always have to originate from writing and words.

Rufus Norris: Often the worst of theatre is when there's a conflict between the source material and the production. It can be quite jarring.

Why do you direct, or design?

Rufus Norris: The playful thing we were talking about is so important. The theatre medium is unique in the combination of inviting an audience into an imaginative playground and having quite an intense emotional relationship to it ... Working in theatre [is] quite high-octane and intense, the rhythm is up and down, the medium keeps evolving. And it's really collaborative. You are surrounded by great thinkers and imaginations and most people are there for the same reason. It's a really lucky way to spend your life.

Katrina Lindsay: Definitely, the sense of play, and engaging our imaginations and then drawing the audience into that, that's very important. Every project is different. It's a very human endeavour. I want audiences to forget themselves and be kids again.

4

First steps of the rehearsal

'Irun a rehearsal room based on trust, people have to get on with what they need to do. It's collaborative and democratic. I try to be [that way]. It doesn't always happen. But the buck does stop with me, and that terrifies me.' Graeae's Jenny Sealey establishes a firm credo for her practice and now we take our first steps into a physical rehearsal process which concerns establishing an ethos and rehearsal room values. What is meant by a rehearsal room 'break-through' is also considered in depth, and some initial exercises are provided as a way of establishing ensemble conditions.

But why should the 'buck stop' with the director, as Sealey suggests? The final piece is ultimately a product, driven by commercial factors and attached to that are conditions of production. Everyone invested in the theatre-making process is aware of the opening night's looming date and time, boldly emblazoned on all publicity material. Ric Knowles, Professor of Drama at the University of Guelph, and author of *Reading the Material Theatre*, asserts against a backdrop of cultural materialism that any creative choices made are bounded by economic and commercial conditions that impact on the work. For Knowles, it becomes difficult to truly take risks, as the notion of 'production, as product [means that] the possibilities for transgression or subversion linger only in the fissures amongst the various processes and practices' (2004: 31). The imposition of strict deadlines means that any transgressions in these fissures may only be possible in certain rehearsals and, as Sealey reminds us, 'we are bound by the rules of normative theatre' and the rigour and discipline is attached to that. Structuring a rehearsal process that aligns a personal ethos and ways of working with the need to 'open the product on time' can be a challenge. As the work in the rehearsal room 'amounts to more than eighty per cent of the creative process of mounting a production' (Knowles 2004: 67), how artists shape that space in terms of its values, ethos and methodologies begins prior to the first day in the room. Michelle Terry is aware of both the materialist nature of theatre with committing to change how rehearsals operate. She exclaims that every rehearsal is about

> hurtling towards the product. The ensemble nature [created as the under-pinning philosophy for a season] was to self-referentially say that we are also trying to practice, and to ask how can you have conversations about process as much as product. Can you have rehearsal rooms where you question who holds the leadership position at any moment? How can you have multidisciplinary expertise, plurality in the room where the agenda is of course to make the work but stay in process as we go? Where is the centre and the focus?

The early stages need to build on that and lay out the direction of travel, both in spirit and in deed.

Ensemble making and tone setting

> An actor's job then is to turn the psychology of a character into physical action. In other words, an actor needs to break down the intellectual infor-mation obtained from the text and their imagination, including thoughts and feelings and translate this information into the physical action of the character in a narrative.
>
> (Zybutz and Farquharson 2016: 76)

If the actor's role in rehearsal is as described above, then the directorial role is to ensure that an actor can be willing vulnerable in a safe and inclusive environment. The word 'ensemble' is used often in relation to a safe rehearsal room, but we must create the conditions for safe and consensual willing vulnerability. Maria Shevtsova helpfully points out that Stanislavski's notion of ensemble 'was a matter of like-minded people with a "common goal", who wanted to be together and were fully dedicated to making theatre permanently together according to this goal' (2020: 7). When forming a company, wanting to be together as a collective is common. When a new production is being mounted with a nascent ensemble, it must find a common way of working, structured around a shared set of values. It is incumbent on the director, as the 'tone setter' of rehearsal, to ensure that actors are empowered to take ownership of the creative process. As Ken Rea reminded me, 'the director can be on the first plane out of town if it's a disaster, but the actors have to hold the production together. Therefore, they have got to find a way of coming together.'

Actor trainer Wyn Jones aims to establish this during training, in terms of how actors think about preparing for their work:

> I'm also trying to get them to understand that the time the rehearsal starts is not the time you walk through the door. That you are always ready to work. It's not just being dressed, it's about the room being ready. On Wednesday I walked into a session and said: 'I'm walking into something here, what am I walking into?' It was a proper working atmosphere.

When questioned as to why this link was important, Jones goes on to say that he is 'quite big on atmosphere and not bringing too much clutter with you. There should be a sense of play when they're not being judged by others or by me.'

The director often encourages the actor to 'let go' in their work, and if the director is likened to a parent who should 'let go' in a more literal sense, then the ownership of the production must move from the director to the actor in the building of the ensemble. In the early stages, there is more dependence on the director, but from the outset, it is understood that the handover of ownership has begun for actors to have ultimate agency. Taking Stanislavski's idea that 'every actor must be [their] own director' (2008: 113), and placing this alongside Katie Mitchell's goal, which is 'for the actors to be self-directing ... [and] able to come off stage after a performance and assess what they have done' (2009: 186), suggests that directors need to find strategies to ensure that actors are self-directing, reflective practitioners through rehearsals.

When Stanislavski directed, he 'pretended ignorance in order to force the actor's independent decision. [Maria Knebel] called it his "pedagogical cunning"' (Carnicke 2009: 203); here actors feel an ownership of a moment, even if they have been led there directorially. From my experience, making explicit that we all know what game is being played at rehearsals is important. Not only does this shine a light on the rehearsal room hierarchy, but it also overtly identifies the director as a leader amongst equals of a team, where 'the buck' does indeed 'stop' as a result of the materialist conditions of theatre-making.

Practical and loving

Asked about her rehearsal credo, Kate Wasserberg explains that

> my process is very practical and the rest of it is love. I give them a parental love, not in a patronising way, but an unconditional love from someone who wants the best for them. I [also] love the play. It doesn't matter what my doubts might have been. I invest in it utterly. I love the characters. I staunchly defend even the worst character and I found that one of the most valuable things [in terms of] that happened when I became a mother. Any character – let's take Ian in Sarah Kane's *Blasted* – I thought about him as a child. I thought about five-year-old Ian, and what made him that way. Then I can love him as I love the five-year-old. I talk to my actors as I am totally on their characters' side. That's natural to me, as I can't get inside the play any other way. It also frees up the actors to not feel like they are defending their characters. Through practicality, problem solving and love, we make that show.

Wasserberg plans her rehearsal process with these core values. and during my observation of *Close Quarters*, one of the cast, actor Dylan Wood, had a breakthrough. Following this, there was this short interchange about the character he was portraying which exemplified Wasserberg's ethos:

> **Wood** Poor guy.
> **Wasserberg** Yes! Get on his side.

(Marsden 2018: 225–6)

Nikolai Demidov, who studied under Stanislavski and later developed his work, states that if you 'take an evil person, for example, he never considers himself evil; on the contrary he's the nice one, and everyone else around him is a scoundrel' (Malaev-Babel and Lasinka 2016: 506). Demidov's words here resonate with the above; here is a concrete example of Wood beginning to work within Wasserberg's frame of actors not having to defend his character, but able to be his champion, regardless of behaviour.

Some directors take a more systematic approach. Mike Alfreds constructs his rehearsal process around the exploration of the world, text and characters, drawing on Laban movement analysis[1] and later Stanislavskian processes such as active analysis and his own 'points of concentration',[2] all outlined in detail in his *Different Every Night*. Contrary to this, Tamara Harvey says of herself that 'I tend to shift and change my process depending on the play and the actors. Fundamentally, for my, [my process] is creating a space where the company can feel free to play to make mistakes and to fail. Often the most exciting discoveries come from those moments of seeming failure.'

The play at the centre

Michelle Terry wants to move away from traditionally structured rehearsals, where

> often the focus, or point of view comes from one end of the room and usu-
> ally on one person's shoulders i.e. the director. That may suit some people,
> but it doesn't suit everyone and it's not always the best thing for the work.
> You have to shift the focus back onto the play. There's such a guiding force in
> a playwright such as Shakespeare, and somewhere within the plays there is

---

[1] Laban movement analysis is based on the work of Rudolf Laban (1879–1958), an Austro-Hungarian pioneer of modern dance. The system is designed as a means of documenting and describing movement, drawing from several fields including anatomy and psychology and used by practitioners including choreographers and directors, but also by anthropologists, occupational therapists and others.

[2] Points of concentration as set out by Alfreds (2010) are something that the actor concentrates on and 'layers' into their rehearsal. For example, they may be in conversation in a scene yet concentrate on a piece of news, or the weather, or a time pressure.

a directorial voice speaking through the words the characters speak rather than stage directions for example. Yet, we are habituated to either lead, or follow, or be managed: how can you shift that? There are as many ways to create rehearsal room structures as there are people: some people do want to be told what to do, some people want to be part of the conversation. Some people want to have agency with no responsibility, some people want to have agency and responsibility but no accountability. So, how can you be open and honest about that?

Moving the play to the centre of the rehearsal room, as opposed to that being the director or lead actor, allows for a change of dynamic where all of those rehearsing are in the service of telling its story. The strongest or most useful idea in the telling of the story should be the one that is decided upon, regardless of from whom in the room it comes, as Kate Wasserberg identifies. The director becomes a chairperson, facilitating ideas, curating material and ultimately deciding upon a road for all to follow.

A genuine collaboration

The director must ensure that any rehearsal room philosophy of working isn't covert but is explicitly executed from the casting and audition stages onward, as well as making sure that deep roots are established through concrete action and modelling ways of working from day one. Wasserberg states that

> you have to know, project and say: 'I'm not the cleverest in the room, I'm not the most talented, but I'm going to do [the directing]. Therefore, being genuinely curious about what other people think is important, as is believing that the work will genuinely be better if you use the talent and ability in the room. As a director you have to be calmly unapologetic when you make a decision, rather than arguing who is right or wrong; but you have to say: 'Thank you for that input; for now, we are going to do this instead'. I say 'yes' to actors whenever I can, though, as they are so often right.

She also aims for actors to be able to overtly see her directorial processes. Actors see her 'reviewing my decisions and saying: "I've got that wrong". I realised a long time ago that a big barrier for me was putting any energy into pretending to know I have all the answers.'

The direction of travel in the early stages is also rooted in the directorial preparation. Ivo van Hove's prep is, to him, 'like a little backpack. I have it with me'. Like Wasserberg, he is keen to ensure he's not closed to new ideas from day one: 'the backpack is there if we get into trouble, or if there's a question. Then I have something to propose. But the backpack is my safety net. It's not there to overwhelm, or to be displayed to the actors.'

Exercises: Building an ensemble atmosphere

Compassion and kindness

Wasserberg structures her rehearsal rooms around the concept of love. Work by researchers Theo Gilbert and Cordelia Bryan on compassionate pedagogy can be applied to the early stage of a nascent ensemble. Compassionate work promotes safety and asks a company of people 'to notice distress and/or the disadvantaging of others and commit to reducing it' (Bryan and Clegg 2019: 155), where kindness is at the heart of the process. In an educational environment, the two questions below form the philosophy, and these can be easily adapted to a rehearsal context:

1. What can I do to enhance the social and learning experiences of my fellow students [actors] in this group work that they will most value in me?

2. What can my fellow students [actors] do in this group work to enhance my social and learning experiences that I will most value in them?

(ibid.: 155)

Rehearsal 'rules'

Mine are as follows:

1. There are no stupid questions.
2. The director is not necessarily the one with the answers.
3. Using the compassionate techniques above, we can all find ways to contribute and not allow monopolisers to dominate.

4. We must 'rise' to the play's demands and aim to embody its emotional, intellectual and creative opportunities.
5. When working on impulse, I encourage actors, using Michael Chekhov's phrase, not to 'swim in cosiness' of their own experience, but to relate to the given circumstances of the play.
6. Phones to be used only for rehearsal purposes. As Heskins states, 'it breaks my heart when someone is acting their heart out and someone's on Facebook. But we do use them for Googling, videoing and recording.'
7. Finally, take risks in order to let go and make rich discoveries. Or, as Tamara Harvey states, 'in the getting wrong we might find something more beautiful than anything you could find if you were trying all the time to get it right.'

Create your own rehearsal rules. Stanislavski believed that 'ethics and discipline are essential for creativity' (Shevtsova 2020: 125). They are also vital for making an ensemble and include a need for actors to be punctual and to enter rehearsals with 'cheerfulness … which is infectious and stimulates collective joy' (ibid.: 127).

Sharing

By placing the play at the centre of the rehearsal process, ownership of the work rests collectively:

1. Have everybody write down several lines that speak to the world of the play, with everybody encouraged to take lines from across several characters and acts. These can be shared and explored.
2. Ask actors to share all their intuitive work on the piece as per the exercise in Chapter 3 on 'Unlocking the clues to locate a world' (p. 78) and 'An actor's first encounter with the play' (p. 103).
3. Create a concept statement together.

Directing strategies for neurodivergent artists

One underexamined area is how to work with neurodiverse actors, including (but not limited to) actors with dyslexia and dyspraxia. Tanya Zybutz and Colin Farquharson's work (2016) examines how we are constantly oscillating in rehearsal and workshop situations between physical sensory mode and intellectual, narrative mode, whereby we ask actors to consider an image, for example, yet this imaginative response remains a cognitive one and needs to be interpreted and then translated individually into a somatically encoded experience. For an actor with dyspraxia, who is unable to switch between the two quickly, a block occurs: they remain in a narrative mode and are thus unable to embody with ease.

Daron Oram (2018), a principal lecturer at the Royal Central School of Speech and Drama, sets out methods to ensure inclusive practices, including: not insisting that eyes be closed when undertaking any work, as this locks the neurodiverse performer into narrative mode, making embodiment less easy; taking notes whenever it suits; breaking down instructions, often called 'chunking', in order to allow for processing; and allowing artists to create their own internal imagery in response to the director's image. Petronilla Whitfield (2020) is currently leading the way on finding new approaches to train neurodiverse actors in Shakespeare. Her use of creating images, both on paper and using the body gesturally helps to anchor text in the memory.

Creative spaces and music

A creative state must be nurtured and tended to. A clear, open space, which is not ghosted by previous productions becomes a home for a new story in development, where its walls can become giant noticeboards for creativity and the world can be created by bodies, sounds, words and scenographic elements. Ariane Mnouchkine allows her spaces to be filled with music, stating 'there should be no rehearsal or creative work without music' (Miller 2007: 114), with actors creatively responding in the space.

Rehearsal spaces

If 'the relationship between actors and the spaces and places in which they work is profound and far-reaching' (Filmer and Rossmanith 2011: 236), then the space should radiate an atmosphere conducive to creativity. Personal experience suggests that actors do not enjoy rehearsing comedy in a cold space, and rooms with an echoing acoustic are not appropriate to rehearsing plays with verbal dexterity and repartee. From the field of art therapy, Shaun McNiff states that 'the agents of transformation are more likely to be in the atmosphere or ambience [of the creative space] than within the person' (2004: 19). For actors to risk take, a creative space should 'emphasise listening, being present, and letting go of tight controls so that things outside our current awareness can come forward' (ibid.: 28). Director Anne Bogart also refers to her working environment, whereby she attends 'to the quality of the room, including punctuality, lack of clutter and cleanliness' (2001: 125). Taking time to consider and construct an environment favourable for creative practice should not be an afterthought.

Approaches to the first few days

Ivo van Hove's approach is as follows:

> What I do basically is one reading, an introduction to the visual concept and the general attitude. I never, ever talk about characters, but I give the actors an idea about the world we will live in together for the next few weeks. The next day, I then start scene one. I always try to rehearse chronologically, so that it's like life. I don't know what will happen within an hour: I know where I have to be, but I don't know what will happen.

Implicit here is his desire for a performance where it should feel as though it is happening for the first time. Kirstie Davis always uses 'big broad brushstrokes [so that] it's blocked by the end of the first week, if not the second, as I can't bear not getting to the end and not knowing what the end is'. When pressed on this, she states that needing to have a sense of the polarity of the play is crucial, as 'the end is really important and can't be left. It has to be satisfying, as it's the lasting memory of the piece. What is the "button" of the piece?' Like Wasserberg, Davis is not keen on a reliance on mental reconnaissance text work at the table either, stating that 'if there's an idea to be discussed, I'll discuss it, of course, but I like to see the actors explore an idea [physically].'

Historically the director has been constructed as an omnipotent being. Wasserberg does not undertake long first-day talks about the concept of the production, nor does she undertake read-throughs. There was genuine, visible relaxation and an audible sigh of relief when, during my observations of *Close Quarters*, she stated that 'we're not having a read-through. Let's read the play, not acting, although you might want to sense your way through it' (Marsden 2018: ll.21–2). These relaxed conditions engendered more active listening since the quick reading of the play was positioned around anchoring the actors into the world of the play and its given circumstances. By not forcing actors to create a character, and instead foregrounding an examination of the world they would eventually inhabit, the actors referred to their characters in the third person and, rather than pushing for a finished result, instead revealed potential starting points through probing the text.

Creating the circumstances

Wasserberg demonstrated that she is a colleague within the process, as opposed to an all-knowing presence, as a mere forty minutes into the first day of *Close Quarters* rehearsals I observed, she was the first to vocalise an individual breakthrough moment when there was a clarity about a given circumstance. In *Close Quarters,* the characters had been together not only for their six months of basic training, but for a further six-month specialist training for the actual mission in Estonia that they undertake in the play. This information on the specialist training was not in the script as a given but was offered by actor Sophie Melville from a pre-rehearsal interview she undertook with an army officer. The impact of the sub-rehearsal was therefore in play on day one, and the impact on the playing of the camaraderie of the platoon, as Wasserberg stated: 'Wow! Wow! Really useful' (Marsden 2018: l.83), lighting up and expressing affirmation through her physicality, with a joyous warmth in her response. She stated to me that this moment was

> really important for me; I draw a lot on characters' pasts, immediate and distant, to inform how I approach a script in rehearsals [so] I was incredibly grateful to Sophie for this piece of insight ... opening up possibilities I hadn't seen before. . . . From day one I am not the only one with the answers and the only person allowed to know stuff. We all need to take responsibility for knowing that stuff.

Wasserberg modelled her own openness to a genuine breakthrough that set the tone for the rehearsal period: a collaborative and ensemble-based one, where no question was too ridiculous to ask, echoing Alfreds who suggests that in a rehearsal room, 'everyone is allowed to be a fool, and no question is too stupid' (2017: 35). Ensuring that the whole room is an inquisitive one, and that the director is not supreme, chimes with Anne Bogart's statement that 'it is not the director's responsibility to produce results but, rather, to create the circumstances in which something might happen. ... With one hand firmly on the specifics and one hand reaching to the unknown, you start to work' (2001: 124). Ivo van Hove said to me that some directors 'think they have to display they are the boss of the production, but I try to avoid this and put the team forward. I'm part of the team [and] during the rehearsal process you might make a mistake, but as a team you are together. A team gives warmth, loyalty and security. You're secure.'

There was certainly a dependency on the director as the *Close Quarters* company began to form with Wasserberg driving the action, yet it was nevertheless demonstrated in this early stage of group formation that the whole company could take responsibility for the theatre-making process. Educational psychologist Bruce Tuckman states there is a natural dependency on the leader (i.e. the director) at an early stage of a group forming where 'coincident with testing in the interpersonal realm is the establishment of dependency relationships with leaders, other group members, or pre-existing standards. It may be said that orientation, testing, and dependence constitute the group process of forming' (1965: 396). The director is naturally looked to and depended on in the early 'forming' stages. By understanding that this must be a temporary role, the director or ensemble leader is able to establish a long-term strategy for rehearsals.

The road map

Heskins is also a director who articulates the importance of having a road map. Knowing where you'll end up helps to find a place to begin:

> In week one, I do the whole play quite quickly, so at the end of the week everyone will go home knowing the story we are telling, beginning to end. Each moment is explored without making decisions. Week two, they then start to make decisions, as we return to start working through act one. But the decisions will be informed by what the end of the play is and what each other is doing.

Echoing Kirstie Davis, Heskins ensures that the whole story is heard and shared, so that the narrative arc is acknowledged. Michael Chekhov advocates that the actor has to have a sense of any polarities between the beginning and the end of speeches, scenes or the whole play, and Wasserberg identifies her need to work through the play quickly, using the first week to solve

> all the practical problems. So, I get through table work as fast as I can. We're normally on our feet by the afternoon of day two. I basically like everyone to know what everything means. . . . We may have had some cool thematic conversations, but then we get up. In week one, we find a rough staging, solving all the weird practical stuff as best we can, such as how do you fold all the clothes, how do you make the chicken dinner, or whatever. At the end of week one, we will stagger it. I'm a great believer in getting from one end to the other and that it will probably be dreadful, but that's fine. We don't need it to be good, as we are finding out what the play is like in its totality.

The totality allows for an understanding of the narrative skeleton, prior to layering. Knowing where you are likely to end us isn't necessarily impinging upon the need to be in the 'now, today, here'[3] of a moment as an actor. Knowing the endpoint's overall atmosphere and tone indicates possibilities for a wider polarity at the start of the play. If, for example, when directing *The Taming of the Shrew* it is the intention for Katherina to submit totally to Petruchio at the end of the play, decisions can be made in relation to how explicitly misogynistic the beginning of the play might be, leading to an ending that is potentially more chilling and nebulous. Using the intuitive frameworks of Anne Fliotsos, if one of the gut responses to this piece is to see in it a potential narrative about abuse, control and gaslighting, then exploring the play's bookends and the polarities of the bounded timeline of the narrative becomes the starting point.

---

[3] 'Now, today, here' is the Stanislavskian term for being present and in the moment.

Regularity, but not predictability

Wasserberg's rehearsal structure during *Close Quarters* was consistent: the actors read through the scene a couple of times, ensuring clarity of meaning of words and phrases, and that basic relationship arcs were understood, core events highlighted and dramaturgy flexed. This then led into 'on the floor' work and the use of Socratic questioning,[4] steering actors to take ownership and discover their own answers, as they cracked the play's codes collectively. As actor Kathryn O'Reilly stated, 'you have to trust also that the director will guide you if it's not working. . . . I love questions. Kate would pose questions and made you think about it' (Marsden 2018: ll.118–21), as opposed to restricting and shutting down the actor's creative processes. An actor's agency is at the heart of Wasserberg's directorial philosophy.

There is a parallel to this in Heskins's early rehearsals. Whilst not analysing the play in a formal manner around the table, there is a sharing of intuitive responses at the end of an early stage layering of the scene:

> One technique I employ is: 'What do we know? What do we need to learn?' We've done the scene and, sitting in a circle, we say one thing we've learnt from the scene and what we need to learn. I try not to answer those questions in that session in week one. I ask the assistant to keep a note of those things, put them up on the wall and as we get to week two, we look at them again. Sometimes they've been answered and with others, we recognise we need to deal with those things.

Overtly committing to these gaps in knowledge, Heskins has found that this can sometimes alter the direction of travel for the overall tone of the production. When directing Elizabeth Robins's suffragette play *Votes for Women* at the New Vic (2018), Heskins was aware that it had not been produced since its 1907 premiere at the Royal Court, when it was directed by Harley Granville Barker:

---

[4] A form of facilitation whereby questions are often answered by further questions, allowing the participant (whether actor in a rehearsal room or student in a classroom) to come to their own conclusions in the 'hope that the [actor/student] might understand it more deeply, having worked it out for themselves' (Oram 2018: 282).

I wanted to do it to celebrate the centenary of suffrage. I did an edit, as it was archaic. One thing that came out of that exercise was that the actors were asking in an early scene in a country house, if they bowed in that time, or would we greet a relative with a hug, and what is the etiquette? I thought: 'Oh my, we'll spend all our time with etiquette manuals'. I thought: 'Let's not deal with any of that and treat people as we would treat people now and if a young relative turns up, you give them a hug'. Instead of bows and giving each other their hands, they would do what we do. It lit the play up. The room seemed relaxed and it became a brighter and funnier play.

To block, or not to block?

Writing in 2012, director and academic Trevor Rawlins suggested that any rehearsal period that doesn't begin with blocking is still outrageously classed as an 'alternative' process. Blocking is a 'traditional approach, [executing] pre-planned moves, whether that is imposed by a director or arrived at through negotiation in rehearsal' (2012: 434). So, what is the problem with blocking? The very word implies something rigid and secure, going against creative impulses. Yet moving towards a form that is shared with an audience means that a physical shape is almost always arrived at. To what extent it needs to be fixed or free is dependent on the play, the genre, personal aesthetics, the rehearsal process and other factors, such as emotional or physical health and safety.

Francis Hodge, back in the 1970s, suggested that we should think of blocking differently, by redefining it as *organic* blocking, whereby the 'seemingly mechanical aspect' (1994: 74) of the process can morph into a different form. By ensuring that the ground plan is fixed in a manner that allows for creative freedom and tension making possibilities, actors can use their impulses within the given circumstances of the scene, to perceive what is happening outside of themselves and to use their environment more and physically respond within. Thus, blocking is arrived at organically. Alfreds does not block a piece, 'except [for] entrances and exits and key conventions [that] are made clear' (Bessell 2001), leading to organic approaches to staging.

Taking the polarity of 'to plan or not to plan' is relation to blocking is dependent on the genre within which you are working. When directing musicals or pantomimes, I have often pre-decided entrances and exits and even roughly pre-blocked certain routines and complex interlocking physical business. The most complicated sequences are then rehearsed early on in rehearsals to ensure that there is enough time for actors to somatically encode this work. Some blocking has to be rigid, due to implications of flown set pieces, pyrotechnics, trapdoors and scenic effects. Timing of comedy or farce has to be negotiated and worked on specifically, as the rhythm of the piece is highly constructed, so as for it to be integral that the audience arrive at a shared response, following a gag line or physical business.

Nevertheless, I leave what van Hove would call the 'backpack' of planning at the door, as I respond to the rhythms, energies and physical agility of the performers: the plan is skeletal. Different subgenres of musicals require different planning and pre-thinking. A two-hander musical, such as *The Last Five Years* by Jason Robert Brown, may require very little pre-blocking, yet *West Side Story* might. Creating images when developing theatre can also be negotiated within the piece. Theatre is, for me, theatrical, and strong bold images are important to me personally. I storyboarded possibilities when directing Dave Simpson's 2017 adaptation of *The Secret Garden* in terms of the playground nature of the set, as I wanted to leave family audiences with strong picture book style images. This is balanced with allowing actors to work on impulse by experiencing the 'now, today, here' of the moment, ensuring genuine responses to both the given circumstances of the play and the immediate circumstances of what is occurring within the production world. Responding to each text differently, with an awareness of the conditions of production, ensures you are a responsive artist: not mapping on a rigid way of working, but allowing creative possibilities. For Leon Rubin, rehearsals are to prepare actors for the public production, 'rather than to try to fix every moment' (2021: 58), thus balancing the fixed elements with the free.

Throughout *Close Quarters*, Wasserberg continually reminded her actors to work somatically through their impulses and listen to each other, marrying Socratic questioning with impulsive decisions to inform the organic blocking of what she called scene 'drafts'.[5] Encouraging a sense of the 'what' and not the 'how' in the first stages of rehearsals allows for an understanding of the world to be embraced and the ways in which people may respond within that world, rather than worrying about an end form.

What does need to be planned, blocked and treated in a safe way, similar to stage combat, are moments of intimacy. These must not be left to impulse and issues of consent must be addressed in a safe manner, both in scripted and non-scripted moments, from touches to kisses to full sexual scenes. According to intimacy director Yarit Dor, her role in the pre-rehearsal stage

> with the director and stage manager [is] to figure out how to handle rehearsal. Is it a closed rehearsal? Some actors will want that, some may not for personal reasons. Who is in the room? Who takes notes especially since video recording might not be possible without consent of all parties and knowledge of where is that stored and how is it destroyed and when? Are notes then voice recorded instead? You should give performers twenty-four hours' notice prior to working on an intimacy scene in general. For a nudity test run in the studio give forty eight hours with a prior agreement with the actors, since some may not want to test out any nudity. If doing simulated acts and nudity performers might want to get prepared with whatever they need to do, such as waxing etc. It gives the performer time. If you only get your call at eight the night before, there's no time for an actor to bring any concerns up. This is a process that needs everyone to contribute to, it can't be a decision solely of the director and stage management team.

Dor is adamant that the choices around intimacy are rooted in the narrative such as

> What are the character's intimacy history? What is the characters relationship? What does the character enjoy or not and how? What do they learn about each other's intimacy, actions, presence, sensation? What do

---

[5] Each time a scene was rehearsed, Wasserberg would call it the next 'draft'. The use of language in the rehearsal room reflects the style of theatre-making. The drafting process (echoing Stockroom's new writing mission) therefore reflects how Wasserberg wants her actors to think about the purpose of rehearsals.

they want to achieve through the intimacy? Do they use it as a tactic? What do they get from the intimacy with the other character? Why did the playwright include that action/interaction? What does it serve? What movement toolkit shall we use? (Just like we do in dance, movement or stage combat: what is the precision, dynamic, energy, effort, weight, touch level in that moment) so you don't jump into generalising kissing? Ask, which character initiates it, is it mutual? Ask the actors to agree to what it is prior to jumping to anything physical.

This is also of particular importance when dealing with free improvisations, as through reaching prior agreement of boundaries, actors are safe in the knowledge of consenting to use specific physical touch through improvisation. Dor also discusses the importance of consent and intimacy choreography:

> I ask them to give me ideas for the moves, rather than pushing them to choreography I have created for them in my head. That is one of the main differences between dance, stage combat, movement direction vs intimacy direction work. That is core if you want to create a consent-based process and a trauma informed/sensitive practice in the room. Rooting it in the character keeps it on a professional level rather than a personal level. We discuss the intimacy of the character, not of the actor. It allows separation and the possibility for closure. Actors need to de-role from their character after a rehearsal session and after a show. Consent, boundaries, agreement, transparency, advocacy, time for brainstorming and open communication all aid in creating trust and a brave or safe space. It invites a person-centred process and it reduces the power dynamic from the director.

Blocking and the psychological

Wyn Jones takes the idea of blocking gradually when he trains actors:

> I don't do it in the first year as I want them to work from instinct. In the third year by the public production block, I am fascinated by the notion of good moves and disguising the fact they are moves. I do find occasionally

that you give a really good grouping or impose very precise blocking and that can make an actor feel something.

Aligned to Stanislavski's notion that every actor needs to be their own director, Jones believes that every actor essentially needs to know how to 'self-block'. In relation to imposing physical moves, Ivo van Hove is not afraid to do this as it may trigger an actor's emotional response:

Ben Whishaw says that in *The Crucible*,[6] in the first scene, I asked him to bang with his fist against the cardboard [set] and then go off. He said later in an interview that that revealed the attitude of how he needed to say the next line. A movement can tell something and take a character further and bring unexpected things out of a character.

Bridging the psychological thinking with the practical essentials is a common preoccupation for many directors. I asked Wasserberg to talk me through what she means when she says she balances concrete physical tasks whilst simultaneously dropping in psychological possibilities:

It's always easier to do something than to think or feel something. Doing something is unambiguous. It's a release of pressure and tension for an actor if they have a concrete and achievable task. That provides context for thinking or feeling something. I'm always trying to avoid the screaming void of a thought hanging ambiguously in the air, because thought without context is not actable. If you are doing something, you are achieving something. Let's do stuff. Move the chair, and whilst we are at it, let's talk about how you feel.

Wasserberg relates this back to creating a safe and open space for exploration as actors

need to own the space, they need to cut it up with their bodies, over and over again, until it belongs to them and that's an end in itself. As I am a reactive and responsive director, as opposed to coming in with a load of

---

[6] Ivo van Hove directed the 2016 revival of *The Crucible* at the Walter Kerr Theatre in New York. The cast included Ben Whishaw as John Proctor, as well as Sophie Okonedo, Ciaran Hinds and Saoirse Ronan.

stuff, it allows me to watch and respond. I don't know what I am going to say until they do something. I need something to interpret. Movement and task-based work is a great leveller, as it allows actors who are more physical than cerebral to assert themselves. I need the actors to have power in the room. Some actors aren't confident in cerebrally articulating their work in a group setting, but once they are up, they are confident in making shapes and have a brilliant rhythm. The longer you sit down, the harder it is to get up. That's why I wrap my ideas around physical actions.

Jenny Sealey echoes this in relation to working physically:

> I don't do actioning. I hate it! I can't do that. I've read all the books. I have been there as an actor, but I like the actors messy. Do something and I respond to what they are doing. I might know what I might want to do, but not the outcome or the form: we need to find that together. It's not everyone's style, but it's mine. I give a lot of power to the artists. I like to play, then we find out the intentions working through it. It's a deaf thing; my stimulus is visual: the pictures, the body language. That's when I get excited and can see the story.

Tamara Harvey describes how the early rehearsal period for *Home, I'm Darling* started with a consideration of the final form, due to the nature of the play, which

> is set in a house and revolves around the domestic detail. In rehearsal we fairly rapidly sketched out a fairly clear physical language for the play, because that was really important in terms of timing and for actor Katherine Parkinson for her journey; [how] pouring a cup of tea for example changes over the course of the play. These activities are fundamental for their character, as well as for the intention and subject. All that aligns in that physical activity.

Some genre thinking about form and content

The form of a British pantomime will often be cemented early in rehearsal, yet paradoxically remains in considerable flux until its opening. The practical form problems are dealt with early on, including complex physical slapstick routines, which, as set pieces, have a basic concrete shape and structure. Music hall sketches and verbal patter are also rehearsed early on for their form. There remains space for the audience's responses, yet as the above examples are tried and tested, there are anticipated replies and reactions and ways to construct an audience's rhythms and responses. Pantomime relies on the audience to be the final character of the piece. Experienced pantomime performer Brian Conley is thinking of the form early on, stating that

> as a performer, I'm not coming in fresh with panto: I know what works, especially my opening spot [where] I get a good gauge of what [the audience will] be like. Don't forget, I've met [with the director and producer] and we've had quite a few meetings in the summer. You're going to tune it up, rather than learning it from scratch. I am a performer who'll bring something to the table, rather than an actor who is given the lines. Then in rehearsal, you need a skeleton, you need a shape. I'd say to any upcoming director, know that panto needs an audience.

For Conley, the form of the comedy which is being 'tuned up' in rehearsal still must have elasticity, until it is in front of an audience, since 'the comedy can all change within the first couple of days of performance; we may have learnt it in rehearsals, but it could be cut'.

Immersive theatre blurs the audience's relationship with its actors and deliberately interrogates and subverts its traditional hierarchy. Many immersive practitioners consider the ethical implications of this mercurial relationship in the early stages of rehearsals, whereby even if the form of the performance piece isn't firm, safeguarding measures are. These measures 'hold' the content and helps to frame the physical interactions between performer and audience. Alexander Wright, director of *The Wolf of Wall Street*, which opened in London in 2019, states that the form of the 'interaction will be by invitation' (James 2019) and that 'boundaries give you freedom, because once you know where they are you have a full space to enjoy' (ibid.).[7] Knowing the form of those boundaries provides freedom within the safety of structure.

---

[7] https://www.thestage.co.uk/features/safety-and-immersive-theatre-where-should-the-boundaries-be-set.

A form is arrived at earlier in most musicals with the need to swiftly integrate actors, singers, dancers and musicians into one organism. Early stages ensure an early integration of the form's separate entities. Choreographer Stephen Mear highlights the importance of both himself and his director being 'on the same page where the vision for the show is concerned. I like to make sure that we work well together, so that it's seamless and you can't tell where the direction finishes, and the choreography begins. I like the dance routines to help [push] forward the narrative'. If integration is left too late in rehearsals, it becomes a case of reverse-engineering, dictated by necessity, rather than making earlier sophisticated choices. Collaboration for Mear in the early stages is of vital importance for a unified form, not only with his director but also with his musical director, as they are

> an important part of the performance for setting the tempo for the dancers. We work together to build the dance routines for the biggest impact and make the most of the music and movement together. Dance should [advance] the story of the piece and there should be a seamless connection between the direction and the choreography. A lot of directors trust me to choreograph the scene changes too, which also helps to give it that seamless effect.

Tamara Harvey articulates that it is not only the genre that needs to be taken into consideration, but an individual actor's needs:

> What I love about directing is figuring out what makes an actor tick: what triggers their greatest flights of imagination and interweaving those techniques. I admire hugely those directors who have a concrete methodology, but for me, that doesn't appeal. For example, you can have an actor in the company who really needs physical work to plot their way through the show or you can have someone who wants to focus purely on the words.

Rehearsal room breakthroughs

Throughout my career I have regularly noticed actors, directors and creatives cry out 'aha!', 'that's it!' or 'yeah, great' and then move on. I define these as rehearsal room breakthroughs, and they take many forms. For several years,

I have been enmeshed in wanting to locate and recognise these moments, to understand what happens and ascertain their efficacy. The dictionary definition of a breakthrough is 'a sudden advancement in knowledge, achievement etc; a development or discovery that removes an obstacle to process' (*Oxford English Dictionary* 1989: II 517). Stephanie French and Philip Bennett's definition of inspiration as a starting point for the rehearsal room breakthrough is 'a realisation of great clarity – an 'aha' moment when something that had been challenging is deeply understood' (2016: 2). Director Hugh Morrison describes the moment of breakthrough as the 'it' moment, explaining its importance through this stark warning: 'Woe betide the director if he misses the moment. ... "It" is something instinctive, something that feels right to the actor and director' (1984: 105). I offer the 'The Four Lenses of Breakthrough', below, in order to gain a deeper understanding of this phenomenon, and I argue that this can be of profound practical use in theatre-making.

The proposition that acting is, as articulated by Jean Benedetti, 'above all intuitive' (Jackson 2013: 246) is all well and good; yet how do actors and directors know when their intuition is 'right' for that moment, and when it supports the direction of travel for the rehearsal? Breakthroughs are often made by actors via an external idea, often offered by a director. Life and business coach Leigh Longhurst makes the point that often when a life coach asks their client a question, a discovery is made (2006). If we substitute 'life coach' for director and 'client' for actor, then we can find a link to a rehearsal room interaction. As director Edward Hall states, 'it's about continually asking questions together' (Croall 2014: 10). This can be traced to practitioners such as Brecht, who started his rehearsals with 'nothing' and an intention 'to work naively' (Britton 2013: 132), allowing for shared discovery through a series of questions: 'Brecht fired off a series of questions which continually queried his collaborators' assumptions as a model of how one retains liveliness in a production period' (ibid.: 135). Questioning and shared enquiry through an openness leads to iterative and ongoing breakthroughs.

To generate a positive interaction, the director's conversations with actors should be guided by a growth mindset of the kind advanced by psychologist Carol Dweck. A growth mindset provision must be generated to encourage actors to 'love challenges, be intrigued by mistakes, enjoy effort and keep on learning' (2012: 176). This, coupled with 'curiosity' (Rea 2014: 237), allows actors the ownership of the text and character. Director Braham Murray's text *How to Direct a Play* makes a beautiful insight that his rehearsals always had 'the aim of making the actors as confident as possible, as quickly as possible' (2011: 52). The supportive atmosphere aimed at correlates with studies in relation to a breakthrough moment, which have proven that positivity has a profound effect on whether insight occurs: 'A recent functional magnetic resonance imaging (fMRI)[8] study showed that people are more likely to solve problems with insight if they are in a positive mood when they arrive at the lab than if they are in a neutral or negative one' (Beeman and Kounios 2009: 215).

'The Four Lenses of Breakthrough'

As detailed in Table 4.1, I have created four lenses through which we can view rehearsal breakthroughs to aim for specificity in terms of what is being viewed as a breakthrough:

1. individual and small recognition moments,
2. individual discoveries,
3. collective discoveries and
4. the 'wow' moment.

This chapter deals with lens one: the individual moments of recognition. Chapter 5 deals with lenses two and three and the 'wow' moment is dealt with in Chapter 6.

These individual moments of recognition as seen through lens one are the small moments of learning and insight viewed when an individual synthesises different pieces of information. For instance, when information from a director aligns with prior knowledge from an actor's individual pre-rehearsal work. This often becomes a confirmation of a moment, where there is a deeper understanding or a strengthening of something that the individual already knows

---

[8] fMRI measures brain activity by detecting changes associated with blood flow. This works on the principle that, when an area of the brain is in use, blood flow to that area increases.

but has lain dormant and suddenly becomes more useful within the context of the production frame. These are moments which, according to constructivist theories of learning, associate 'new information with ideas already known, they [then] assimilate the new [information] into their existing knowledge ... scaffolded onto existing knowledge, skills and expectations' (Whitfield 2020: 19).

Individuals thereby only become fully aware of a fact when meaning is attached to a moment where meaning is being generated, as this is a crucial start to exploring deeper layers of responses to the text. Breakthroughs also occur for actors when sharpening and embodying their given circumstances as they began, as Demidov put it, to 'give [themselves] up to the circumstances of [the] character's life' (Malaev-Babel and Lasinka 2016: 564).

Table 4.1 *The Four Lenses of Breakthrough*

Lens	Description	Definition summary	*Oxford English Dictionary* definition
One	Individual moments of recognition	The individual recognition moments that happen for an actor or a director in rehearsal	Recognition is 'the mental process of identifying what has been known before' (1989: VIII 341)
Two	'Aha': an individual discovery moment by an actor or director	This is a moment of individual breakthrough where new knowledge is gained through discovery.	Discovery is 'the action of discovering. Verb. 1. Find something unexpectedly in the course of a search. 2. Gain knowledge about or become aware of' (1989: IV 753)
Three	'Aha': a collective discovery moment	This is a moment of shared breakthrough (e.g. between actor and director or actor and actor), where new knowledge is gained through discovery	As above
Four	The collective company 'wow' moment	This is a breakthrough moment where there is a collective 'rightness' and ownership, not of a small moment, but of a larger bit, scene, or the entire production, following a run-through or performance	'Wow ... chiefly express[es] astonishment or admiration' (1989: XX 595)

Exercises: Early stages methods

Movement

Does movement need to be foregrounded? Are there military or stylised sequences that need to be embodied? Are there any period movement, dances or manners that could be explored? Even if I am setting a play, such as a Restoration comedy, in a contemporary context, exploring the language of the fan used by the female characters, or the different bows dependent on hierarchy, can allow a way into the world and the status games at play. The job is to then transpose the original coded gestural language and movement into a contemporary context.

Relationship threads

In early read-throughs and run-throughs, have the characters who are discussed and mentioned get up and allow them to play in the scene, so interactions can be established, and relationships achieved?

Active reads

Using the philosophy of active analysis, have a scene or bit read by the actors and follow this with questions and answers in relation to meaning and a discussion of any key events, plus basic intentions and relationships. Then ask the actors to either read the scene physically in the space, working on impulse, or with texts down, improvising the scene using their own words, which relate to the section's dramaturgical structure and givens, or using any remembered words from the text. This isn't about line recall but about engaging with the spirit and fabric of a scene or bit, as well as with the dramatic architecture.

Renaissance runs

Following the group rehearsal idea of original Renaissance practices allow the actors on the first morning to work together without the director. Then run the play in the afternoon. This will produce a rough and ready physical telling of the story and places the actor at the centre.

Beginning and end

The director chooses a substantial amount of text and neutrally reads out the lines at the beginning of the play and then the end of the play. Have everyone write down what they intuitively feel about it and draw images or write down any words or phrases that leap out. By looking at the bookends of the piece, the company is aware of the bounded nature of the story and any key polarity changes for characters, mood, atmosphere, intentions, learning or morality.

Sharing the story

Everyone collectively tells the story in the third person. They should do so at speed, jumping in or over each other, stopping others if they have missed something. The language and words used will give a clue as to what individuals feel is important, or what precisely resonates with them.

Event and image

Have the actors create group tableaux of the key events of each scene. What is to be foregrounded? Is the beat of the story clear? Can anything be shifted to tell the story in the way you'd like it to be received?

Open questions

Ask questions about the play as artists in the room at various stages. What do I know? What do I think I know? What do I want to find out?

Questioning answers, not answering questions

Directors should use Socratic questioning in the early stages of rehearsal, not necessarily answering the questions, but using questions to allow the actor to explore possibilities.

Études for the world and relationships

An étude is a 'sketch', a pre-performative improvisatory rehearsal device where possibilities are drafted. With its roots in the French *étudier*, meaning 'to study', an étude is a way into work individually, somatically embodying ideas and/or experiencing with another actor. Études, which are 'exercises of the imagination' (Shevtsova 2020: 139) may be non-verbal or verbal, explore the scene itself or any previous circumstances. By rooting the given circumstances and core events through the études, the actor is able to begin experiencing. An étude often becomes a rough first sketch of the scene.

Voice

I personally draw on Kristin Linklater's practices when approaching a play, combining imaginative responses to a somatic experience of sounds and words, revealing the world. In a classical play, the words are the world, and in the early rehearsals I often spend time with vowel sounds which generate atmospheres.

Feeding in

Another method to free the actor from the text and to connect to and with one another is that of feeding in. This may be another actor or stage manager feeding in the lines neutrally to an actor quietly as they follow them in the space. When the line resonates to and with the actor, they interpret this line psycho-physically and, by keeping full attention on their scene partner(s), they remain rooted in the world and the given circumstances of the moment.

Integration of scenography and stage management

For actors to holistically perceive what is happening outside of themselves, many practitioners aim to build and integrate as much of the scenographic world from day one of rehearsals. Ivo van Hove suggests that the whole of the rehearsal period can be reframed as a technical rehearsal; for him, there should ideally not be a separate 'tech'.

Whilst this may not be financially achievable for many, it is possible to work with the spirit of this. Theatre design can be acted 'in front of', in a similar vein to the Restoration playhouses as suggested in Chapter 2, yet scenography repositions this to also include the relationship with the body (i.e. the performer) in the playing space. For Kate Wasserberg, 'the version of that for the actor is that they've learnt to put a new coat on and it feels like theirs; so, when they put it on, it looks like they've owned it for a year, as opposed to a coat handed to them in technical rehearsals'. Sound designer Gareth Fry asserts that 'it is increasingly common to have the sound designer and/or a sound operator present for most of the rehearsal process'. Fry is adamant that this relationship with the actors is integral in rehearsals as, for him,

the rehearsal process is where the rhythm and dynamics of the show are developed. Sound design often sounds 'tacked on' if you try to add it too late in the process, when the performers have already established their rhythms and dynamics. You end up either trying to crowbar sound into pauses in the text, or breaking across their rhythms, or just having it sit entirely in the background, because there isn't any space left in the foreground. By developing the sound design in the rehearsal room, as the actors develop their performances, we're able to create the two together in synergy. This means we can work sound design into the foreground of the show, with the actors working with it.

Stephen Mear's relationship to set and costume designers is essential to effectively deliver the creative work and needs to be built into rehearsals where possible, as they 'set the time and place of the piece and the costumes can be used to accentuate a dance movement. We need to also make sure that the dancers can dance freely, with minimal restrictions and work on any props needed. This is usually tried and tested in rehearsals.' Heskins discusses how, when she directed *Around the World in 80 Days* for the New Vic in 2013, the acting company also had agency in design elements:

For example, the play called for a journey by elephant. Lis Evans, the designer, had offered us elements to potentially create an elephant, but I also wanted to explore it in rehearsals. Lis had given us a brilliant kit to play with, props and costumes (like a dressing up box). I ask for props to be in the room early, so they are part of the world of the play. We have a busy room. I remember clearly that week one Thursday that 10.30 to 11.15 was scheduled to be 'solve elephant' and we had forty-five minutes to do it. That was terrifying, but there are thirty-three scenes in that play, so there's a lot to do. I said to the eight actors: 'in four groups of two: make an elephant: use anything you find in the room, or across the building, or even grab passers-by in the street. Bring back an elephant! You've fifteen minutes! One group had found an Inverness cape in the corner of the room and they discovered it could be twisted and turned to make ears and a trunk. The two were brilliant puppeteers and it was a stunning elephant and we all thought it was great and yet so simple. For that process, it's all offers. It's sharing, as the person who invented the elephant didn't make it in the show, but they had made that offer and put it in to create this lovely element. Ideally everything should be like that.

Wasserberg is famous for the relationship that she has with her deputy stage manager (DSM), who keeps the 'book' in rehearsals of all the blocking and is the conduit between the rehearsal room and all other departments, organising the daily rehearsal processes. For Wasserberg, this begins with a simple premise that she wants to be present with her actors and engage with their work: 'I never, from day one, look at my script. My collaboration with my DSM is so important, as they become the person who looks at the script so that my head is up, and I am with the actors. I work with DSMs who have a feel for text, who understand it.' The role of the DSM is creative as well as operational, and the rehearsal room's smooth running is dependent on directorial openness and trust in the DSM to undertake their role effectively and take ownership of the room.

A summary of Chapter 4

Uniqueness is vital in the deciding of processes: the uniqueness of the genre, the piece itself, the background and individual needs of the company members and the conditions of production including time, budget and space, amongst others.

First rehearsal steps whereby the company forms are tentative at best with a new company. The forming stage within a permanent ensemble will have been reached, yet the newness of the latest project or product remains to be navigated for transient company and established ensemble alike. First steps are taken through the confidence of everyone bringing a personal backpack of pre-rehearsal preparation. There is an overwhelming consensus from those I interviewed on an exploration of content over form and a need to get a sense of the whole play, so that the overall story can be examined and owned, by moving the play to the centre of the room. All of the interviewees articulate the need to have as many of the scenographic elements in the rehearsal room as practically, physically and financially possible. First steps within the rehearsal room can begin to be quantified through the 'Four Lenses of Breakthrough', with the small, initial moments of recognition forming the first of the four lenses.

Chapter 5 moves on to the middle stages of rehearsals: the challenges and opportunities for this liminal stage, where actors are often coming off book, and content is segueing into form.

Interview: Sir Alan Ayckbourn on directing

One well-known practitioner who has written in detail from an insider's perspective about his own work as a director and playwright is Sir Alan Ayckbourn. I interviewed him about his work as a director.

As a director, you've been described by academic Paul Allen as 'a cross between a schoolteacher leading a particularly enjoyable outing and a host at a party'; by John Hudson as directing actors 'in a rather sideways way'; and by Malcolm Hebden as 'letting actors come along at their own pace' and directing 'by stealth'. How do you personally describe your directing style?

I usually describe my style as 'sheepdog'. That is, initially keeping one step behind the actors, allowing them to indicate the direction they have chosen themselves. The second phase is collaborative, where I show approval, encouraging their correct choices and gently frowning upon wrong or overly simplistic ones. But at the first hint of a totally wrong basic choice, which is rare if you've done your casting right, I am ready to race ahead, barking eagerly to indicate gates they may have missed, fresh fields they might not have been aware of or even, as a very last resort, revealing the final destination. But my maxim is always to allow the actor to lead. In an ideal relationship, my approach needs to be subtle enough for them to believe that they've made 95 per cent of the choices purely by themselves.

Do you approach directing different genres differently? You've said in the past that 'the approach depends on the play'. Do you have a common structure or a set of methods, regardless of genre?

Not really. Drama, light comedy or farce, the approach to character should be more or less the same: truthful and consistent. Of course, truth is an elusive thing and there are several versions. But once you've established a starting point, be it delicately stylised or heavily naturalistic (and that really does depend on the play and how you, the director, plan to approach it), but once, orchestrally speaking, the key signature has been established, it should be religiously observed with scrupulous consistency. Until such time, that is, as you mutually agree on a dramatic key change.

Your pre-rehearsal writing process has been well documented in interviews and in your book. Could you describe your pre-rehearsal work?

Since I work principally in the round, I find blocking in advance to be rather non-productive. Along with the designer, I have already decided the basic geography, the disposition of the exits and entrances. It is then up to the actors to occupy and explore the space we have created for them. In general, I find actors are somewhat put out if they feel that every decision affecting their performance has already been made before they even enter the rehearsal room. As a director, don't be afraid of spur-of-the-moment spontaneity.

You say that 'casting is everything'. Could you unpack that a little?

It is a terrible feeling for a director – and even occasionally an actor – to have to acknowledge halfway through rehearsal that someone, somewhere, has been badly miscast. At that stage there is precious little either can do but tacitly acknowledge that a mistake has been made before starting on a series of measures, best termed 'damage limitation'. There are various reasons that this occurs, ranging from a mutually different approach to the character, down to a sheer lack of ability to play it. Motto: 'Make the right choice early'.

You are well known for speaking about the writer (i.e. yourself) in the third person, when rehearsing your own work. What do you think are the opportunities and challenges inherent in directing your own material?

The advantage of directing my own material is that at least the work gets interpreted as I envisaged it. The disadvantage is that the buck very definitely stops with me.

What advice would you give directors of your work?

My advice to directors tackling my work for the first time is to respect the truth and trust the structure. To paraphrase an old British Rail slogan, 'let the play take the strain'. Sit back and enjoy the journey and, please, never be tempted to lean out of the window and wave to the audience.

Very little is written about tech, dress and preview stages from a directorial point of view. How do you approach these stages?

Techs, aside from casting, are the most important period a stage play has to undergo. After the (comparative) calm, leisurely flowing waters of the rehearsal room, your craft is all of a sudden caught in the rapids as new crew are press-ganged aboard, each of them with their own important, specialist agenda: lighting sound, props, costume, special effects, etc. Until now, all have been working on something which will have been – unless they're lucky – a single rehearsal room run, or a script they have only read. They have not been privy to the countless decisions, large and small, which have been made over previous weeks in rehearsal. To compensate for this, a director requires two things. The first is a very diligent DSM, in constant communication with all these departments on a daily basis from the very start. Secondly, where possible, anticipate the tech maelstrom which awaits. Get ahead of the game by, for instance, incorporating the sound early; or, if there's a difficult prop, costume or piece of scenery, try to incorporate it whilst you're still at the rehearsal room stage.

5

The piece grows: Delving deeper in the middle stages

'The first time is a big splash of paint on the wall. So much might change and it's about seeing what it might be. I can't see in minutiae straight away, I have to go from broad to detail and bit by bit, as the weeks go on, there's more and more detail.' Here Kirstie Davis describes the middle stages of rehearsal as concerning detailing, following broad brushstrokes. Davis shares this method of a broad initial exploration of content, as an attempt to understand the narrative arc of the story and test the production frames, with many other practitioners. Matthew Xia parallels this process, thinking of rehearsals as a 'well-made swimming pool that has a deep end and a shallow end. And we walk from the shallow end to the deep end over a period of four weeks, honing.' Not obsessing over fine detail in the early stage is important as the final production will 'end up looking like a Rembrandt or a Basquiat, or some piece of great art. But it's going to start by looking like a really badly-drawn circle on a piece of paper in chalk.'

Moving the piece from being a badly drawn circle to a Rembrandt happens in the middle stage of rehearsal. The early stages can feel awash with creative ideas and exploration; the final stages start to consolidate, building confidence and strength through running the piece. This middle period is a liminal stage with actors coming off book and where directors often worry about whether the piece holds together, with early decisions tested for efficacy. The middle stages should be ones where the actor is more fully engaged in what Demidov calls 'authentic experiencing' (Malaev-Babel and Lasinka 2016: 46) where an '"authentic truth" [is] living naturally in unnatural conditions' (ibid.: 60) on the stage, as 'the Russian word "experiencing" (*perezhivanie*) [is] the term [that Stanislavski] chooses to describe what actors feel when the exercises completely release their full creative potentials' (Carnicke 2009: 129). Carnicke simplifies 'experiencing', defining it as 'an actor's unbroken concentration on the events of the play in performance' (2009: 133). So what layers are being added at this stage to move actors into a place of experiencing and finding 'truth'?

Creativity and flow

'Flow' is the popular term for 'optimal experience' and can help in approaching this middle period. In acting, this feels like an 'onstage exhilaration where all internal and external elements [come] together into a perfect efficiency' (Polanco and Bonfiglio 2016: 205). In the latter stages of rehearsals, I wrap this feeling into the 'wow' moment, discussed in Chapter 6. Seeds need to be planted in the early and middle stages as conditions are created to generate this state, whereby the 'actor responds truthfully in the moment without the infiltration of self-conscious thoughts' (ibid.: 206). Exponent of this theory Mihaly Csíkszentmihályi outlines that we experience flow when we have a clear goal to achieve and the challenge is consistently married with the skill base of the individual undertaking it at that time. As skills increase, so too must challenges. Therefore, new challenges and offers need to be made by the director as the production moves towards the deep end of the rehearsal pool; the actors too must posit new challenges for themselves, both within rehearsal and in the sub-rehearsal.

Flow is achieved when there is absorption in the task, with immediate feedback, no fear of failure, a distortion of time, a lack of self-consciousness and attention focused in an autotelic (self-motivating) manner. Throughout this state, much personal enjoyment or happiness is sensed by the individual following the event. This is where one is 'flooded with gratitude' (Csíkszentmihályi 1997: 32) and it can be related to Stanislavski's sense of being in a creative state as well as the proven sense of enjoyment following flow. A positive sense of 'rightness' following an achievement such as a successful run-through of a scene is linked to this experience.

Flow can support the creation of an environment for rehearsals where skill levels are high and challenges match or stretch the needs of both the individual and the collective company. For example, casting could consider the skills of the actor in relation to the challenge of the role. Rehearsal room practice must increase in targeted challenges, so that as an actor's skill increases in relation to the knowledge of the text and embodiment process, challenges from the director are specifically raised. Too much repetition in this middle stage can stymie challenge. It is useful to recall George Bernard Shaw's remark, cited earlier, about the 'schoolmastering' director and the fact that 'repetitions on the spot do not improve, they deteriorate every time' (West 1958: 283). Rehearsals must increase in challenges; otherwise, according to Csíkszentmihályi, boredom will occur. This balance between challenge and skill is a 'fundamental condition of Csíkszentmihályi's flow' (Polanco and Bonfiglio 2016: 209): if it is 'too easy it leads to boredom; if it is too difficult it leads to anxiety' (ibid.: 212) and in the light of creating inclusive and compassionate rehearsal rooms, this balance is crucial. If, in the polarity of 'to plan or not to plan', the director forges ahead with pre-prepared rehearsal techniques without responding to immediate needs of the room, there can be a problem.

Flow and motivation

Flow is also related to intrinsic self-motivation. In a 2002 study into actors' experience of flow and their motivational characteristics, Keir Cutler and Jeffrey J. Martin discovered that the motivations of actors when achieving flow are not extrinsic. This is supported by Teresa Amabile's research at Harvard Business School: she believes that 'intrinsic motivation ... still applies as conducive to creativity' (Rickards 1999: 33), which may reduce the need for an unhealthy continual positive feedback loop if the motivation of the actor is to 'please' a director within rehearsals, as opposed to experiencing with their fellow actors. Csíkszentmihályi posits people feel at their best when what they do is voluntary and therefore directors should allow actors to take ownership, as with little intrinsic motivation, 'entropy' (Csíkszentmihályi 1997: 28) can occur. Ownership must certainly have moved to the actors by this middle stage. Researcher Chris Fields notices that there is a pleasure derived from personal discoveries that are not driven by a leader (or a director) and that an individual 'recognition of a solution' (2011: 1162) is triggered by intrinsic motivation.

Flow and the creative state

To fully embody and experience, Stanislavski wished for actors to enter into a 'creative state' (2010: 293), whereby actors 'truly enter sacred [physical and psychological] space to do this work' (McNiff 2004: 30). During this, an actor's 'inner and outer creative state brings him to the state of "I Am Being": an ideal when an actor 'knows instinctively what to do' (Bennett and French 2016: 3) and that in every performance the actor is 'fully experiencing and embodying the role' (Whyman 2016: 158). John Britton, like Stanislavski, proposes that a creative state must be induced in a company, whereby the 'precise and subtle use of the senses is essential' (2013: 344), reinforcing the idea that the 'actor's inner creative state' (Stanislavski 2010: 293) must be nurtured as must a conducive atmosphere for creative endeavours and optimal experience.

Hefferon and Ollis (2006) outline some factors influencing flow in a creative environment for dancers and I expand on how this may relate to a theatre rehearsal room:

1. A performer's confidence. A supporting and compassionate environment nurtures confidence and risk taking.

2. A connection to and with stimulus. In a dancer's case, this is often music; for the actor, this is their text and the world.

3. A familiarity with their performance space and stage. Creating the scenography in rehearsals enables actors to live within their environment.

4. Their relationship with the choreographer and artistic directors. The relationship between actor and director must be based on trust and shared beliefs; a strong and safe relationship between actor and director does not impede play and risk taking.

5. Positive mental attitudes of their fellow performers and directors. The creative state must be engendered through kindness and the elimination of harsh external judgement, echoing Mitchell who believes that actors in theatre need 'positive feedback' (2009: 129). This recalls Wasserberg's need to 'love' her actors, which means that she would 'only praise and tell them what they are doing right, if I really had to choose'.

6. A pre-performance ritual such as 'tuning up' for a scene.

Terence Crawford developed the 'road runner' theory of acting, where an actor is 'to pursue one thing at a time' (2011: 140). For me, this could be pursuing a new challenge as skill increases. Yet to do this, the director must be sensitive to when a challenge is needed, such as a new rehearsal method or a point of concentration stimulus. The 'director needs to be fully alert and present in the very moment, as both director and actors try to figure out the depths and details of the situation in a direct encounter . . . with the playtext' (Ostermeier 2016: 165). Being alert to when something is needed is part of the directorial craft, whilst the actor's role is to be open and responsive to these possibilities and to be honest in articulating a problem or requesting a new challenge from the outside eye.

Exercise: Middle stage challenges

Time pressures

Behaviour differs in relation to time and circumstance. A documentary play I directed, *The Fight for Shelton Bar*, examines the closure of the steelworks in Stoke-on-Trent in the 1970s. Ted Smith, head of the action committee, has an extended monologue to the workers. I felt that the delivery had become too safe: the actor's skill with the rhetoric and structure of the speech had plateaued. The discovery was then made that in reality, this speech had been delivered for the third time, to a different set of workers, with the speaker not having slept for seventy-two hours. Understanding this time pressure of battling against severe tiredness unlocked new energy.

The Young Vic's archives contain materials pertaining to Tim Supple's 1998 production of *Twelfth Night*. One of Supple's concerns was to understand the time frame of the play, writing that 'the action takes place over a few days in May'. (1998a). Explicitly working on the timescale meant that there is a pressure cooker emerging for the action to be housed within. Under these conditions, a need for solutions to be found swiftly intensified and this pressure lends itself to comedic misunderstandings.

During *Close Quarters*, many breakthroughs were made by clarifying the timeline during the middle stages. Highlighting the fact that the characters had not had much sleep over a period of five days intensified the action, ensuring that grogginess and snappiness came from embodying this circumstance. I observed a pressurised, high-stakes, chamber environment when the piece was replayed.

Highlight the time pressures of the overall play or a specific situation in your play. How might this affect the behaviour of the characters?

Objective clarity

In the middle stages, returning to the early thinking and clarifying, sharpening or changing objectives to be more dynamic through an understanding of the whole play becomes a new challenge. For Fabio Polanco and Diane Bonfiglio, 'objectives may prompt focused concentration, because the objectives are challenging enough to require significant attention to accomplish ... the objective provides the actor with a clear direction and means by which to measure success' (2016: 211).

Research challenges

Tim Supple's direction of Edward Kemp's adaptation of William Faulkner's *As I Lay Dying* for the Young Vic in 1998 involved him specifying challenges for each actor, according to the production archive. Ian Taylor was to research and understand 'the seasonal work of a Mississippi Farmer [of the] 1930s, also different types of farming/trading' (Supple: 1998b). Dan Milne was to go fishing: 'investigate a legal place for Dan to try it out!' (ibid.). All actors were to visit a farm and Thusitha Jayasundera was to 'milk a cow [and] research cotton picking' (ibid.). Layering in research allows actors to locate themselves within the given circumstances of the world.

What research challenges can you create?

Looking to 'get on their side'

Remember Demidov's words? 'Take an evil person, for example, he never considers himself evil; on the contrary, he's the nice one, and everyone else around him is a scoundrel' (Malaev-Babel and Lasinka 2016: 506). During the middle stages of rehearsals as embodiment deepens, I begin to ask the actors to talk from a first-person perspective, rather than from a third-person perspective. This allows the actor to be their character's guardian. As a director, spot when actors are not 'on the side' of their characters and are judging them solely based on their own lived experiences or moral compass. As an actor, are you distancing yourself too much and commenting on your character?

Feeding in the psychology

Wasserberg is keen on creating a physical shape first, a series of concrete actions. Then, whilst 'they are working physically and the actor's brain is occupied with all that, you also feed in other ideas such as "he's actually trying to tell her he's always loved her". The best conversations in life happen when you're doing something else, having a deep and meaningful with your dad, doing the washing up.'

Where could you feed in such a direction in your work?

Questioning characters

Josie Rourke's use of first-person structured questioning whilst working as an assistant director on Stephen Sondheim and George Furth's *Merrily We Roll Along* at the Donmar Warehouse in 2000 is a less freewheeling approach to hotseating.[1] It is clear that the questions were relevant to the actor's imagined circumstances, especially if writers Sondheim and Furth had not supplied the answers. Explicit examples include:

> Franklin, when exactly did you stop composing? What made you want to produce movies? Gussie, did you train formally? How old are you? At what point in your career did you marry Joe?

> (Rourke 2006c)

What specific questions would you ask of the characters in your play?

Metaphors as triggers

During *Close Quarters* rehearsals, metaphors were often employed by Wasserberg, in order to stimulate imaginative responses. At one stage she stated, 'you're running downhill here … Armstrong, you're pushing the stone down the hill here' (Marsden 2018: l.891).

---

[1] Hotseating is a well-established exercise where the company asks questions of an actor 'in role'.

Reminiscent of Uta Hagen's notion of substitution, if material 'fails to stimulate you sufficiently, [then] you must search for something which will trigger an emotional experience' (Hagen 1973: 35).

Think as a director how you might use metaphors.

More rehearsal room breakthroughs: Individual and collective discoveries

Chapter 4 introduced 'The Four Lenses of Breakthrough' and detailed lens one: the small moments of recognition. Lens two is the 'aha' breakthrough moment, whereby an actor or director makes an individual discovery. Breakthroughs observed through this lens are classed as new discoveries and can accrue from the smaller moments of learning that have formed through lens one. This 'inspiration can be described in terms of a discovery: a dormant thought, feeling, or response suddenly re-emerges, preparing us to meet the world in all its turmoil' (Sidiropoulou 2019: 5). A deeper understanding happens for the director or actor, and new knowledge is gained. Again, its usefulness is to be aligned to the needs of the production frame(s) and is often verified by the director. For an inspirational moment to occur there needs to be a catalyst, 'in the form of something impromptu, a detail, an action, a moment of genuine truth' (Benedetti 2010: 331), which could be a directorial note or a rehearsal room challenge.

Lens three is another discovery moment but is a shared breakthrough between artists and celebrates the collective nature of theatre-making. For Wasserberg, a discovery is a moment of 'locking in, where the thing you all know in a cerebral and intellectual way is given breath and is alive. It's also where the space between two actors or more ignites with a truth'. Discoveries are again verified (often by the director) through an external recognition of the usefulness of the breakthrough aligned to the production frames. Lens three moves the emphasis away from individual moments to the collective, flattening hierarchies and supporting the notion that discovery can occur between people at any point in the process. Examples throughout this text illustrate how these discoveries are triggered by the collaborative interaction between designers, writers, directors and actors. Whilst these are rightly chaotic and unpredictable, they are important for the ongoing development of the rehearsal process and need to be recognised and unpacked when they occur.

It is worth positioning breakthroughs in relation to Csíkszentmihályi's five stages of creativity: 'preparation, incubation, insight, evaluation and elaboration' (2013: 79). If rehearsal breakthroughs are mapped onto Csíkszentmihályi's stages, the 'aha' moment would therefore need to be evaluated as something worth pursuing (which may also include verification) prior to a period of elaboration, where an idea is developed. One should not be too literal with these phases as they 'overlap and reoccur several times before the process is completed' (ibid.: 83); there may indeed be a 'thunderous "aha" made up from a chorus of little "eureka"s' (ibid.). The term 'evaluation' seems a formal concept, yet ideas are implicitly evaluated all the time in rehearsals, often against the production frames within which everyone is working.

Searching for a truth

Truth is an important benchmark to test the efficacy of a breakthrough moment, which is defined relative to the needs of the play, the genre, and the production's frames, as there can be no singular truth. Robert Baker-White positions rehearsals as a 'site of truth and authentic knowing' (1999: 23); for Dominic Dromgoole, the strength of acting lies in its being 'judicious and true in the playing of people and relationships' (2017: 34). Bella Merlin describes truth as a 'tricky word and an even trickier concept' (2011: 114), and how actors and directors know when a 'truth' has been reached is a messy and non-linear journey. From an actor's perspective, Merlin goes on to define truth in relation to a breakthrough where the actor says, 'Ah! Now I get it. Now I understand why the character says those words and executes these actions' (2015: 58), finding a rightness for the moment.

Distilling what is meant by 'truth' in acting means grappling with something nebulous. Are we looking for Merlin's 'lure' to unlock that truth? Or are we following Stanislavski's notion of truth being 'what we sincerely believe in our own and in our partners' hearts' (Merlin and Packer 2020: 154)? Donna Soto-Morettini, in *The Philosophical Actor*, takes a philosophical and syllogistic approach to truth. Stating that truth is 'elastic' (2010: 20) and arguing that actors should not be trapped by a single definition, Soto-Morettini's search for truth is related to her need to discover what makes something click in rehearsal, when there is a 'sense of feeling that a scene is going well' (2010: 30). As far back as 1968, Peter Brook pointed out that 'truth in the theatre is always on the move' (2008: 157), as genres and playwriting styles shift. If there is a sense of something working, then it is truthful relative to the context of the play, its genre and the production frames. If truth is on the move, each rehearsal period must discover its own relative truth.

Simon Godwin states that the director's role should be one of monitoring truth; when this occurs, the play 'works': 'When the play works . . . it's like even I am seeing it for the first time . . . [It's] probably something to do with spontaneity, which is essentially the aim; to get to a level of relaxation that a line, a looking, a moment, a way of listening can just be fresh. That's the truth' (Godwin: 2015). A director's benchmark is that truth on stage should 'evoke belief' (Stanislavski 2010: 18) for an audience and as truth can only be relative to the 'context' (Soto-Morettini 2010: 36) of the production, its genre and its style, in order for the audience to believe in the world, whether that world is Chekhov, pantomime, tucker green or Behn. In his text *Acting Stanislavski*, Gillett states that actors must 'play people fully and truthfully within the demands of the particular language and style of each play' (2014: xxiv). In the genre of British pantomime, children in the audience must believe in the relative truth of the mythical story and outlandish characterisation, for example, even though, logically, there is little real-world verisimilitude. Katie Mitchell retells a story of a neuroscientist observing an early career production of hers, who observed that there

> were two different types of acting going on: one was lifelike and the other was 'more heightened, self-conscious and theatrical'. He could cope with either, he said, but the moment that the brain struggled most was when the actors lurch[ed] between one style and another: in these moments, he lost all engagement with what was going on in the action of the play.
>
> (2009: 179)

A useful rethinking of truth comes from Demidov. By combining truth with experiencing, his 'authentic experiencing' (Malaev-Babel and Lasinka 2016: 46) is where an ' "authentic truth" [is found] living naturally in unnatural conditions' (ibid.: 60). A cohesive acting style must be arrived at within the relative and authentic truth of a production in the middle stages.

Actors finding truth within the subtext

Actors often make breakthroughs when links are made between the dialogue delivered by their characters and any potential subtext,[2] which alters the tone and physicality of a character in a particular moment. Kate Rossmanith argues that to discover the subtext of the scene is to understand and embody the 'underlying emotion' (2003: 114) of a moment, thus creating believability for the actor where a sense of truth can emerge. Patrice Pavis advanced that meaning can be made 'between different semiotic systems such as verbal and non-verbal, symbolic and iconic' (1992: 29), suggesting that a truth emerges from what the company or individual believe to be an appropriate subtextual choice. For Pavis, the 'non-verbal behaviour has so great an influence on the spectator's understanding of the ... text' (ibid.: 32), highlighting the importance of the non-verbal signifiers to generate meaning. Yet words are the final stage of communication. An actor ideally needs to begin with an immersion in the world and to experience the conditions of the moment, prior to the playwright's words being uttered. Yet, in rehearsals, we often begin with the words. Stanislavski stated that 'the line of the role is taken from the subtext, not the text itself' (2010: 118), and many études that were developed at the various studios of the Moscow Art Theatre were designed to interrogate this. Non-verbal étude work was one format, whereby actors connect with the experience of a moment working within the given circumstances supported in developing true experiencing. For Pavis, there is a difference between the 'dramatic text' as written and the 'performance text' of what is both visible and audible, including non-verbal communication (NVC), which can be driven

---

[2] Subtext sits beneath the text and is the unspoken feelings and thoughts of the character that often radiate through tone or non-verbal communication.

by subtext. Both Michael Chekhov and Stanislavski highlight the importance of an actor radiating subtext and inner feelings to an audience through NVC, as without this communication nuances of the moment may become shallow, or altogether lost. Radiation must 'give out everything [the actor] has inside' (White 2009: 33). Certain rehearsal room decision moments are reliant upon agreeing on the appropriate level of radiation, to reveal inner thoughts and feelings to an audience, whilst maintaining an appropriate theatrical truth, whereby a fellow character might not pick up on these clues.

Rick Kemp raises several salient points in relation to acting practice, which impacts on decision-making in rehearsals: 'an actor's task . . . is to dig beneath the surface, explore the forces that are in play, the desires, fears and emotions that underpin an exchange . . . and then make these forces manifest through the vocal, spatial and gestural means at their disposal' (2012: 79). Kemp also suggests that the 'meaning . . . of the scene' (ibid.: 45) is linked to working on NVC and subtext, arguing that the actor's main challenge is to turn written text into an 'embodied expression' (ibid.: 63). He concludes that the subtext is to be explored in rehearsal and that when 'consciously-chosen NVC appear[s] credible' (ibid.: 31), then there is a rightness to the theatrical moment within the production frames. The notion of credibility also must be decided upon, mainly by the outside eye of the director through verification of these choices.

Actor Ruth Wilson articulates the importance, for her, of the freedom director van Hove gave in directing her through physical actions when she played the title role in *Hedda Gabler* at the National Theatre in 2016. I asked van Hove to elaborate on how his method of the physical 'score of actions' works in practice and why he thought, for Wilson, these apparent 'constrictions [makes her] more creative' (Bennett and Massai 2018: 12). He replied that

> theatre is not only a language of words. People, if we consider theatre as a human art, are live and present in the auditorium and in theatre the art is the person on stage. So, for me it's very clear that we need to see people doing things: reading a book, strolling by, thinking, playing games, making love, killing. Everyone has different movements and they express them-selves not just by what they are saying. Audiences look at them and believe

there is a story to consider from their physicality. What are they thinking about? a movement can tell something and take a character further and bring unexpected things out of a character.

Opening up the dimensionality

When questioned about psychology, van Hove warns of not reducing the character to one single archetype, for example, 'a mother':

> I have a problem with pure psychological thinking, as when you do that, you could play a character that's one-dimensional. I was inspired by the French author, Amin Maalouf, who wrote *In the Name of Identity*. He develops the idea that we always reduce human beings to one thing. The book is about ethnical identity, as he's Lebanese and French. He says we have several identities: ten, twenty, thirty identities. In theatre, we tend to reduce characters to one or two identities, which I refuse to do. Some actors have a problem with my way of working, because I resent a purely psychological thinking, as it's not how we are as humans. Every day there's something unexpected that we have to react to. Every day, even when we have boring lives. Sometimes you react in a way you think you never would, such as getting angry over small things and you think: 'Why am I doing this?'

Decisions made during early stages concerning character should be re-examined in the light of working through the play, ensuring complexities are honoured, personalities are not reduced but become complex and even ambiguous if required. Playing the scene through the lens of different archetypal identities as an exercise can offer choice, dynamism and complexity. Hippolyta, Queen of the Amazons, for example, who has been captured in war by Theseus in *A Midsummer Night's Dream*, could easily be played as 'a warrior' in early rehearsals. Rehearsals in the middle stages could build on this by exploring her as 'a survivor', 'a nemesis', 'a wife' or 'a diplomat' to see what other possibilities unlock.

Integration in the middle stages of scenography

Chapter 4 advocated the importance of ensuring that designers integrate their work meaningfully rather than working in parallel to rehearsals. Designers Jess Curtis and Max Jones both share the belief that the British system of finalising the design prior to rehearsals can hinder a more fluid, sophisticated creative process. Jones is clear that part of his job is 'to get it "right up front" as . . . there is pressure on the designer to be successful before rehearsals commence, due to the build process. You don't get time to play and that's a flaw in the British design process, as everyone else is allowed to explore and evolve work.' Curtis states that 'in the UK you can't change the macro, but you might be able to change the microcosm and that comes from rehearsals'. Turning the challenge of current processes into creative opportunities is possible for Curtis and Jones but only ideally if they are present in rehearsals and can respond to the work. The ideal situation for Curtis is to 'spend all of my time in rehearsals, as they clarify everything beautifully'.

A more fruitful and collegiate manner of theatre-making is one where all the creatives are in rehearsals together throughout. However, if working at the pre-planned end of the polarity, what opportunities are there in the middle stages for design to respond to a deepening understanding of the world of the play? Curtis wants to use this middle period to 'flex those micro-choices around each actor: what they wear or touch, asking, "what is their mini-universe?"' Jones echoes this pragmatism, stating that 'the staging conceit remains the same, but details may shift, such as costume ideas based on casting and what they're doing. You can tinker with content, but it's more difficult to tinker with the architecture'. During the middle stage of *Close Quarters* rehearsals, Jones introduced an idea to Wasserberg and actor Bradley Banton, suggesting Banton, playing Sergeant Adeyemi, should have a conversation in scene two with Captain Sands whilst counting out bullets. I asked Jones about his decision-making in that moment: 'it's a way of emphasising the danger of the scenario. That's a nice example of a visual signifier on a small scale. You can have operatic-scale signifiers, but you're looking for a way to adapt small details that have a huge amount of weight. That evolves from rehearsals'. Keen to emphasise the importance of open collaboration, Jones asserts the directors I work with always come and have a chat about my take on a scene from a visual [perspective]. That moment I was thinking: 'What does that dialogue mean?' Or 'what is the tone of that conversation when it's said with an implement of death?' Captain Sands and Sergeant Adeyemi are talking about the careers and lives of twenty-year-old soldiers. I'm thinking about what the heat is under that conversation. That's how I design, where visual stage language can amplify the psychology of the moment. That's the designer's language.

Sonic landscapes also feed into the world of the production. As Gareth Fry attests, 'for some shows, the world is complex, busy and perhaps far from our everyday experience, so [being in rehearsals] becomes a valuable tool to develop both the sound design of the world and how the actors inhabit that world in rehearsals. Many actors have commented that having sound in rehearsals allows them to inhabit the world of the show'.

One rehearsal layer I introduce in the early stages and deepen during the middle stages is identifying and creatively responding to what pressures are being placed on the character's circumstances from the external world. This relates to the pressing issue[3] of a scene. In Lorca's *The House of Bernarda Alba*, pressing issues may include heat or the continual (off-stage) presence of Pepe el Romano. Fry gives a specific example when designing the sound for Katie Mitchell's production of *Women of Troy* at the National Theatre in 2007, where

> the outside world is often putting immense pressure on what is happening onstage. In *Women of Troy*, the offstage world they hear is their entire city being torn apart, people dying and other people being shipped off to become slaves. That's an immense external pressure. By having those sounds in rehearsals, the actors are more quickly able to immerse themselves in the world of Troy, and to more viscerally feel those pressures.

---

[3] A pressing issue is defined by Bella Merlin as a 'subject that underlines a dialogue, propelling it – either secretly or implicitly – in a particular direction and . . . it's the preoccupation which can drive a character's objective' (2016a: 79).

Thinking more deeply about ethical considerations

Ian Manborde of Equity is insistent that there needs to be a balance struck between freedom within rehearsals and the health and well-being of the company. Questioning what constitutes good practice within rehearsals, Manborde recognises that one of Equity's challenges 'is not wanting to impede the work and the process, whilst recognising there need to be safeguarding issues. There needs to be a recognition that there could be psychological harm, particularly around sexual scenes; if [that recognition isn't there,] then it's problematic'. Psychological harm can also manifest itself dependent on the part played. Michelle Terry describes how she 'was talking to Kathryn Hunter about playing King Lear and she said she had physical reactions to the play twenty years after she played it, just reading the play'. Expanding, Terry explains that 'if you're playing Rosalind from *As You Like It* every night, it's wonderful: you fall in love and it's a beautiful thing to carry around with you every day. But if you're playing Othello . . .' Terry believes in the importance of an actor checking in on themselves and a company checking in on each other, 'allowing time for those conversations' in rehearsal, time to de-role as much as inhabit a character and noticing and acting on any distress and ideally not allowing it to develop into something that could cause harm over the course of a long run.

Matthew Xia similarly advocates a sincere and explicit duty of care in rehearsals, where there is a concrete demonstration of ethical approaches, rejecting notions that ' "everything is allowed" and "everything is permitted" . . . It's a workplace! We think we have a duty of care in our industry. But then we get into the rehearsal room and we traumatize and bully and scar and ask people to dredge up deep-seated, packed-away trauma from their childhood, or two weeks ago. And that's massively dangerous'. So, what are the philosophies underpinning Xia's rehearsal strategies?

This is a borrowed quote from Lyndsey Turner, genius that she is: 'All I need, from everyone I'm working with, in every space I work with them, is for them to be a professional, adult artist'. That's it for me. What would a professional, adult artist not do in the workplace? They wouldn't put their hand up your top. OK, but what if the stage direction says: 'He puts his hand up her top'? Well, this is a dance now. We're into choreography, we're into intimacy direction, we're into illusion. We're into the imagination.

Illusion is a concept Xia refers to often; with his background in magic, it is no surprise that this informs his directorial aesthetic. Against the backdrop of professionalism and a duty of care, Xia uses the playtext as primary mediator to stage these moments safely and ethically. He begins by

investigating it fully. Why has the writer put it there? Do we need it to be as physical and true as it is on the page? If yes, OK, then let's go down that path. Who is best to help us get there? Hannah Patterson's *Eden*, a play I made at Hampstead in 2019, had two girls who had been in love when they were younger and rediscover this in a night of passion on a beach. The text says: 'She puts her hand up her top, and she grips her breasts'. If you just have two actors go at each other on stage, you're going to end up with a lawsuit. You're going to end up damaging somebody. I think people have gotten away with all sorts of mad power-trips for years and years and years in this industry and continue to. Policies appear, but the stories don't go away. So, for me, it's like it's an office. It's a workplace: it's really simple.

Xia also removes himself from any method that places emotional memory at the heart of the process. He jokes about asking the actors: ' "When was the last time you hit someone? How did that feel? OK, so put that into this moment". No! No, please, don't!'

Piecing, stumbling, staggering and running

During the middle stages of rehearsals, the piecing together of various sections and scenes, as well as running through acts and the play as a whole, frequently occurs. If these become a place to push for results, there is then a danger of short-cutting the process and challenge outweighs the skill. As opposed to simply using the catch-all term 'run-through', I posit several stages and by offering a more nuanced set of terms, practitioners are able to match the challenge to the skill at these points:

1. Piecing: It is valuable to piece together a bit worked on in a rehearsal call, as opposed to leaving it akin to an unbuilt Lego set, strewn across the floor. This gives a chance for actors to embody some of the slower processual work and to test the efficacy of any decisions.

2. Stumbling: This is an increased piecing together of an extended section, or indeed the entire play. A stumble-through allows the actor to sense the arc of a section and its journey, as well getting a sense of sustaining scenes. It also permits the actor to sustain what Bella Merlin refers to as dynamic listening[4] and allows actors, particularly in farce, pantomime, musicals or the classics, to gain an awareness of the stamina needed for the piece and how to pace themselves. As with the piecing stage, I always find that stumble-throughs are more useful for the actor than the director, and many directors will actually stumble through the whole play at the end of the first week of rehearsals. I have, however, heard these referred to as 'run-throughs', which often does nothing but engender fear and dread in the hearts of the acting company. These stumbles are also useful to ascertain whether anything is overcomplicated. As Kirstie Davis states, 'if all the actors are doing is battling against something, there's no point. I'll throw it away if they struggle. I've probably tried to overcomplicate it.'

3. Staggering: This bridges a stumble-through and a pressurised run-through. Whilst at the stumbling stage there may be many stops and starts, a stagger-through allows for continuity wherever possible. I might also give specific points of concentration here, such as honouring the stakes, sharpening the emotional and physical imagined journey between scenes, or focusing on any time pressures people are under. Following this, I undertake a notes session.

4. Running: A focused run-through in the rehearsal room allows the actors to get a real time sense of the full piece. Where possible, scene

---

[4] Dynamic Listening is one of the four guiding principles Merlin espouses in her *Complete Stanislavsky Toolkit* (2011) which encourages actors to really listen to one another, including listening to pauses. This dynamic listening follows the pattern of: action (I do something to you), reaction (I respond consciously or not, having perceived what is outside of myself), decision (what I do consciously or not in relation to that experience).

changes and transitions are also undertaken in real time. Aiming for several run-throughs in the final week, with time for notes and working in-between, allows ample opportunity to sharpen or alter moments.

Visitors to the rehearsal room should be told at what stage things are at, to reduce expectations for actors to 'push', resulting to representational acting. Scheduling staggers and runs with advance warning is vital, as there is an increased level of anxiety for the company, and to surprise a cast with the announcement of a run-through does nothing to generate a creative state. An actor needs to be prepared physically, mentally and vocally for these. Insisting on a full focus on the work, with mobile phones turned off and distractions at a minimum, is respectful as all energies concentrate on the collective endeavour of telling the story. The wider team such as marketing personnel, other creatives, administrators and producers will also want to know when they can observe these and should be invited to all stagger-throughs and run-throughs as a common courtesy.

Noting and self-noting

What should you note when watching a stagger or run through as a director? Directors should give full attention to the action and work of what is happening in front of them as opposed focusing their attention on their scripts. The DSM (or a free actor in the space where there isn't the luxury of stage management) can have a directorial eye on the text and check for cues and paraphrasing. By not having to focus on their text, the director is able to get a sense of the piece through the eyes of the audience in the moment and observe the space between actors and the quality of their connections. Ignite gut responses: Did you laugh? Were you bored? Is the storytelling clear? Is the storytelling dynamic? Are the stakes high enough? Is the character connected to the need and want of their situation? Are actors pre-determining results or living truthfully within the given circumstances of the moment?

I mainly try to scribble notes down between scenes and acts; if I can't remember a note, then it probably wasn't important. Notes and feedback give a mark in the sand, allowing decisions to be made concerning the next stages of rehearsals. Josie Rourke's directorial notebooks reveal that she makes few notes in rehearsal room run-throughs, with her notes on the first run-through for *King John*, at the RSC in 2006, amounting to only four sides of A4, with considerable blank space between. There are broad brushstroke notes, aiming to continue to explore content and not lock in form, as well as precise notes for individual actors, such as her note to Patrick Robinson, which reads 'Patrick: you are solving a moment of crisis' (Rourke 2006b). Targeted notes are, as Rourke demonstrates, vital for actors to understand the specificity of thinking.

I ask actors to note themselves following a run, to begin a habit of self-feedback as they progressively take ownership of the process. Many of the comments that I might go on to make have already been acknowledged by the actor and reveal where there might be any misaligned thinking between us, which can then be more easily and openly navigated.

Some genre thinking

During the middle stages of a musical theatre rehearsal, the company should be developing a nuanced way of travelling between dialogue, choreographed or physicalized sections and sung text. I look for whether an actor has been affected by the underscore, when moving from spoken text into song, for example. A musical's middle rehearsal stage can ascertain whether certain routines or sections need further work in relation to embodying the choreography.

For comedy or farce, more stumble-throughs and stagger-throughs may be scheduled as a director needs to determine whether the verbal and physical comedy is being delivered with ease, and whether the physical comedy is sharp and not overcomplicated. Not being afraid to simplify and go back to basics when something isn't bedding in well is crucial. When rehearsing Restoration comedy, as well as certain of the heightened comedies of Oscar Wilde, the middle period of rehearsals can ensure that a mannered style isn't subsuming the character as human being. All too often at this middle stage there can be an emptiness, where period gestures, codified physical language or heightened delivery supersedes any human connection beneath the artifice. This is especially so within Restoration comedy and some Wilde, where real pain and misogyny bubbles beneath a thin layer of fanciful fans and beautiful bows.

When directing theatre for young audiences (TYA), the stagger-throughs may benefit from young eyes watching the rehearsals. Is the target audience engaged? Are there enough of what playwright David Wood terms 'suddenlies' (Foot 2006) to hold the attention of young eyes and minds? These 'suddenlies' can take the form of a new character, a sound effect or lighting change, a costume swap, a new prop or puppet. Similarly, when directing pantomime, I observe the mid-rehearsal stagger-through through the children's eyes as they are in the chorus and are present in the room. I question: are they vocally and physically participating in the appropriate ways, as demanded by the genre? Do I need to sharpen the structure of comedic set-ups? Is there a healthy balance between physical and verbal humour? Are they bored?

Concentrating on classical or verse-based drama, I determine whether the language is becoming embodied and whether there is a balance between the heightened nature of the verse text and a sense of 'large truth'. Having worked through the play at least once, I am also interested in whether the narrative polarities of both the play and the journeys of individual characters are being honoured, as there are considerable transformations, changes and differences in terms of emotions, positions, attitudes, events and world views. Within classical texts, these are often across single speeches, scenes and acts, just as much as they are across the whole play. Finally, I am also sensing whether the stakes of these plays are being fulfilled as plays by writers such as Lorca, Shakespeare, Molière and Cervantes embrace themes of life, death, suicide, murder, love, passion, hatred, secrecy, jealousy, revenge and vengeance. Are the stakes of what is to be lost and won being honoured and are the key events affecting the characters?

Finally, in relation to the delivery of the language against the polarity of 'to plan or not to plan', this stage can ascertain whether certain early choices are being cemented too soon and if any pre-decisions are halting the genuine experiencing and dynamic listening cycle of the actors in the scene.

A summary of Chapter 5

The middle stages are a time of continued creativity and increasing flow. Disparate pieces give way to sections of the piece that can be stumbled through, staggered through and ultimately run together. Noting is crucial at this stage, as is knowing when – and how – to note as a director and self-note as an actor. As skills increase, so must challenges; where these challenges can be augmented by the integration of design and scenic elements, then so much the better. Building the ensemble is crucial, as connection and familiarity deepen, not only through collaboration but shared ritual and play: a notion taking us right back to our first exploration of the history of rehearsal and of storytelling itself. A crucial part of this ensemble building – and an element that has sometimes been neglected in the past – is company well-being. Artistic needs and freedom must be balanced with the well-being of individual company members. Both those interviewed and those whose published work has been drawn on emphasize the importance of truth during this process; however, it is important to note that truth is nebulous, elastic and relative, inextricably linked with genre and framework, but requires cohesion, whether through uniformity of acting style, or a sympathy between the designed world and the storytelling. My 'Four Lenses of Breakthrough' introduced in the previous chapter continue to be in play during these stages, often with collective discovery coming to the fore as the ensemble coheres and the piece begins to flow.

Chapter 6 now moves on to the final stages of rehearsal process, as the piece arrives at a form. The chapter also looks at how, in practical terms, the director can help the actors towards their task of needing to replicate their work on cue, each night of the run, whilst not sacrificing immediacy, freshness and clarity.

Interview with Roy Alexander Weise

Roy Alexander Weise is joint Artistic Director of the Royal Exchange Theatre in Manchester. I talked to him about his journey into theatre, his ambitions for the theatre, inclusivity and diversity and why he makes theatre.

Tell me about your journey into theatre.

I don't come from a family of artists. I'm sure that they do see the value of art, but they don't see the value of their children being artists. I'm from a really working-class background: both my parents were immigrants. So, we're first generation. We're like the first generation of British in our family, and neither of my parents were university educated either, and I went to Archbishop Tenison's in Oval and I was always into music. Music was massive in my household. And I was, like, 'I'm going to be a singer songwriter.'

And one day, I, really randomly, on the way home from school – I mean, literally about thirty seconds after coming out of the gate and walking down the street, thought, 'I need to use the toilet'. And there was this building, and I was like, 'I'm just going to go in and ask if they have a toilet'. They were like, 'Yeah, fine', and when I came out, they said: 'Oh, we have all of these classes. This is a theatre.' And I thought, 'OK'. I didn't know anything at all about theatre, but I was a very open child, and I feel like I threw myself at lots of different extracurricular things – whatever was free, anyway – I threw myself at that.

And then I got asked to be in this play called *More Light* and played the emperor, and I remember, I got my hair done into really small plaits and it was a real event. It's an old East Asian tale about an emperor who dies, and all of his wives who mourn. So, you've got this massive chorus of his all of his wives. And I literally died in the first few minutes. And then I just played dead. The whole play, the entire play, just lying on the floor, dead. And it was quite an experience, and a bit of a challenge. I was a very chatty, fidgety kid. But it taught me a lot of discipline, and I really enjoyed it, and hearing the drama going on around me, while I was playing dead.

And then, a few years later, not long after I turned sixteen, my mum suddenly passed away, and it was massive and devastating – as devastating as I think it could be for anybody. And then, I remember the day after I found out that my mum had died, I went to the theatre, and it was the only place after that I wanted to be, because I felt safe, and I knew that there was a space there for me.

A few months after that, I got asked to play the lead in the first ever production of Enda Walsh's play *Chatroom* as part of NT Connections. It's about cyberbullying, effectively, and about bullying in general, and about identity and finding your place, and finding your own safety, but also about the way in which this boy was trying to find closure to what he understood was quite a traumatic childhood and move into the next stage of his life. It was a kind of coming-of-age play. And I did that play, which had this wealth of tension and conflict and emotions. And I feel like having this story structure to exist within, night after night, in performance. I started to feel myself understanding what I was going through, and I started to understand my grief. I was sixteen, and I really realised the power of theatre. And I decided at that point: 'This is what I want to do. This is exactly what I want to do.' After drama school I assistant directed for about seven-and-a-half years before I got my first show. In 2016 I won the JMK Award and directed *The Mountaintop*, which is the play I'm about to open at the Royal Exchange later this year [2021] in its third iteration. But after that, it was a very steep climb, because a year after that, I was already working on my first show at the National, and it was just crazy. But yeah, in those seven-and-a-half years, there was a lot of hard graft, a lot of wanting to give up, a lot of going away and coming back, in order to fight against the odds; to actually succeed and build a career.

It sounds like that pivotal moment at sixteen was about making sense of what was happening to you in the world at that point. For me, storytelling is about sensemaking isn't it? Is that why live theatre is the medium for you?

I feel like I found the best articulation for this only last year, actually. So, I got asked to run a masterclass in directing at the Troubadour Theatre in Wembley and had these amazing young and emerging actors, directors and writers in this big workshop with me. And we heard this massive commotion outside, and we all go to the window and we all stare outside the window. And there are two cars that have almost crashed into each other. And both the drivers are getting out, and they're about to fight. And all of us are absolutely gripped and frightened for them. And then, the conversations that started happening were all about what we would do if we were there: 'Just get back in the car, get back in the car! Don't pay any attention to him!' And I could really hear everybody exercising that muscle that theatre allows us to exercise, which is sort of like a scenario-and-strategy in preparation for when we experience some of these really challenging things in real life, so that we start to learn about how we might approach things. But at the core of it was that we were all bearing witness to this event, live. And I feel like it really reminded me of moments when a murder happens in a play or, even something like somebody saying, 'I don't love you.' And an audience gasping, and us bearing witness to that thing together; that somehow, in the sounds that we make, the ways in which our bodies move, collectively and individually, we all begin to understand that we're not alone.

And I think one of the things about emotions is that we all experience them differently, and in such different orders; we all process them so differently. But nonetheless, to know that people experience an emotion similar to one that you are [experiencing], is a subconscious community building-thing. We know that we're not alone in that moment. I sort of feel that in the world that we live in now, and the society that we live in, Western society in particular, individuality and individualism that is such a massive part of being.

Theatre allows a community of strangers to become a community of people. And I can't really let go of the possibility, therefore, that we have with this art form to give people the tools to understand those people who were strangers when they entered that room. And it's even more acute here at the Royal Exchange because we have this arena where you can't watch a play without watching somebody else. And I think that there's something so incredible that I'm continuing to learn about that collective act of bearing witness, and how powerful it can be for the individual and the collective.

How do your values marry with the Exchange's values?

There was a year when I just got really fed up with theatre in London, and I was really struggling to find shows where I could see the black experience. And I went on the Royal Exchange's website. And lo and behold, two shows on in the main house and the studio with all black casts. And I was like, 'Wow!' And it was Talawa's production, Michael Buffong's production with Talawa, of *All My Sons*, and Michaela Coel's brilliantly epic one-woman show, *Chewing Gum Dreams*. And I remember going to the Royal Exchange and watching these two shows. Obviously *All My Sons* is Arthur Miller, and he's not a black man, but to see performances by black actors, and then to see a story originated by a black actor. My family are Ghanaian and Jamaican, and Michaela is Ghanaian. And so much of the story was about growing up in a very Christian Ghanaian family, and I grew up in a very Christian Ghanaian family, and so I just felt my life was being reflected back to me in the most potent way.

And I got asked to read for the Bruntwood Prize. And I have a massive passion for playwriting and originating new stories, yet also see huge merit in classical work, and the ways in which we can really zoom out of the micro a moment or a time, and experience the macro of what it is to understand that story in relation to where we are today, and where we hope or want to be individually and collectively in the future. I love classic work for that. But I think there's something so incredible about the way in which new writing is like the heartbeat of a nation in a moment. The fact that the Royal Exchange really invests in and is excited by radical adaptations, radical classical work, and brilliant and bold and fresh new writing and new voices; in terms of the actual styles of work and forms of work, it really sat well with me.

I had moments at the beginning of my career where I was trying to understand where I would go, and I thought: 'Well, I'm just going to be one of those artists that's on the periphery, making work that's really important to me and to the people that I want to see it. And I don't care if it's above a pub or in a car park or wherever. I'm going to steal or borrow the space that I need to let to tell the stories that I need to tell.' And then I remember getting asked to do *Nine Night* at the National Theatre, and I asked my brother, 'What makes you go to the theatre? What plays have you seen?' And everything that he listed was in the West End. Everything that he listed was on the side of a bus, basically. And I thought: 'Well, that is a way to reach more people.' And I think that art can pack a real punch, and art can give people the tools to question the world around them. And so, we don't have to make propaganda, that is, like, smashing politics over people's heads. But we can make brilliant entertainment that challenges in simple ways. And so directing *Nine Night* was an amazing thing, because it really allowed me to understand what it is to make a piece of popular art and in a really intentional way and so I really started to believe in mainstream art through telling this kitchen-sink mainstream drama. And that's one of the things that I've really enjoyed about the Royal Exchange: being able to hold the duality of complex 'high art' and really accessible work.

One of the really big things that got me excited about the Royal Exchange is its desire to connect with ordinary people; the desire to constantly push the boundaries of who this space is for, who belongs here and who can take up space. I now understand the power that an artistic directorship holds, because essentially, the organisation's values do become the values that Bryony [Shanahan, co-artistic director] and Steve [Freeman, Executive Director] and myself set. Brilliantly, these values are not very far from the values that already exist in this company: they're just an extension. What our values are now is very particular to this time and what we need to in order to facilitate social impact through the theatre.

Have you found then that your role as co-chief executive and artistic director has been able to shift dominant ways of working?

Yeah, absolutely. We've made some really massive, bold changes to our structures, the ways that we're working; we're continuing to do that, continuing constantly to evaluate it. We want to be a theatre that is constantly outward- and forward-facing, and future-facing, and not an organisation that ever gets wedded to any one particular idea about what it is supposed to be. And of course, identity is a really important part of that, and audiences want to know what your identity is. I feel like the identity of the Royal Exchange is open to all. The work will challenge you and give you the tools to engage with the rest of the world, and your neighbours, and those strangers that you sit with in that auditorium, in a very simple way. But obviously, that branches out and bleeds off into so much more nuance as you unpack it.

The pursuit of inclusivity and access is also urgent. The revolutions that have been happening in the world in the last year and a half [Black Lives Matter, #MeToo et al.]; we've paid really close attention to them. And, of course, there's so much revolution happening in our sector, and so much uprooting happening in our sector. We're trying to make a company that can work and function a bit like a rehearsal room can: ready-to-go and nimble; reactive, but also strategic at the same time. It's a place where all the voices are valid, where all the voices are dramaturgs, and where everybody has a stake in the organisation, and the organisation has a stake and a responsibility to everyone. That's a part of it as well. To really shift that culture. We've made a bit of a kind of a change in priorities. So, the Royal Exchange structurally existed, if you looked to our budgets and you looked at the way that we spent money – and it's hard to get away from this even still – but it was so clear that our investment was in the art and in the productions, which you could argue is an investment in the people as well. But then you looked at our budgets for audience development. We looked at the hike in prices in tickets before the pandemic, and whom that excluded. It made us put accessibility and inclusion at the heart of what we do and how we connect with Greater Manchester, and really sowing seeds, and building amazing bonds, and discovering what the values of the communities around us are, and the ways that we can connect with those values, and make those connections, through a two-way exchange.

It feels like it goes back to the origins of the organisation, too: the 69 Theatre Company?

Absolutely. And the democracy of the current space, the democracy of performance in that space and voyeurism in that space are key. Bryony and I had a conversation with Marianne Elliott, whose father, Michael Elliott, was one of the founding directors of the Royal Exchange Theatre, when it was the theatre that had five artistic directors. But one of the things that Marianne told us is that the founders wanted the audience and the performers to enter from the same space, so that the gods and the villains and the pauper all shared the same space and entered the same space. And so status was level and it was possible for anybody that entered that space to imagine that they could be, or that they are, anyone of the characters that they encounter in a performance or production. And that was just such an incredible, enlightening thing to hear. That democracy of who owns the space is absolutely something that's important. I guess the last thing is that given the Royal Exchange as a building, its history and its connection to the transatlantic slave trade, there's also something about the occupation in this space. If we left – if our theatre company left – it would probably become a big shopping mall. And I don't think that there could be anything worse for society than for it to become a retail space or an office space. So, there's something about the occupying of this space. And we totally understand that, like that relationship with the transatlantic slave trade, people have very complex relationships with us in the theatre. But we realise the huge value in reclaiming, as well. And that's a really, really important thing for us.

I know that you've been a real vocal advocate for diversification of audiences. Could you talk me through how we continue on that journey?

This work takes a lot of time, it takes a lot of money, it takes a lot of patience, it takes a lot of vulnerability, and it takes a lot of bravery, which is why it's a really difficult thing for us to fix, but it really takes an individual and a collective organisation really turning themselves inside out, shaking themselves out like a pocket to see what exists there, what preconceptions, what biases, what misjudgements exist there. It's not just about getting people in to do the work, it's what support you give also, and also how you make sure that you don't patronise.

One of my big pet peeves is the idea that we think that we can just knock on a community's door, and invite them to come and watch a show, and then disappear. Why should they invest in us if we're not investing in them? And I think what that investment looks like is really spending the time to understand the values of the people, really understanding that you – that we, as British theatre – have to be humble.

At the core of the conversation is people *really* understanding why diversity is important and *really* understanding how detrimental it is to our society that we allow capital-fuelled-and-driven machines to tell the stories of who people are for the sake of, like, flash entertainment, and headlines, and news, and the misconceptions that have been told, and the lies that have been told about who the variety of communities are, on screen, on stage . . . So many people have been missed out and missed off and not been seen. And I think, in a society for people to feel invested, they've got to feel a connection to the democracy that they're supposed to be a part of. We have to allow everyone to really see how they are connected and plugged into the society that they are a part of, through the stories that we tell about all of the people that exist in our societies and communities.

Sometimes, we get one black person, or one Asian person in the cast and we feel like we've done some good work. Our rooms, our spaces, our theatres and auditoriums have to reflect who is on public transport. In the major cities, at least, where there is huge diversity. I look outside in Manchester, like Market Street, just across the road from where we're based, just off Cross

Street: and there's everyone, every language, every sound, music, different styles of dress and we see different ways in how people move and navigate life.

And we don't have that in our theatre. And that's not just because people don't want to come to the theatre; people just do not believe that this space is for them. And I think having now understood how much storytelling and theatre and live performance can enrich my life and the lives of people around me, I really understand what it is, in some ways, to be privileged. It should stop becoming a privilege to have access to art and entertainment and self-expression. It should feel like you *can* be a part of it, to feel like you *can* tell your story.

The last thing that I would say is that discrimination has taken centuries to build. And it's not going to take just a few decades to unravel. Think about the world that Martin Luther King lived in, in 1968, the year that he died. And what was happening to people then. He was saying, 'Let me live.' And we look at where we are today. That's, what, sixty years? And there's absolutely no way that we would have fixed it quickly. This has to be done in our lives, our next generation, and the generations yet to come. And I think the sooner people realise that, the more that they realise how much of a priority it needs to be. Because it's not going to be something that one season of work, or two, or three, or one theatre organisation, or even one country can fix.

So it's working with what you can do, within the micro of the theatre, and take time to have that exchange with the communities that you serve, but seeing it as a long-term approach?

Absolutely. And when we go, it won't be done. That's for sure. Let's think about how far the journey of Eurocentric feminism, the journey that that has taken over the last century, for instance. And yet still this iPhone 12 Pro Max I'm holding is made for the hand of a man. Medicine, modern medicine, is still tested and made for the male anatomy. And there's still so long a journey to go there. So, we have to think about it comparatively and realise the huge amounts of work that we've got to do and where we really need to pay attention to the progress of the world.

6

Growing up: Final stages and the emergence of the form

'"How can that moment be better?" "That's boring!" "How do we fix that?" "Oh, gosh, I want to leave!" Your job is to look at it and go: "Is it boring?" Then work out why, then stop it from being that!' Matthew Xia's inner thoughts in the later stages of rehearsals place boredom thresholds front and centre: is the story being told dynamically? For Xia, 'fixing that' concerns moment-to-moment sharpening and clarifying. This chapter presents exercises and ideas which, it is hoped, will support actors and directors in identifying what elements to enhance, as well as when to recognise to leave things alone. Kate Wasserberg gives her actors even sharper attention at this point, critically responding to the work in front of her: 'I pay attention to what's happening in front of me and I am alive to seeing if the decision I insisted on last week is still working.' Not being afraid to let go of, adapt or change elements at this final stage is paramount, as is holding your nerve as public performance looms. In that final week, Wasserberg aims to continue to discover and play, whilst also aiming 'to do a run every day. It's discovery and run every day. The actors have multiple opportunities to run, and I have all the props and costumes, so they are confident with the practicalities.' This is the balancing of impulse and technique with trusting gut responses in order to progress, whilst drawing on technique to develop and enrich prior work.

Regardless of genre, rehearsal strategy or text, one thing is certain: a form is reached. Content has been explored and a form may have organically developed through the earlier stages of rehearsal. Returning to the polarity of 'to block or not to block', whether a piece is deliberately loose in its physical blocking or whether it is one whose structure is highly controlled, such as a mega-musical, a form is always arrived at. In a commercial theatre environment, this is often required of the actors and director by the producer; this is especially true of a revival, a musical or a pantomime, whereas a two-hander play may have a less concrete physical form in terms of its staging.

Whilst form often relates to blocking, in a much more nuanced manner form is reflective of directorial decisions, specifically in relation to the polarity of auteur directorial concepts versus the invisible director. If a high-concept production is rehearsed with an auteur at the helm, the form will be filtered through this vision. Even the most anarchic of production concepts has an internal logic and works within the frame of this. Even in the most freeing of rehearsal processes, there will be certain technical parameters around moments of health and safety, such as intimacy, fights or scenographic considerations. A rehearsal process that foregrounds actors working on impulse may still wish to reach or sharpen certain stage images or have elements and events that require honouring for clear and dynamic storytelling.

It is up to you to decide on the form, and to know this in advance of rehearsals. Directors should communicate this clearly at audition or casting call stages. Actors who have an explicit understanding of the rehearsal process within which they work have a comfortable and safe knowledge of the expectations and parameters around which the process coalesces. Knowing this is vital; if this hasn't been made clear, tensions can manifest themselves. A seemingly free early rehearsal process that allows for the input and ideas of actors that at this stage becomes a totalitarian state in miniature is not conducive for actor ownership, final embodiment and the overall creative atmosphere.

The actor fully embodies and letting go

The actor now should preferably have embodied cerebral understanding. The intention is that 'what is in the head [has moved] to the body' (Wright 2001: 28) and the directorial role is to ensure that this is transpiring. Beginning with the premise that 'all acting is embodied' (Kemp 2012: xvi), if this is not manifesting itself, swift action needs to be undertaken. Directorially ensuring that everybody is arriving at their destination at a similar time is a crucial skill and this psycho-physical embodiment is essential for ownership of the role to take place and for actors to 'let go' and experience truthfully within their immediate circumstances. Actors should likewise raise concerns with their directors.

Psycho-physical acting, as outlined in Chapter 1, debunks the myth of 'cerebral versus somatic' approaches to rehearsal. Psycho-physicality can be said to be the 'totality in which the actor fully experiences and embodies the role, and is present in the moment, drawing on sensory information and experience, as opposed to simply sorting out the movements as might be done in early stages of rehearsal' (Whyman 2016: 158). For an actor, there is a need to reach this stage with the minimum possible rehearsal clutter, whereby lines have been learnt, givens are understood and moves are somatically encoded, in order that genuine experiencing can occur. Demidov states that when actors 'rapidly [engage] with their character's circumstances ... the actor begins to merge (synthesise) with [the] character's persona, with all of his given circumstances, [and their] personality will change' (Malaev-Babel and Lasinka 2016: 510). Ivo van Hove suggests that 'great actors are open to a process, stepping into a rehearsal like in life, not knowing what the next line would be, not knowing the next line of the conversation: that's really important'. This is the Holy Grail of the acting and rehearsal process, in order to reach the 'I am', which 'donates the actor's attentive "existence" in the "very middle of imagined life" ... and his/her "living it authentically" rather than just playing it' (Shevtsova 2020: 102). This is the elusive 'letting go' moment for the actor, trusting prior discoveries and being in the moment. Many directors ask their actors to 'let go' (Daboo, Loukes and Zarrilli 2013: 40) with the aim that actors connect with one another, perceive their immediate given circumstances and respond accordingly. Ken Rea believes an actor should choose the 'high risk peaks, having risked the troughs along the way' (2015b: 101) as to take risks *is* to let go where, for Demidov, 'effort is gone ... as a path to the working of the subconscious' (Malaev-Babel and Lasinka 2016: 533). Plotting in stumble-throughs and stagger-throughs at the liminal middle stage of rehearsal can act as a benchmark in terms of whether this can ultimately be reached collectively in the final stages, and whether the actor is trusting their psycho-physicality.

Courage is also related to risk, as 'going there takes courage' (Ginters 2006: 55). This aligns with the notion of 'willing vulnerability' (Merlin 2013a: 24) and this inclination is supported by Mihály Csíkszentmihályi, who details that creativity involves the 'willingness to take risks' (2013: 72); the unconscious supersedes conscious thought where early to mid-stage embodied rehearsal work is trusted. The scaffold of earlier rehearsal work supports the actor as they make genuine moment-to-moment connections in the now, today and here, as actors trust their prior decisions.

Chris Johnston, in *The Improvisation Game: Discovering the Secrets of Spontaneous Performance*, argues that one of benefits of an ensemble company is that actors who are familiar with each other can be braver earlier, since this bravery 'makes the risk-taking process much less fearful' (2006: 137) as 'risk is a key ingredient in the act of violence and articulation' (Bogart 2001: 48). To return to Bruce Tuckman's work on group cohesiveness, embodiment and letting go can be seen to be part of the 'norming' stage. Tuckman defines 'norming' as being when a 'cohesiveness develop[s], new standards evolve, and new roles are adopted. In the task realm, intimate, personal opinions are expressed. Thus, we have the stage of norming' (1965: 96).

Anne Bogart's metaphor of the 'attack' highlights the need to take risks. She articulates how, in the Japanese language

> when attacked, you always have two options: to enter, *irimi*, or to go around, *ura*. ... To enter or 'to choose death' means to enter fully with the acceptance, if necessary, of death. The only way to win is to risk everything and be fully willing to die. ... To achieve the violence of decisiveness one has to 'choose death' in the moment by acting fully and intuitively.
>
> (2001: 49)

Pitting this against the polarity of 'to plan versus not to plan', letting go relates to living truthfully within these dynamic listening cycles, whereby actors do not consciously draw upon their rehearsal room planned work, but allow themselves to be present, scaffolded by previous decisions and to respond to the action and given circumstances of all that surrounds them. Not planning what might happen is essential to letting go.

Clarity of storytelling

Let us return to Matthew Xia's question: 'How can that moment be better?' This can be answered in part by sharpening the clarity of the storytelling, moment-to-moment. Dan Rebellato states clearly that theatre professionals should not

> repeat the silly but persistent idea that theatre is entirely created in the minds of the audience. The theatre artists shape, for the most part, the performance object and these decisions are crucially important; however, the audience determines its significance, meaning, affect, resonance, understanding, reach, function, ambiguity, playfulness, profundity and power.
>
> (2013: 14)

One example of storytelling clarity during *Close Quarters* was the layering in terms of how the audience would potentially contextualise and make sense of location and emotional energies at the start of a scene, particularly as the set was a metaphorical playground rather than a mimetic space. The clarity of the characters being in their bunkroom sharpened with each rehearsal, as the visual signifiers were increasingly defined by the company as a whole: shoes were polished, water bottles drunk from, beds made; there was a degree of comfort and security with the characters being present in their own setting. This was in tandem with the actors impulsively undertaking those activities with a particular quality reflecting their internal psychology: shoes were polished vigorously, water bottles were drunk from rapidly, beds were made with anger. Another example is from one transition sequence choreographed by combat company RC-Annie, where Wasserberg felt there was a lack of 'rightness'. To sharpen the story beat, she gave a simple direction to the cast imploring 'urgency, urgency, urgency, urgency, urgency', which aligned the specific movements to the acting intentions, encouraging them not to 'think of it as a movement sequence but think of it as getting ready to go [on patrol] ... and let the scene flow through the movement' (Marsden 2018: l.258). The tension in the sequence when replayed was palpable, as collective embodied notes radiated through the actor's bodies.

Kate Rossmanith's notion of 'rightness' is trusting that feeling and allowing an overt path towards sharpening story beats. Working on the polarity of impulse versus technique, being attuned as an actor or director to feeling impulsively that there is something 'not right' and then being able to articulate this to the company is central to unpacking a moment and moving forward.

Exercises for the final stages

Atmospheres

Building on the work of Russian acting practitioner Michael Chekhov, explore whether atmospheres are being both created and perceived. Some characters are subsumed by dominant atmospheres and others hold their ground. Some characters wish to change atmospheres and others wish to maintain the status quo.

Articulating inner lives

This is a well-known exercise, where an actor speaks their inner thoughts continually, even when other characters are speaking. There must be genuine dynamic listening and I ask actors to really commit to their inner thoughts and feelings and to get this into their bodies and voices, so it can be a very loud exercise! I also ask actors to frame their inner thoughts via three questions: 'what do I think about that?', 'what do I feel about that?' and 'what do I want to do about that?' Following the scene, we discuss the exercise and if I have heard something that I do not feel is useful, or if something has not been included, I ask the actor to feed that into their inner life thinking next time.

Emotion or action?

Demidov uses the phrase 'motor-storm' (Malaev-Babel and Lasinka 2016: 55) to describe actors who believe they are experiencing but are actually 'acting' acting and emotionally overplaying. Tamara Harvey explains when she is watching her actors, she is 'least interested in performers that are concerned with their own emotional state. I'm interested in the active side. What are you trying to make the other person feel? How are you wanting to change the other person? Please don't feel you need to portray your own emotional state, or I might weep from the boredom.'

Problems and solutions, allies and enemies

If you feel as an actor feels though there is nowhere else to go, try exploring the following questions from your character's perspective:

What are your main problems?
Do you keep them internalised or articulate those?
Where might the solutions be housed? Within you or others?
How will you go about gaining your solution? In the specific scene, in thought or action?
Who might your allies be; who can help you?
Who are your enemies; who is hindering you?
When does any of the above shift?

Solutions might not be found within the immediate circumstances. Iago in *Othello* plants a seed in the first act and realises its ultimate result by the fifth.

Kate Wasserberg's danger week

Wasserberg explains that

this came about when I was directing *Aristocrats* by Brian Friel at Theatr Clwyd in 2013. By the end of week three we had made the piece: It was clear, humane, beautiful and detailed. I said to the actors at the end of week three: 'We have a show. It's banked. I hereby invite you next week to offer me the craziest, wildest, bravest, most terrible, wonderful ideas that you have. We are going to trust each other and you're going to show me. Go with everything. Some things will remain in the production and others won't.' We would decide that together. I didn't make them do anything they didn't want to do, and if they tried something and hated it, they didn't have to do it again. I wanted them to delve deeper into the pain, fire, wonder, humour and glory of these characters. They were throwing drinks over each other, climbing onto stuff, making beautiful pictures. It became operatic. It sunk into the bedrock of the detail of the show and it elevated it. I've kept that rehearsal method [in the final week], as you can get to a place if the play is manageable, and the cast is able and there's no obstacles; you can have a show by week three if you get a move on, don't waste time and don't paddle around in concept. Then they can go into fifth gear, and it unlocks something brave, fierce and wonderful. 'Danger week' is a deliberately silly name to make actors feel swashbuckling! They

> might offer some ridiculous things, and a lot may stay in the show; those become the moments audiences remember as they are surprising, brave and audacious. Because they've been in the skin of it for three weeks, everything that is offered grows out of that. It's not random, silly stuff, but a further extension of the thought they already have.

Specificity of structure, punctuation and syntax

Unless working on a production that specifically seeks to deconstructs a play, most text-based rehearsal processes embrace the need to get as close to the playwright's text as possible. Even when using improvisatory techniques such as active analysis, études need to be constructed to support the actor to become word-perfect, ensuring specificity. Often when actors are 'stuck', returning to the text and mining for clues can unlock moments and new breakthroughs are made. Using the text as the mediator of problems and re-examining the structure, punctuation and syntax, often leads back to a path of 'rightness'. Director James Macdonald states 'what you're always trying to put on stage is the spirit of the writer' (2008: 149). Yet, if the writer is not alive or is not part of the process, what then? To what extent should the writer be revered? The contracts issued by the estate of Samuel Beckett, which grant performance rights for the author's play, state categorically, for example, that 'there shall be no additions, omissions, changes in the sex of the characters or of the performers as specified in the text . . . or alterations of any kind or nature in the manuscript and presentation of the play as written' (Keramidas 2008: 198). As if directing from beyond the grave, this statement leaves no doubt as to Beckett's intentions.

When Macdonald discusses breakthroughs that 'make most sense' (2008: 152), these can often be linked to finding possibilities within the theatrical potential of the language. The potency of the choice is to be unearthed from the text, just as an archaeologist carefully dusts their layers in a trench. In relation to stage directions, playwright Simon Stephens desires they 'provoke creativity and charge imagination' (2016: 263). The playwright need not be physically in the room to help the actor, since embedded textual clues implicitly direct the company. Clarity of thought (and speed of thought) for the character comes from a detailed textual analysis and honouring what Alfreds terms 'logic text', whereby actors and directors 'make sense of the text at its simplest, logical and grammatically structured level' (2010: 196). Jean Benedetti sets out the need for honouring the punctuation as the text's 'musical pattern' (2008: 88), whereby meaning is generated from the punctuation and structure.

The script is the map

During *Close Quarters* rehearsals, actor Dylan Wood and director Kate Wasserberg shared a breakthrough during their final stages. Through a snowballing of ideas, debate and discussion, a moment was unlocked by returning to the text's specificity. After a rejected kiss in Scene Six from Ali Cormack, following Brian Armstrong's advances, the following dialogue is exchanged:

Armstrong   Why are you so angry?
Cormack   You know what happened last time. Imagine if the others –
Beat.
Armstrong   How would they know?
Beat.
Do you think I'd *tell* them? Those animals?

(Bowen 2018: 53)

Wood stopped suddenly after reading that part of the script and Kate Wasserberg asked, 'Are you feeling stuck?' (Marsden 2018: ll.1554–5), to which Wood replied hesitantly: 'No, no, I'm not feeling stuck . . .' (ibid.). Perceiving that there was something Wood was unsure about, Wasserberg took a rare look at her script and exclaimed 'Oh, oh, oh, Kate's written it in the text – there's emphasis on the "tell"' (ibid.), after he asked where to place emphasis on the line. Wasserberg did not give a line reading, but gave a wider context, stating: 'you've really liked [Cormack], secretly really liked her for a year. You'd never ever betray her trust. But this is so special' (Marsden 2018: ll.1557–8). This resonated with Wood immediately, as he started playing around with the emphasis of each word of the line. Placing emphasis on the word 'tell', there was a sudden general exclamation:

Wood   Yes!

He shouts, jumps in the air; DSM Bethan Dawson and Kate Wasserberg simultaneously cry out 'yeah!'/'yes!' Wood is beaming and grinning.

I heard it . . . I heard it . . . I heard it!

(Marsden: 2018: ll.1561–3)

Using an examination of the text's own inner logic as a springboard, the shared breakthrough allowed for a moment of clarity in the meaning and therefore the truth of the moment. Wasserberg explains that

> the writer always knows! So often when we can't crack something, it turns out we simply haven't gone back to the text. The text nearly always contains the answer. Here, the stress on the line gave us a completely new context, one that we had missed. So, it wasn't about thoughtlessly following the stress indicated, but using that to decode the thinking behind the line. When the writer isn't in the [room], the script is the map.

Thus, as Mike Alfreds notes, 'by analysing the structure of the words, by reverse-engineering, you begin to discover the thoughts that bring them into existence' (Bessell 2019: 91). As I watched, Wood and Wasserberg unlocked a pivotal moment by placing the text at the very centre of the rehearsal.

Running

For Heskins, the final stage ensures that the play is worked through again, 'not in the same small units, but piecing it together to get a sense of pace and momentum'. This momentum comes from a sustained sequence of run-throughs, allowing actors to embody the play in 'real time'. Where possible, scene changes and transitions are also undertaken with stage management working in coordination with the actors to achieve this. The run is, of course, a chance to consolidate. But it also needs to be a place of sustained organic growth and discovery rather than inadvertently cementing pre-decided choices that may not always necessarily be the most useful or dynamic.

Directors need to consider the emotional well-being of their acting company, as anxiety levels increase with the prospect of a run-through, with some actors placing an unfounded level of expectation upon themselves to achieve and thereby push for results. Wasserberg helpfully expresses this in the form of an analogy where 'the director is safely on the ground and the actors are on a tightrope. I don't want them to fall off'. Actors, unlike other artists such as painters and writers who can incubate creativity at their own pace, must be able to 'switch on' at the cry of 'action' or at precisely 7.30 pm. Simultaneously, this switching on must not completely rely on predetermined, conscious, cerebral ideas. Switching on may sound difficult, but directors must support actors so that they can do this with ease and several methods help towards this. Firstly, thinking of performance (and therefore run-throughs) as an extension of the acting process is important. Philosophically, this can create a sense of tumbling from one stage to the next for the actor, segueing seamlessly from early stages through to previews and opening night. Whilst it does not eradicate the pressure completely, by ensuring that these stages are not heightened unduly or unnecessarily means a continued sense of ease. Secondly, if the rehearsal room is not made private and visitors are welcomed throughout, a run-through in front of an audience becomes a natural extension of established practice and the hinterland between rehearsal and performance becomes a comfortable, blurred line, rather than an alarming demarcation. Finally, as argued throughout, creating as much of the scenographic world in rehearsals means that a technical period becomes a seamless extension of the rehearsal process, rather than too sudden a gear change.

Giving notes at a run-through as a director

Following a run-through, notes are traditionally given, and sections worked. Director Poppy Burton-Morgan stated in *The Stage* that 'with the exponential increase in mental health issues and anxiety, note-taking has become increasingly charged. It's easy to forget that huge numbers of performers are dyslexic or neurodiverse and that can make notes sessions highly sensitive' (2019). Being honest and direct does not mean eschewing sensitivity and tact. Embracing Wasserberg's tightrope analogy is of use here as the actor, following a run, has been in a state of a vulnerable heightened awareness, along with their fellow performers. A highly critical director, who infantilises the actor in notes sessions, will exacerbate any anxieties already felt. Having actors self-note following a run, as outlined previously, is just one of the ways for a director to glimpse an actor's thinking. My golden rules for directors when noting run-throughs are:

1. Try not to spend an entire run-through writing. Observe, sense and respond.

2. Don't note an actor for the sake of it.

3. Ensure that there is sufficient time to give notes. If there is not enough time for a meaningful engagement, hold the notes session at another time.

4. Decipher your notes to ensure clarity.

5. See a notes session as a discussion with the actor. Listen if there is a different opinion, to understand why there is a different stance and make a judgement call.

6. Ask actors for their opinions and ideas.

7. Actors being lectured at does not support the neurodiverse performer. Can notes be worked physically? Some overall thoughts may be given prior to working some key sections physically, so that notes become somatically encoded.

8. Notes should be helpful and include ideas around development, improvement and support. If you do not know how to turn the note from something philosophical into something concrete and meaningful, be honest about this and use the collective expertise of the company to solve something.

Wasserberg's notion of loving the actors filters through to notes sessions and run-throughs:

I'm asking actors to make an offer and to see if it works in notes. If you don't tell actors what's working, they can't help to solve problems. If you are constantly criticising, what are they aiming for? How are they supposed to know what success looks like if they only know what they are getting 'wrong'? It's like when you're in love and everything flows; I want actors to feel like that. I want them to feel loved and beautiful, successful and at their most charming and charismatic, regardless of who they are playing. Then actors will fly and give a performance to me they've never given anyone else. I'm after the greatest performance an actor's ever given. You don't get that through criticism and mind games.

Exercise: What to note – a directorial checklist

Boredom

If you are bored at any point, acknowledge that and remedy it. Do not blame the actors but ask what you can do to create dynamism and energy.

Not 'why?' but 'what for?'

Considering asking the actor 'what are you doing this for?' as opposed to 'why are you doing this?' This propels the character to imagine their future and see potential for changing their life direction. Asking 'why' roots behaviour in the past, which isn't always the most useful or dynamic choice.

Endgaming

Is there any 'endgaming' occurring? If the actor playing Alfred Ill in Friedrich Dürrenmatt's *The Visit* begins to play the opening act with a sense that his life may be over by the play's resolution, a run-through should be able to pick that up.

Same play, different production?

Are the actors all in the same production? Is there a consistency of style? It is important to have differences when these are rooted in the character's given circumstances. Yet, if one actor in pantomime is playing it as though it is a Chekhov play, there will surely be trouble.

Pressing issues

Are the pressing issues of the scene, such as time or environmental factors, being honoured? Offering an imagined circumstance can add a point of concentration to a scene and raises its stakes.

Physical actions and qualities

Are physical actions aligned with inner thoughts or feelings? What might happen if, for example, the letter writing (physical action) is undertaken with tension (quality), or the ironing undertaken with joy?

Contrasts and polarities

Are the actors honouring the polarities at the beginning and end of a speech, bit, scene, act or play? What events change this? An internal intrinsic motivation, or an external stimulus?

Stakes

Are the stakes high? Are the characters fully engaging with what is to win and lose at each moment?

Directorially, Wasserberg plays the long game in relation to her notes. She explains that she does not keep 'an amazing notebook that [will] become an artefact' but prefers to 'make work in space and time. I might scribble something on a paper that might get thrown away. I tell it to the actor and that's where the work lives.' The long game is played because she feels that

> there's something in the way that the text and the work of the rehearsal room filters through your brain, where you see something in week one and think: 'That's a week four note'. I might write it down to keep it in my mind, but if I don't keep noticing it, it's probably not a note, so I try to put all my energy into seeing what's in front of me as if for the first time, every time and giving my fresh, new and present response rather than a series of recollections that I've already seen.

By seeing each run afresh, run-throughs do not become about ticking elements off a 'to do' list but rather a vehicle for sensing how the story is being told in that moment and what to prioritise moving forward.

Gillian Hanna's script archive indicates that when she received notes, such as when playing the titular role in John B. Keane's *Big Maggie* in the 1993 Birmingham Rep production directed by Gwenda Hughes, these were all entered onto the same script: a living site for all her thinking. Practical notes against a line are rooted to a psychological motivation: 'Shake hands, get out of the way so we can talk business' (1993). This action links to her need to shut down the niceties expressed by character Mr Byrne about her husband's death, in order that she can move onto business in relation to the monument she needs building. Hanna's script notes read as a psychological score, using simple words such as 'BINGO!' (ibid.) when she wins a point against her daughter Katie, followed by 'Survival' (ibid.) or 'Security' (ibid.). Her notes do not relate merely to what her character does physically but are responses to the actions of other figures around her in the play, such as when the character Gert uses a 'delaying tactic' (ibid.) on Maggie. There are no explicit notes on Maggie's response, but believing what is being done to her was important.

Directors too will receive notes, from artistic directors and commercial producers. Have an open mindset and welcome these when delivered at the final rehearsal room run-through. I negotiate this to happen at a penultimate run-through, as then there is a chance to implement them as the notes are a welcome creative tonic at this late stage. Often, an artistic director's knowledge of their audience demographic and expertise of the dynamics of the stage space (such as acoustics or sightlines) is of immense practical value as the transition from rehearsal room to stage is made. Artistic directors fundamentally give support to the freelance or associate director's overall work, pointing out some of the broader brushstrokes, rather than fine details. Commercial producers are also extremely supportive. Yet, with personal money on the line, sometimes major alterations are suggested or requested, cuts are posited, songs changed, or choreographic dynamics altered. Producers care for the product just as much as do artistic directors, and it is wrong to think of a producer as a non-creative; it is the director's job, however, to work within their brief.

Some genre thinking

For comedies and farces, ascertain whether pace and verbal repartee is sustained. As an actor, plot in conservation points where you know you can breathe and relax. Is the 'big truth' required matched to the frame, concept and playwright's style? Finally, check in on ensuring consistent ease with the comedy.

Run-throughs for musicals should be checked for seamless integration and relationship between music, movement, dialogue, lyrics and choreography. Check whether a song is diegetic, where the character knows they are singing a song, or non-diegetic, where the character is not aware they are singing, but the song is an extension of their emotional state. Are they being honoured as such? Sometimes we need to 'see' the character acknowledging the movement from dialogue to song and a run-through can determine whether this is being delivered. As a performer, reattune to the music, separating this from the lyrics. Are there any musical elements that you haven't heard, which might provide further clues to emotion and behaviour?

In pantomime, final run-throughs can check the balance between story and anarchy. If the story is blurred or subsumed by anarchy and jokes, it can be an unsatisfyingly homogenous experience. All the genre's flavours need to be experienced. Some less experienced pantomime performers at this late stage begin to blur their role's tropes. For example, an actor playing a character who carries the story may begin to tell jokes or become diegetic in their approach. As a performer, check in on yourself at this stage and make changes prior to being given a note.

The strongest classical writers tailored work to actors and so plotted in energy conservation points. As with the above, use the run-throughs to plot these in and know when to keep things simmering, as opposed to bubbling. Act Five often needs an energy of its own, and I have seen actors running on empty by this point. Final run-throughs can also verify the extent of any paraphrasing that may be occurring. Not respecting the logic text means that rhythms and meaning can become skewed and veer off course, making attention to this at this late stage paramount. As an actor, are you truly 'letting go'?

'The Four Lenses of Breakthrough': Lens four – the 'wow' moment

As a director, I have witnessed and felt many moments of 'wow' throughout my career, yet in some processes, I have never experienced one. Building on the work of Gay McAuley, who also uses this term, I personally define them as a collective celebration, or a sense of relief in achieving something profound or meaningful, or a collective way of expressing the unlocking of a moment. The shared 'rightness' that both Ariane Mnouchkine and Kate Rosmmanith propose is evident, palpable, recognised and radiated in this moment.

A rehearsal period embodies the 'complex nature of collective creativity' (McAuley 2012: 8) and so a 'wow' moment certainly cannot be forced or predicted; however, conditions can be created conducive for them to manifest themselves. The ground should be prepared in the early and middle stages of rehearsal to achieve an optimal flow experience. The 'wow' moment sees the actors experiencing an 'exhilarating, efficient, complete connected moment in performance' (Polanco and Bonfiglio 2016: 206) where all 'cognition is focused on the work in the moment' (ibid.: 209) and when multifarious individual and smaller strands coalesce into one; this could also describe the moment that Ivo van Hove explains as the production arriving firmly at its destination. The 'wow' moment sees actors letting go, when, as Demidov suggests, any 'effort is gone' (Malaev-Babel and Lasinka 2016: 533) and is described by Tiffany Stern as when elements 'all click and come together, when the sparks occur'. During this moment, actors are not working with conscious effort, but rather there is a 'quality of ease' (Merlin 2013b: xiv) in an actor's performance, as they embody the cerebral notes and discoveries, connecting to and with each other in a state of flow.

Snowballing, flow and reaching a 'wow' moment

Creative 'wow' breakthroughs grow out of 'separate flashes and moments' (Stanislavski 2008: 104) where there is a snowballing of smaller moments towards a major 'wow' run-through. If rehearsals are akin to a snowball gathering its layers, then a 'rigorous rehearsal . . . details, layer upon layer, the minuscule happenings that occur between the actors, which slowly coalesce' (Cortese 2019: 260).

The cumulative effect is ideally to reach a 'wow' moment, since these manifest themselves when genuine experiencing is reached within the 'here, today, now' (Merlin 2014: 214) of the story, where an audience member 'no longer know[s] exactly which actor is in support and which actor initiated the action: they are simply together' (Evans 2015: 87).

Arts Council England chief executive Darren Henley states that the creative process involves 'constant repetition with incremental, minute improvements' (2016: 23). This concept is useful, as to pursue a 'wow' moment can be self-defeating. A 'wow' moment should also have a feeling of ease, and referencing Stanislavski's text *An Actor's Work*, Daboo, Loukes and Zarrilli describe the state following the creation of a merging of actor and character as a 'third Being . . . as easy, effortless and pleasurable' (2013: 165). In a rehearsal, there is often a feeling of 'exhilaration that often accompanies flow' (Silberschatz 2013: 17), echoing Stanislavski's frustration when breakthroughs are not made due to a lack of a creative state.

By constantly aiming to balance the rehearsal journey, where 'challenges continually increase in sympathy with actors' skills' (ibid.: 20), flow occurs that may lead towards an organic and unforced 'wow' moment. Yet, to actively seek this moment is a fallacy: 'many people have figuratively stood in thunderstorms, waiting for the lightning to strike, but creative ideas evolve from existing memories and impressions . . . They arise from the interweaving of billions of microscopic sparks in the vast darkness of the brain' (Brandt and Eagleman 2017: 46).

It is worth noting that progress is always being made, through the snowballing of minutiae, whether there is a 'wow' moment or not.

A summary of Chapter 6

The final days in the rehearsal room sharpen, clarify and detail. But it is essential to recognise what can be enhanced or further refined and what should be left alone. Growth must always be balanced with consolidation. Breakthroughs will continue to occur: indeed, the work of previous weeks will potentially provide sufficient structure for a 'wow' moment to materialise. Form will have been arrived at and pace and momentum of the piece reveal themselves as it begins to flow. Multiple runs – incorporating as many scenic elements as possible – allow the actors to embody and experience, both promoting truth in terms of the storytelling, and allowing them to grapple with the practicalities of those scenic elements. A resonant image is that of scaffolding: this has been constructed in the earlier stages, and now this is built upon and overlaid. Within ethical bounds, scaffolding allows for a letting go, for play, for risk, such as Wasserberg's 'danger week': a novel way of capitalising on this.

Chapter 7 now moves on to the complex stage where the production leaves the rehearsal room for the technical and dress rehearsals. Beyond that, it considers the further stages in the lifecycle of the production: the first night and the continuing run, and what role the director has, once ownership has been passed to those performing.

Interview: *The fight directors as collaborators – Rachel Bown-Williams and Ruth Cooper-Brown of RC-Annie*

This interview is in full due to the flowing nature of their interwoven dialogue.

Talk me through the role of fight directors.

Rachel: We have to choreograph violence within the play that is safe, effective and repeatable. Our work tips over into areas that aren't violent, like fainting, falling, impacts or lifting people. We also provide gun consultations which included staging and safe working practices for all involved.

Ruth: There's no average human being, we tailor all our work to the abilities of the performer. Working with them to create the choreography we don't layer a pre-choreographed fight over a scene, saying 'here are the moves off you go'.

Rachel: We work and devise with the performers using their bodies to create a fight. I started off with a pre-decided fight early in my career, as I didn't have the capacity not to do that. I wanted to go into a rehearsal room with something. I thought, what happens if I blank? Even now, there are days where I feel I haven't got much, but you have a target to work towards in the rehearsal

room. Sometimes it's feels like it's not great and sometimes it's
brilliant, but it develops as you go.

Ruth: It's exciting to work collaboratively in the room responding to all
          creative input within the parameters of the scene. The actors may
          offer you something unique on the spur of the moment that you
          won't have thought about which might then become the basis of
          the whole thing.

Rachel: And at its simplest level, on the first visit an actor won't be able
          to perform the fight with all the bells and whistles straight away.
          They need time to bed it in and rehearse it. Our next visit, we will
          build on the work laid down previously. The benefits of working
          as a duo are, that there are two bodies in the room, we are
          working at the moment on *The Lion, the Witch and the Wardrobe*
          [The Bridge Theatre] with large casts and a big battle sequence.
          One of us can look at organising everyone and the other can look
          at detail. In battle scenes, we can look at different sections of the
          stage at the same time.

Ruth: We bounce off each other – One person can be thinking whilst
          the other is doing, or one of us can be talking to the director or
          movement director as the other is working. It's like film, one in
          the role of director and one as the first AD [assistant director]
          and then swapping them over. Also, a more obviously advantage
          is that we can demonstrate it. We can both fight it and get a sense
          of it physically, where it needs to go, what works.

Rachel: For example, when working on the sword fight for Macbeth
          (played by John Simm at the Chichester Festival Theatre), we'd
          both fight with an actor so they can get a sense of the correct
          distance, targets and accuracy and we can feel how it feels for
          them from the inside of the action.

*If a director works with a fight director for the first time, what would be
your advice?*

Ruth: Collaborate and communicate honestly. You need to get on
          the same page from the start. Everyone needs to be complicit
          and in agreement so there's no jarring later on, as that's an
          uncomfortable experience in a rehearsal room. So, get a meeting
          early on, talk and check in throughout the process so we're all
          working to create the same vision. As every job is different.

Rachel: We've worked with some directors who've not worked with fight directors before. I think it's OK to not know everything. When you say, 'I don't know how you work, what do you need?' That's brilliant; that's really helpful.

How does intimacy training work alongside the fight directing?

Rachel: Intimacy has always been an inherent part of our work as fight directors

Ruth: Whether that be a scene of a sensitive nature, an act of violence or a scene involving blood or gore, we need to consider the effects on the performer. We have to find the comfort level for an actor in any potentially uncomfortable, sensitive or triggering scene. It's about emotional well-being as much as intimacy; it's not just about sex or closeness. Everyone needs a safe space, every member of the team. You just don't know peoples past experiences or how vulnerable they are.

Rachel: We choreographed a strangle in *The Duchess of Malfi* (RSC, 2018) starting with the technical elements. As it was a complex scene with many variables. Including a stage covered in blood. So, we are layering and building from a basic outline.

Then the psychological is layered later?

Rachel: It depends on who you are working with. If you're talking about intimacy rather than violence in general, we have to come from an emotional level as that informs the moves that you can do; so you can't just come in and block the fight then layer in the emotional side; you have to do it at the same time. Sometimes with elements that are more sensitive, you may build the framework of what it is, detaching the emotional thing to begin with, that is, your hand goes here, you do this . . .

Ruth: A more technical exercise . . .

Rachel: That doesn't come from an emotional point of view.

Ruth: We are mindful that intimate and violent work can be triggering. We establish boundaries and process to help the actors to protect themselves and enable them to fully invest in the performance. They have to perform this eight shows a week and we have to be mindful of that.

*You say in **The Stage** (12 September 2019) that you want to look after people 'physically and emotionally' in the fight situations. Can you unpick this further?*

Ruth: It's about communication with the actor all the time. It's about the well-being of the whole person. As we are often doing physical and emotional work, we are often dealing with the climax of the play. The actors need to feel safe, in terms of what they can offer and share. They must have control of that.

Rachel: It's everyone's responsibility for well-being. The plays that we have worked on with Katie Mitchell are hard hitting and often challenging for the audience. This is a hugely considered aspect of the work.

In the same interview, you say stage combat is just acting with props, can you expand on that?

Ruth: That was a bit 'tongue in cheek', but there's a truth in it, in the terms that; you don't stop acting when you fight. Whilst a scripted fight is an important element of a character's journey in the play. The fight is just one part of that story.

Rachel: However, if your character is meant to be skilled with a weapon, they will need to have some understanding of that. If you have an actor who doesn't smoke, you can tell. You have to look like you know what you're doing, so when working with weapons it helps to have some skill or training to build on.

How would you advise directors to collaborate with their fight director(s), pre-rehearsal, rehearsal and then through tech to opening?

Rachel: If there is a lot of fighting in the play consider holding a fight audition so you can assess an actors' skill. This helps us determine how much time we will need based on the actors abilities and also gives the actors an insight to see what is going to be required.

Ruth: Allow sufficient time, start early, get your fight director on board before you start rehearsals to help with planning. Things often take longer than you expect for example: if the characters have special skills then we may need to need to allow regular rehearsal time in to practice those skills so that they are ready for the rehearsal room.

Rachel: In tech, we set the action on the stage this is often the first time the characters are doing it in costume, so we need to make sure everyone is comfortable. This includes tightening angles and sight lines. On *King John* (RSC, 2019), the tech was the first time we are able to look at the food fight with the actual floor, to see the traction on the floor and if we have managed all the potential hazards.

Ruth: We bear all that in mind while fight directing in rehearsals we have to be open to change. You come into tech and there's may be limited time. Ideally, we are there for the whole process to see the action in context.

Rachel: I was there for the whole of *King John*. Which was a very complex show with lots of violent elements and with many effects including, a food fight, strobe lighting, blood effects, fights on moving tables. It was important we were there to see where the blood and food may land and how it would affect the next scene, so being there all the time was imperative.

Ruth: During tech, everyone's in the room: everyone's creative ideas and everyone's input; so we can all communicate and pull all the creative elements together.

7

Independence: From technical rehearsal through to the run

You've been in the safety of the rehearsal room, you know how it operates, you even have your favourite chair and spot. Then you move to the stage. Unless you have had the luxury of building the production in the performance space, transitioning from the rehearsal room is one of the most dynamic, exciting, nerve-racking, vulnerable and effervescent periods of the process. Several types of transitions may be experienced. If the rehearsal period has integrated scenography, this transition can often be a fluid one. If these elements have not been incorporated, but the director and creative team have nevertheless been open and explicit in sharing production decisions, actors have been able to envisage the bigger picture. However, if there are numerous surprises and alterations, expectations differ and the technical period can be fraught with difficulties and tensions.

This chapter posits some philosophies that may allow the production to be birthed with as little pain as possible and considers how the production matures following a director's departure.[1] Actors continue to make discoveries throughout the production run due to a deeper embodiment and as the performance is a 'continuation of the rehearsal process' (Stern 2000: 92), the technical and dress rehearsals become part of this creative continuum.

---

[1] For in-depth how-to guides on running technical and dress rehearsals, Stephen Unwin's excellent 2004 text *So You Want to Be a Theatre Director?* and Katie Mitchell's 2009 book *The Director's Craft: A Handbook for the Theatre* are highly recommended.

Chapter 3 indicated the need to structure the overall rehearsal process, and director Matthew Xia warns against pushing for results, allowing for incubation time for each of the various stages:

> I use every bit of process to get out what I need to get out of it at the time I need it. You only need to be ready for the thing you need to be ready for and this is something I stole from Joe Hill-Gibbins. So, it's no good trying to be ready for the technical rehearsal at the end of rehearsal week three, if you've got another week to go.

Plotting collaboratively

Prior to the arrival of the actors at the tech, plotting sessions are held where we see the director, deputy stage manager (DSM), lighting, sound, audio-visual (AV) designer and others huddled in a row in the stalls, lit by Anglepoise lamps taped with blue gels, working through the play sequentially. Operators are furiously 'plotting' the technical elements, cue-to-cue, into the appropriate board and alongside the director sits the DSM, feverishly writing cues for these into their prompt book. I encourage the wider creative team to fully collaborate in this process. Stephen Mear states that, as a choreographer, one of his major collaborators is the lighting designer, as 'working with them is important, so that placement is done correctly, to maximize an effect that [creates] an atmosphere and sets the mood'. By being present at overall creative discussions, including plotting sessions, the creative team's work is therefore not diluted by a director. I also encourage the use of haze in the air from the plot, to sense the full potential of lighting's architectural structure and atmosphere. Josie Rourke eloquently discusses why haze is used in her response to a complainant, concerning high haze levels during a preview of her 2005 production of *Much Ado about Nothing* for Sheffield Crucible: 'One of the things haze does is to pick out beams of light that the audience would otherwise only see reflected on surfaces and bodies. It gives a painterly and sometimes even architectural quality to the lighting of the production. Without it . . . the space would seem bald, spare, even uninviting' (2005).

Sound designer Gareth Fry aims to achieve the majority of his creative work by the plotting session and 'by the time we move into the theatre, I'll often have about eighty-five per cent of the sound design completed, with the remainder often being scenic transitions that we can't work out until we physically have all the elements to play with'. Every member of the creative team has a short amount of time to execute their work during the plotting and technical process, and compromise is needed. Designer Max Jones notes that

> every creative's individual moment is the most important in the world. I really care about my design, the lighting designer really cares about their work, the movement director really cares about their work; so, it's not just about where the work meets but also where people meet and how you negotiate, recognize and be sympathetic to the fact everyone is aiming to be the best they can be.

Out of the need for creative collaboration for Jones, 'sometimes, for the collective good, you might choose to back away [from], or to push, a certain idea; the collaborative process is constantly that of negotiation'. Directors who embrace the creative knowledge of their team are often held in high regard. Wasserberg believes that it's 'my job in tech to let my team do their work. My designers should show their ideas and make their offers. As directors we respond and we tweak, but I'm not there to tell them what to do.' She also believes in giving considerable agency to DSMs who, she says, are 'brilliant at foreshadowing practical issues; if you let a DSM work at their highest level, they will solve those problems for you, as they are the only other person who has consistently watched the process'. As a neophyte director, suffering from imposter syndrome, I felt that I should have had all the answers. Now I have the experience and confidence to admit that I have absolutely no idea how to solve certain issues and ask for everyone's creative thoughts.

A creative and collaborative technical

Once lighting and sound states exist in principle for the majority of the piece, with scene changes rehearsed, the next stage is a technical rehearsal, piecing the entire production together with the actors. Wasserberg insists that 'an important part of my job is not letting the actor get to tech and be thrown into panic and confusion.

Tech shouldn't contain many surprises and we've solved problems before.' Part of my practice is to say to the actors that if they can solve a problem and it doesn't change the overall look or feel of the piece and doesn't fundamentally change what anyone else is doing, then permission is granted to implement this without asking. If they can solve a problem, but it may significantly affect something that someone else may do or alter the look or the feel of the piece, then talk this through with the company/production manager, or myself, before implementing. Allowing actors agency means I have fewer problems to solve and they own their decisions. I find it incomprehensible if rehearsal processes promote freedom and independence throughout, then remove these at this period.

One inherent pitfall is perceiving this stage as one devoid of creativity. Kirstie Davis advocates ensuring that it feels 'like a natural extension of the rehearsal room'. Asking Davis what happens when she needs to make a fundamental change at this stage, she states that 'if we keep to the original grain of the idea, then any changes aren't about the play going off kilter; it's simply that there's another way of doing it'. By ensuring that the frame holds the production ethos and aesthetic, changes and adaptations then remain rooted in a world.

Wasserberg believes that the role of her DSM is creative, as 'they are literally enacting the rhythm of the play through the way they call it' and the conductor of the piece from this stage, steering the pacing and rhythms established in the rehearsal room. If 'the writer is like the composer, in terms of music, then the DSM is the conductor as they, eventually, call the show'. For Wasserberg, they shape the cadence of the piece with intuition and specificity:

> You look up, the music comes in, the light comes up and as it hits brightness the hazer starts. If they don't have that rhythm you can't achieve that. Especially if an actor comes in later, for example. If the DSM can't pick up that change in the rhythm in relation to cueing the show, there's a problem. They need that sensibility.

Close Quarters: The discoveries continue

One of Wasserberg's major creative discoveries was during the first technical session of *Close Quarters*. As a memory play, the initial intention for the opening image was for the protagonist Findlay to materialize in a spotlight centre stage and begin her soliloquy. However, practical access problems in the space meant that the actor simply could not find her mark in a complete blackout. Wasserberg suddenly saw the possibility of a using backlight to cast a shadow through the actual dock door of the studio at Sheffield Crucible, being used to signify an entrance to a sawmill, as Findlay stepped through to deliver her opening soliloquy.

A problem became an opportunity, further establishing the production's memory play frame scenographically. If creation for Anne Bogart is 'one hundred per cent intuitive' (2001: 51), then Wasserberg intuitively identified this as she believes that 'we keep discovering through tech and previews anyway'. Here was a moment of genuine discovery. Wasserberg immediately consulted her sound designer, who then created a haunting motif underscore based on the melody of the folk song *Over the Hills and Far Away*. Wasserberg describes the importance of this breakthrough for her:

> The best advice I have ever been given about directing from Terry Hands was to look at what I have in front of me. Not what I thought I would have, or hoped I would have, or am frightened I don't have, but what I have. This was that: the idea of apparition didn't work at all, but we had this incredibly beautiful space created by Max Jones, and I wanted the audience to discover it along with Findlay.

This became the production's powerful and arresting opening image, supporting Brook's notion that 'the first thing that the theatre has to do is to make us wish to go on watching' (Todd and Lecat 2003: 33).

Interview: Ivo van Hove on scenography, technical and dress rehearsals

Talk me through your approach to scenography.

People think of Ivo van Hove and think I'm the face of the production, because I give the interviews. But I always say that 'Ivo van Hove' is a team. Most of the time I have long-time collaborators, such as Jan Versweyveld in [terms of] scenography and light. I've worked with video designer Tal Yarden for twenty years, I've worked for a long time with An D'Huys as a costume designer and with two or three dramaturgs throughout my whole career. They are loyal, and loyalty gives me a basis where I can fail. That's important. That's the same in the rehearsal room. There should be a safe rehearsal room, so that actors can do stupid or ridiculous things: it's important to fail in order to find something. Also, there's an idea of a team that we work within. The whole creative team is there in the rehearsal room: they are part of the rehearsal period. Some actors find it awkward because I'm not the only one who talks to the actors; the dramaturg talks to the actors, Jan talks to the actors, without consulting me. We are a team. Bryan Cranston loved that [in *Network*, at the National Theatre]; he loved this way of working, as it's not top-down. At the end of the day, I make the final decision, if that has to happen; but most of the time, it's not necessary, as we feel the same, which is the opposite of making compromises. Teamwork is crucial.

And because you've built the world in the rehearsal room, you're not starting to build this in the tech?

Indeed. I never need to do that, as we've been extending the tech time in rehearsals. My secret is that I don't make the design of set and lights an artificial thing to be added, as the cherries on a cake at the end of a rehearsal period. When you make a soup, you don't add ingredients in afterwards; you add them at the same time, otherwise it could be a failure.

Audience thinking

For director and performer Simon McBurney, 'theatre is created in the minds of the audience. It's an imaginative act' (Innes and Shevtsova 2009: 166). Rehearsal rooms, from personal experience, often chime with directorial phrases such as 'this needs an audience' or 'who is the audience to you?' For director Peter Snow, many of the rehearsal decisions he made were linked to an understanding of his target audience when directing *Metamorphosis* for an indigenous Australian community. With English as their second language, the production form developed as a result of creating the piece for this audience as 'it emerged quickly … that we would play it as farce, *Keystone Cops* style … If we were to play to different language groups … we thought we should concentrate on physical action' (2006: 44). Understanding the audience demographic informed the production's frame.

It can be vital to meet what Marvin Carlson describes as the audience's 'ghosted' notions and expectations, discussed in Chapter 1. For pantomime, Iain Lauchlan states that the actors must 'fulfil the expectation of the audience and connect with them' (2020: 244). There are expectations from a pantomime audience which are anticipated throughout the rehearsal period and 'ghosted' by the historical and cultural antecedents of the genre. Rehearsal rooms therefore keep the audience at the heart of each decision that is made, as director and actors construct the conditions for when the production meets with its final character, the audience.

Previews and dress rehearsal audience reactions give a sense of the piece's final rhythms. Josie Rourke describes the previews as a 'work in progress, and this is reflected in a lower ticket price ... you are therefore more likely to encounter a finished product if you book following its press night, which is also the night on which the creative team concludes its work on the show' (2005).

Returning to some genre thinking, when rehearsing the Edwardian comedy *Charley's Aunt* by Brandon Thomas, I felt sure that the following end-of-act business constructed with the actors was hysterically funny: 'Lord Fancourt puts skirt over his head, falls back into Spettigue's arms; Spettigue catches him. Jack kneels at Lord Fancourt's feet and holds down skirt, hiding feet with hat. Tableau. Curtain' (Thomas 1998: 77). Opening night was going well. Audiences were laughing; what philosopher Henri Bergson would recognize as the coiled spring of comedic tension was tightening, like that of a jack-in-the-box. We reached this point where the jack-in-the-box spring should release and audience laugher ensue, yet the audience barely offered a titter. Believing in the importance of that moment to punctuate the end of the second act, the next day we raised the stakes by playing a bigger archetypal truth; we 'buttoned' the comedy and earned the response.

On the opening night of the Agatha Christie mystery *And Then There Were None*, audiences laughed at a section I needed to remain serious. It was a shock as no one had laughed in rehearsal. Upon reflection, due to the very nature of the surreal plot and a cluster of killings in quick succession, coupled with some melodramatic stage directions from Christie where lines are to be expressed 'with a sudden outcry' (2014: 97), unexpected laughter occurred. We had honoured the stage directions, but to the letter, rather than the spirit. The following night we softened those elements, which ensured a lack of laugher during subsequent performances.

Matthew Xia also explicitly focuses his attention on the audience at this stage, since 'in preview one, I'm mainly watching the audience. By preview two, I can forget about the audience a bit and look back at the actors. I can compartmentalize where my attention is at different moments, to make sure that I'm using each part of the process for what it's there for.'

A director calls: Maintaining the production

It is natural that 'the longer an actor performed in a given role, the stronger s/he "owned" the role' (Hanssen 2020: 144). During the run, the director will return and note the show. For van Hove, 'it's the only thing I don't like about my job, but I've found my peace with it. Going back to look at a production is not my favourite thing. I've not quite found a solution for this', yet he nevertheless supports the natural progression of deeper embodiment, balanced with appropriateness of ongoing choices, expressing that his role is to 'support its journey after opening night'. Echoing the philosophy that the actors have ownership, he defines the run as 'the actor's journey. When I come back, I'm the stranger, the foreigner'.

When directing *Pilgrims* by Elinor Cook, a 2016 co-production between HighTide, Theatr Clwyd and Vicky Graham Productions, director Tamara Harvey decided that 'the play is about who has the right to tell a story and how stories are told, [so] we never set anything and the rehearsal process was all about trying to see the many different ways possible to change and shift the storytelling'. Yet during the run, this open frame had been replaced by actors subconsciously settling on a fixed form. Harvey states that she 'would often say: "I saw that before – now try something new."'

Matthew Xia is also keen to allow for expansion and development from previews through the run, but, as with Harvey, within the production's frames:

I want you to be able to go out there and replicate quite cleanly what we have found, so different every night but within some really strict parameters. I've been back to shows before where people are taking off items of costume in the middle of a scene. And they're like: 'I just felt hot and I thought it was. . .' I'm like: 'No, no, no, no, no, no, no! We have a colour-coding that's working, and there's a designer who's decided that there's something going on here with this bigger image that's happening. So please keep that show' . . . Define the parameters of character and intention and objective and action, and occasionally give a small spectrum of action for a particular moment, so that people do feel like they can play and go out and it's like a live game of baseball or football every night. But it's a well-rehearsed one. I think it's unfair as well [if], whilst you keep finding things, you are now denying your audience the experience that we decided we were going to hand over to them.

Therefore, a balance must be found of remaining within the production frame, without denying the audience an experience of the choices made, with spontaneity and freedom expected of a live event.

Jens-Morten Hanssen's distinction between performance and production is useful for directors and actors. Hanssen's framework allows for the liveness of the theatrical form to be honoured, whilst simultaneously ensuring Xia's 'handing over' to the audience is achieved:

Performance is characterized by ephemerality and non-repeatability: it emphasises the theatrical event as such and its impact on the spectators at a particular point in time and space. The term 'production' on the other hand suggests a more or less fixed mise en scène and points to the fact that there are, after all, elements that tend to remain more or less constant throughout a performance run: for instance, set, costumes and performance space. (2020: 149)

A summary of Chapter 7

Though the safety and familiarity of the rehearsal room has been left, it is apparent that the most helpful way to think of the stages of technical and dress rehearsal, as well as the opening night and beyond, is as a continuum. There is no reason the technical cannot be as creative and collaborative as the rehearsal room and no reason why breakthroughs cannot continue. This stage is one of embodiment, and experience, where the production can fly within the parameters collaboratively determined and laid down in rehearsals. For the director, this is naturally a complex time: ownership is being passed on. Metaphors of letting one's children fly the nest are too easy, but they are probably apt here. When the director returns, it is as a visitor, but nevertheless one with responsibility: the guiding hand of the rehearsal room may still very much be needed, especially where play has become too unconstrained, or where audience reaction has proved otherwise than anticipated.

In Chapter 8, many of the voices that have been heard throughout now come together in an exchange, woven together from numerous interviews. Together, they explore common themes, envisaging the future of theatre in the twenty-first century, as well as interrogating the hierarchy, casting, safe spaces and what training can offer to a new, emerging generation of practitioners.

Interview: Paule Constable on the role of the lighting designer

Paule Constable has created lighting designs for productions at the National Theatre, the Donmar Warehouse, the Royal Opera House and Théâtre de Complicité, amongst others. She has won five Olivier Awards and two Tony Awards for Best Lighting Design of a Play for *The Curious Incident of the Dog in the Night-Time* and *War Horse*.

Talk me through your aesthetic.

As a lighting designer, you are a reactive person, rather than creatively proactive; more crafts person than artist. The first major decision I make is whether I'll do a project or not. That's based on who I might be working with. I am vulnerable in the nature of how I best collaborate; I have spent a lifetime learning what I need to make my best work. Once I'm in the design process, my personal feeling towards a piece is seen through the filter of what the director and designer want to do and how they want to tell the story. Whether they choose to do a play on the moon, or in a house, or with no scenery at all, my job is to come in quickly off the back of that . . . and decide how light can be part of that story. I have habits and things I am drawn to, but my work tends to be simple and stripped back. Where light is an active participant and it's quite present. Once the director and designer have created the context for the piece then it is for me to join the conversation and consider the question 'how': 'how does light come into that space and why is light part of this conversation?' My collaboration starts very early on, but it's not one where I impose my own aesthetic. I do have choices I make: attitudes to colour, angle and quality of light . . . but that's to do with my response to something once it's got a sense of a form. My aesthetic does tend to be stripped back and, in a way, I think it's fascinating how every role, not only with actors, is about casting. I am not appropriate casting for many things and I know what I'm bad at. I've done a few musicals, but [not] jukebox musicals or big events, [because] I don't understand light for light's sake; [it has to be] light that's forming and interacting with what's going on onstage and with the audience in an active conversation.

What is the primary function of light?

The function of light must be seen through the lens of how the director and designer have agreed the landscape to be. You should never make a passive decision, even if your decision is no apparent lighting change. Then you think [about whether] it's really fixed and still, or are you just making the audience think it's fixed and still? You shape their experience . . . in such a way that they don't consciously understand; they may follow it, but they aren't overtly aware that light is doing it. If it's really fixed and still, then they sit back and there's one gesture and actors move in and out of that in a way [whereby their] decisions are based on light. But there's no rule to that; that is the creative decision that is made. [Deciding] what the light is going to do: that's an active choice based on the piece and the interpretation.

Who are your chief collaborators?

My key collaborators early on are the designer and director, but [chiefly] the designer. Once we've got a sense of creating a landscape for something, it can help me to decide how involved I'll need to be in the rehearsal process and [need to] be around to steer those rules I am creating around what light does through the rehearsal process. A director like Marianne [Elliot] is really good at something like that. [Designer] Bunny [Christie] on *The Curious Incident of the Dog in the Night-Time* came up with the idea of the graph paper and I articulated that with light; it was clear that we were creating simple rules. Marianne takes on board what you're saying about the physical language of the play through constant conversations and identified early on when we might need to 'lift the lid' off something in the script: the whole point of [*Curious Incident*] is that it's experiential and we wanted the audience to sometimes be looking at it and other times be immersed within it, experiencing what [the protagonist] Christopher was experiencing.

So, you listen out for those hooks, so you can build your work within that frame?

Exactly. We are all looking for clues. It's forensic. You are looking at the source material that designers and directors are using and what inspires them. There will be certain things that will really resonate with me. That might be something an actor does in rehearsal, which I'll bank in my set of tools, along with what the reason and nature of that moment is. I can't do arbitrary. I come from the devised, Complicité background, where you're constantly looking for clues; there isn't a structure of the piece, but there's always a world for the piece. So, if you can't define a moment, it's defined by the wider landscape where things can happen. I stand within that landscape.

So, your background with Complicité feeds directly into text work?

I have three main influences. [Firstly,] devised process. [Then] opera, which is … a scale of expression I find inspiringly bold and which made me more front-footed as a designer, more willing to have a voice in the room. Finally, my background in rock and roll, which gives me a bold aesthetic. I'm thinking back to my Complicité days, where I was also production manager and ASM. I became a member of the company, but ultimately my response to the work is with light. How Annabelle Arden and Simon McBurney worked in the early days was to break down the traditional roles [so that] we were creating something together. If you only turn up on the last couple of days in the rehearsal period, you add pressure to everyone in the room who might think: 'Fuck, we're about to go into tech!' I am interested in the whole process of making work. When I did *Ivanov* at the National Theatre with Katie Mitchell, it was in traverse, in the Dorfman space, so the light could only come in from the two sides of the space. When Ivanov and the Doctor had a conversation, I spoke to the actors about how there is a choice to be made about which window the light can come through: the light doesn't come through both. I was interested in the power relationship between them. I said that I thought the light would be behind Ivanov, [if he wanted] to have the best evening light on his book, but that then put Ivanov in silhouette, and that changes the relationship to the Doctor, with whom he has an antagonistic relationship. If I make that choice and I can talk to Katie and the actors about that choice, then light becomes part of the architecture they can play within.

How do you ideally like to work during the plot and tech?

I like to plot things, make things and put things together. We look at it once there's something for the director to respond to and shape with me. So many directors want to respond to something. But it depends on time, as we never have time to do proper plotting sessions. It's never a good idea when the lead maker, the director, is seeing the space in light for the first time as the performers are arriving. That's too late. With most directors I try, even if it's showing them the first few cues in the desk, to ask: 'Am I going in the right direction with this?' Then there's time for them to look at the light, without having to deal with a million other things. Give them the big, broad brushstrokes first, then you can carry on plotting through the tech as that trust builds.

So, just as rehearsal is content to form, should it be so for you?

Exactly. It's the same process for me. If there's a scene with, say, a naturalistic space with light coming through a window, I will start with light coming through a window, then let's see what else we might need, or not. With a bold statement, it allows for a director to see the rules of light. Then you ask: 'does it need filling in, or do we undermine that moment with light?' It needs a gesture to begin to create the landscape, then explore what else it might need. In production and tech periods, the lighting designer is in a hot seat. You are having a creative conversation, but you are in the middle of a technical world as well. I've also learned that you can get stuck on something, but I say: 'can we accept that it's rubbish? [Let's just] get it in place for the actors'. It's like a sorbet: palate cleanse, start again, try something different. Perhaps in a day or two you might find an obvious and easy solution for that bit you are really stuck on, rather than staring at it, thinking, 'What is it? What is it? What is it?' over and over and over. I am good at keeping the tone of a tech quite light and sometimes you need to move on.

And directors need to trust that process?

I like to get a rough [sketch] quickly for everything, to sense the whole thing, rather than picking slowly through it. Don't try to achieve perfection.

Otherwise, you'll spend six hours working on the first two minutes, then you'll run out of time.

Do the dress and previews mean more to you, as you see the arc of light?

Yes, as you see everything relative to everything else. You can't just look at moments out of context. [Designer] Lez Brotherston once said to me: 'You light at levels that would make a beginner panic.' But I believe it's better to under-light something and see the shape of it, than to chuck acres of light at something. And yes, that is an act of faith. You need people to trust you to work like that. I like to do a preview at night with quick headline notes, then meet up the next morning to work through what's working or not. The more you [build] a relationship with a director, designer and group of actors, the more you can make those bits that are terrible and say: 'We'll come back to it.' Otherwise, it's easy just to throw front light at it, it turns to mush and it's dull.

What is the biggest piece of advice you would offer to a director as to how they should work with their lighting designer?

When I meet young directors, what they talk about is their fear of their lack of knowledge. I think it particularly exists around lighting, as [lighting is] apparently technical and is slightly invisible. Early on in your career you can be dependent upon technical staff to deliver your ideas. That can be difficult when you're trying to learn what your voice is as a young director. The director might have a sense of what they want, but they don't know how to say it. So young directors [sometimes] come with the baggage of: 'I don't know what to say to people.' I think one of the key things is to liberate people from [this fear] about the technicalities of lighting. If you work with someone who calls themselves a lighting designer, their role is about interpreting what you are wanting to say with light. So, the act of interpretation is to be made by them and the conversation for the director to have should be around the bigger things.

With a new director, I want to know what they like, what makes them tick. We go for dinner and I get a sense of how they work, what interests them. Then it's about picking up the clues. I must pick up those clues and deliver them in the form of lighting. It's not a failing for the director to not have that knowledge. People used to say, 'Flash me through your rig, so I can tell you what I want.' That's not creative, as lights on their own are not particularly interesting. I also joke with student lighting designers that I can smell a show before I can see it. The director, in terms of the aesthetic of something, should discuss the smell of something, rather than the delivery of it. What does it feel like? What does it smell like? Give me clues, but don't feel that you should give me an answer. In previews and notes, I love directors who talk generally: 'that's a problem', 'that bit's not working', 'is it a bit under there?' 'are we serving that in the right way?' and so on. That encourages better collaboration, as it's about earning your own response and finding a collective response together. There's a sense of ownership through a shared vision.

Ultimately, the sort of theatre that interests me is something that unleashes something; it reveals itself. You give it space to be, rather than controlling it.

How should the lighting designer, programmer and director work together in tech?

The relationship with my programmer is my key relationship in the theatre. I don't touch a desk anymore. I really want them to be my second pair of eyes and ears. There are a couple of programmers I've worked with for a long time; I enjoy [it when] they might suggest something. But that's a rare thing, to have an intimacy that is that close. . . . But I worry about everyone having carte blanche with [making suggestions]: it can't be a free-for-all. But you want your programmer to be your closest collaborator on everything, to see things you might not see, but to filter that not through the director, but through their relationship with you.

What is the biggest piece of advice you would offer to an actor to work with light?

I was thinking about *Phaedra*, which I did at the National with Nick Hytner. From the moment we hit the stage I had had to make clear decisions about where the light was coming from, that came from decisions I watched Helen Mirren making in rehearsals. I'd watched her rehearse and made decisions about where dark and light could be sculpting light around her choices in relation to Bob [Crowley]'s set. [During] her speeches, when she chose to walk in and out of the light, I saw her playing with this physical relationship with the light that she needed. It was a beautiful thing but challenging. From the moment she hit the stage, she was looking for it, making it part of [her being] in the piece, moment to moment. If there's a visceral sense of dark and light, as in *Phaedra*, it's about drawing away from light, but it's Helen Mirren, so you can't plunge her in gloom, or you might get fired! But there's a contrast between direct light and then the ambient light as the piece moves on. I love it when I find an actor who responds to light. I also find it completely extraordinary that there are actors who are unaware of light. They are brilliant actors, but you can put them on a dark stage, put one light on and they'll stand a metre to one side of it.

Should drama schools place an emphasis on teaching and exploring this?

I think it's really good for people backstage to experience other things, such as acting, and I think actors should have a sense of what the other disciplines are. It's understanding what we are all trying to do together. If you put yourself into a collaborative room, then that will be collaborative with the actors, the creative teams and with everyone else, you would hope. There needs to be a sense of the shared vision and an awareness of the demands that everyone is experiencing. Good design is a distilled response to something and there is no such thing as 'it's just light'. You take that process to distil it into as small a thing as possible, as much of an essence as possible. That, I believe, makes for better work. You have to ask what a piece needs, and a distilled response is the overall aesthetic to something, and you have to be in rehearsals, to keep the rules and definitions you've considered alive in the conversation.

And your rules sit within the directorial and design rules?

Yes. A designer is creating the visual aesthetic and the director is creating the world within that aesthetic.

8

Next stages: Industry viewpoints

This final chapter sees a tonal shift, handing over to some primary voices at the heart of our industry, as well as those training our future practitioners. Imagining a flowing dialogue between the individuals allows for common themes to align and coalesce.

On theatre as an art form in the twenty-first century

Theresa Heskins: Our leisure activity is personalised and our consumption is individual. In my house, I watch my iPad in the bath and my partner watches network television! Theatre is an important place to come together to create a community, asking us to think about ourselves in relation to other people. It asks us to philosophise about what society we are looking at, but then asks us to think about what we would like our society, friendships and relationships to be like with what we see on the stage. In theatre in the round, your backdrop is made up of other members of your community; every play that you watch is about the other people in your community, so that informs it. I love that imaginative act of co-creativity.

Kate Wasserberg: We are more than ever in need of communal social spaces. We are more than ever in need of a live, real experience that isn't perceived through a screen in our hands. Theatre does unresolved complex narrative brilliantly: there are multiple views, and you don't have to pick a side. You are allowed to feel complicated about a play. You can feel conflicted. You can love the people you are watching and empathise with them, without being tribal in that response. Theatre can encourage complex empathy and exercise your empathy muscle. A colleague at Stockroom recently referred to theatre as an 'empathy gymnasium'. I think you go to the theatre and practice seeing people and listening to people. We don't listen to each other anymore and theatre is an act of listening. We think about having an opinion instead of encountering a world.

Theresa Heskins: I'm a massive democrat and theatre offers a democratic way of being; that's of increasing importance as we become more solipsistic.

Kate Wasserberg: Theatre can't be boring. Theatre is special and rare in our lives. Our responsibility as theatre-makers is enormous. It's got to be good and it's got to be profound. It has to be great fun, a rollercoaster ride, as good as a movie. Theatre has to nourish us.

Michelle Terry: Theatre's the opposite of isolationism; it can only be done collectively. It's always a surprise: you don't know who you're going to be sitting next to, or about their class, or religious beliefs; not in all theatres, but when it is cheek-by-jowl like that, you have to reach across consciously or unconsciously to reimagine the world. Theatre has that responsibility to question, but not necessarily [the responsibility] of solving the problems.

Ivo van Hove: We now crave seeing live human beings in the art form which theatre can deliver. We have delivered this for centuries already and this will go on. In our age, the element of the live experience of people on stage will keep attracting audiences. They will crave getting away from computers and televisions and need to see a live person on stage and be together with other people in the auditorium. A thing that's actually there – people telling stories, actually there in front of your eyes – this will be the greatest attraction also after Covid-time. On the other hand, the theatre is different from other forms as it can give us something that we don't have in our daily lives; that's why I think naturalistic theatre might not have a place in the twenty-first century. Theatre should deal with the big issues of our lives and a live human being telling a story in front of our eyes; that will be of real value in the twenty-first century.

On being an artistic director

Theresa Heskins: I thought of myself as an artist; now, I'm a businesswoman. That enables me to curate an artistic programme for a diverse community. Also, it's about being part of a national industry and having a responsibility not to cultivate taste, as that's intrusive, but to help people develop their own taste. The New Vic audience [in Staffordshire] deserve all the elements of form and theatricality and how theatre is made [just as much as do] people in London, Edinburgh and Manchester. They come for the story, but they should [also] have the forms of promenade, physical and visual theatre, contemporary clowning and circus. That's one thing I've been able to do as an artistic director.

Tamara Harvey: Running a theatre is about being a community; our arts centre is the community's only connection with the arts and our base is one where people can come and be, come and ask questions, have conversations and have a coffee. In a world where we feel more isolated and where there are fewer places to come together, theatre feels like a really important part of society.

On curating a season

Michelle Terry: Greg Doran [Artistic Director of the RSC] said something recently about Shakespeare always being relevant. I think that's true, as the preoccupations of Shakespeare's time are the preoccupation of ours, since they are human preoccupations. The question is then how you curate a season. It felt clear to me, with Brexit, that this is a time when our nation is in a state, so we need to do state-of-the-nation plays and [look at] what history can offer us as a comfort, or a tonic. So, it's a time when identity is in constant question, representation and intersectionality is being interrogated and we have a canon that allows for those questions to be explored. The Sam Wanamaker Playhouse offers a very different lens to the very mythic, epic landscape of the Globe. It's an implicatory space, so when you put a play in there, you need to work harder to achieve the participation which is so present in that live interaction with the groundlings in the Globe, how do you allow these plays to be a conversation? A provocation and a question? Rather than having to feel like you have to provide a solution. I think: 'What are the provocations and questions of our time?' There is something around gender. What is the spectrum of gender? There was seemingly something more fluid in their approaches to gender even though, ironically, women weren't allowed on stage. How they were able to explore gender through the plays feels present and prescient now. We were always going to complete the History Cycle and we'd always planned to do *Henry V* and *Richard III*. With anti-literal casting, how does that offer a different perspective on, say, the she-wolf, Margaret? Who is playing her? Who is playing [the role of] Richard III, which is often seen through the prism of disability or the trickster prism, where that Machiavellian [quality] is a game and it's heroic? How do we question these notions? So suddenly, there's a season around she-wolves and shrews and who gets to decide who is a she-wolf and who is a shrew? In Thomas Middleton's *Women Beware Women* you question whose ambition, whose power, whose cruelty it is. Where misogyny is always about male overpowering the female, there is the feminine power over the feminine, so it felt an obvious piece to produce. The domesticity of that play [in 2020] in the Sam Wanamaker Playhouse felt appropriate: its savagery in an intimate setting was there and it felt like an important time to explore it.

[*So, you're aligning the questions of the play with the questions of our time?*]

Michelle Terry: That's right. Part of the job description of my tenure was how we are creating and making work and, in particular, theatre bespoke to the architecture of the space, which is what the Renaissance playwrights were exploring. What can we do here that can't be done anywhere else? That is about the architecture of our spaces.

On creating new models of rehearsing

Lucy Kerbel: Years ago, I interviewed a group of actresses and one actress told me the director said: 'You earn your right to speak up in the room based on the role you play.' Her point was that, within the dynamic of the cast, the bigger your role, the bigger your opportunity to speak up when there are conversations. If you play a peripheral part in terms of the action, you have less of a voice. That conversation shows how far we have come, but it's not all there yet. I sat in a room during a production of *Hamlet*. During table work, the actress playing Ophelia said something. The director turned to her and said: 'Shut up, love. You're just the totty.' That was mixed with misogyny too. Conversely, I was fortunate to work with Katie Mitchell and I observed that, in the early part of rehearsals during the exploration of the text and the language of the production, everyone in the room had equal value and equal voice. During the improvisations and exploratory work with the language and the characters, an actor could be playing a maid and they would have the same weight in that process as the senior actor in the lead, who was also the 'name' [that sold] the tickets. I thought that was very special, making everyone alive within that part of the process. Having seen that work so well, I see no reason why everybody can't do that.

Kate Wasserberg: Theatre does have a bullying problem and sometimes it manifests itself sexually. We must stop behaving as if there isn't a disregard for people's feelings or a need to always be right. We elevate people to the point where they can do no wrong, then we give them a pass because they are charismatic and talented. I believe that hierarchy in a rehearsal room is necessary, but what that means is that, as a director, it's my job to lead and make decisions. Therefore, I have to behave the best in that room . . . no matter what kind of day I'm having, or how much sleep I've had, or what pressure I am under, I have to always be courteous, decent, caring. I have to act with integrity. I have to love and care for the people in the room. If you can't do that, don't be in charge. First and foremost, we must remove the idea that it is ever okay for people in charge, or for important actors, to intimidate or upset other people because they are under pressure. I have to empower people in that room and give them agency to escalate complaints. We must stop giving people who we may like a 'pass'.

Michelle Terry: What we have learnt over the last two years and before my time is that, to put it crudely, the system and the machine (by which I mean budgets and rehearsal structures) have been designed and are designed for predominantly white, predominantly male, predominantly single, predominantly childless, predominantly privileged people. The knock-on [effects] of those assumptions filter into budgets, rehearsal rooms and decisions. There's no judgement on that; it's just historically what has happened. That is where we must start to unpick the systems and that's the long-term endeavour. We had no idea just quite how embedded those decisions and structures are. You end up with ableist structures. I'm not just talking [in terms of] a sign language interpreter or [whether] wheelchair users can get into the space. I'm talking about who you need in a room, in order to make the work. When you look at who the custodians are of the knowledge of the play, everyone comes in with different understandings, but usually there's a small team called the 'creatives', who are the custodians. That's a lot of pressure on a small group of people, so how do you shift responsibility for the work? That creative team disappears on the opening night. Therefore, all that imaginative excavation of the plays happens with a very small group of people and that excavation or archaeology is often years in the making. So when you get to the first day of rehearsals, the people who are having to make the work are having to step into other people's dreams; dreams are really hard to articulate and, if you're not careful, actors don't really have an understanding of why the decisions have been made and yet have to represent those decisions for incredibly long runs.

Jenny Sealey: I define [Graeae's work] as 'work in progress', still discovering the form of productions and realising there are areas we haven't embraced, including work with deafblind people. We are still understanding the world of neurodiversity and the explosion of gender identity, so there's an evolution of the world and we have to evolve with it. Artists who have come to us who are disabled and identify as 'they/them' means we then have to think about casting, especially in a gender-heavy play: we need to look at how they want to be cast in the play, or how we can tell the story of that play differently. As a company, we've never said: 'We know how to do this.' We've just had a week with twenty young people, a gloriously diverse group: all passionate about theatre. It was an interesting group in terms of one person's [need] to have things clarified several times before they felt informed enough to do the exercise. This process of reclarification however overwhelmed another person, rendering them confused and unable to grasp the exercise. We now have juxtaposing needs. Fatigue was another issue, as was lighting: there was a moment where a visually impaired person said they couldn't see, and I couldn't see my interpreters, so we had to work out how to compromise, as some people couldn't have too much light. It was a real challenge, but we need to aim always to cater for all. At what point do we agree as a group what the compromise is and how can we make 'compromise' a healthy informed equal process? The theatre world isn't ready. Some things are changing: job/role sharing for those that have children. That also fits in with actors who have chronic fatigue or physical needs [where] doing a show only every other day would be beneficial for their ability to do that job. If you have chronic fatigue and you want to do musical theatre, it's about managing expectations also. There are ways of doing it, but theatre companies and venues need to think outside of the box. We have such a normative way of doing things and that is old and tired now. There's so much to change. In relation to the casting debate, if it's a play around mental health, it could be said that, [in terms of] casting someone with lived-in experience of mental health, it might not be the best play [for them] to be in, but this is the conversation that has to be had. It should not be assumed that someone might not want to play a character that has a similar experience to them. So, there's so much to consider.

On safe spaces and ethical considerations

Ivo van Hove: Safety is very important. No one feels threatened or feels that 'if I do something wrong, Ivo will be angry'. That's not what I do. That allows for collective discovery in rehearsal: that's what I try to establish.

Ian Manborde: Equity's *Safe Spaces* campaign is about safe rehearsal, audition and performance spaces. It examines who has power in the space and who manages this strategy. It fundamentally rests on an understanding, working in theatres, where *Safe Spaces* fits into broader duties of health, safety and welfare. If you take theatres, there are risk assessments, often with a duty to look at what kind of workplace you are and in what ways workers face exposure to harm; what safeguards are in place? Because of the unconventional, peripatetic nature of the sector, there's been a downplaying of safeguarding for performers. Since the #MeToo movement and Weinstein, it's even more about saying: 'We cannot expose anyone to harm, whether from the public, co-workers, or people in senior positions.'

Tamara Harvey: I hope I've always created a safe space in the rehearsal room. I also feel very strongly that the work we create in the rehearsal room is owned by everyone in the building and people should be able to see in and come in. When I arrived at Theatr Clwyd, the rehearsal windows were blacked out, so we took off the blackout material. On day one I say to the full company and staff: 'Please come and spend time with us if you'd like to.' Ideally, that safe space should widen to include everyone in the building who is part of making the work. It's also useful and important as an organisation that we say: 'This is a safe space and a safe building. Please talk to us if anything is making you unsafe.' No matter how safe you think the space is, someone else might not [find it so]. It's never been part of my methodology to see how far I can push people, to the very limits of their emotions. I'm not interested in breaking people to see what 'exciting thing might come out'. I don't think we should be doing that, and I'm not trained for that. I'm not a psychologist or a counsellor. I think it's arrogant and wrong if you think that's your role as a director. I feel very passionately that my role as a director should never be about breaking people.

Rachel Vogler: The whole thing about improvisation and rehearsal room techniques when rehearsing for a play [means that] most training providers and rehearsal rooms cultivate the environment where confusion is a default mode. I think it's dangerous when the answer to everything is 'yes'. We shouldn't underestimate the impact of this 'first rule of play' that drama school students across the country are taught. It's not establishing boundaries, familiar language or a code of conduct. They are vulnerable and nervous and yet the answer is 'yes'. Every game must have rules, especially when the people playing the game are wanting to please, and if they are wanting to please, then rules are really important. Rehearsal rooms are where power is condensed in a small space. If people say there are no rules, then that is where power may be abused.

Ian Manborde: It's not about saying: 'You can't do that' if the play needs it, but thinking about how you get to a point [where you can] create the safe space, particularly around direction.

On education and training

Ian Manborde: One of the issues that crops up around rehearsals is the lack of prior thought around how to forewarn people about issues and themes that may challenge them psychologically. Some of the work we do is around better choreography and direction of sexual scenes whilst not saying you can't do them. A scene may give an option to act in such a way where one person is unprepared for something and the other goes beyond what is required for that particular scene or scenario. For us, how should such rehearsal scenarios be better directed? It must be clear what the boundaries are, what the purpose is and there must be a point where a person can say: 'That's more than is needed in this scene.' We don't want to go down a route where you cannot do the work, but we recognise that in highly creative work there's an unconventionality, making safeguarding and welfare so important. There are basic questions as to whether psychologically, emotionally or physically [people] are harmed and if they have to be, then why? Having gone through those questions, you get to a more comfortable position, where you can do what you need to do, but limit exposure to harm. Think through what the outcome might be, of asking people to do a particular thing. There's sometimes a lack of thought in rehearsal and performance that gives rise to formal cases and the damage it can do is at a psychological level. People in education at universities and drama schools need to have a level of awareness in this area.

Matt Wilde: Overall, it doesn't mean that because they're students, because they're younger, somehow liberties can be taken and that I'm going to rehearse them twelve hours a day, or I can yell and bark at them, or speak down to them, or condescend or belittle them, because they're students. That's not right. So there needs to be an understanding of creating a safe environment. We were doing some intimate work on *The Mysteries* and they were doing lots of physical, intimate work, lots of company collaboration, contact improvisation. A really simple traffic light scheme worked, by saying: 'Green: I'm happy for you to touch me and pull me and throw me; amber: I'm not sure about that; red: I'm not happy with that.' Really simple forms of communication to say what you are, or are not, happy with, in terms of physical work. And the same goes for verbal, too, in terms of a piece that's discussing sex, for example. It's about what is appropriate to ask and explore. You should never feel pressured to share personal details and material if you're not comfortable with that. And I think that, again, comes back to robust safeguarding issues. I had a student who identified as non-binary who came to me and they said that they weren't happy with some of the language that some of the staff were using. Unintentional language [such as]: 'OK, let's have all the lads over there, all the girls over there, OK, guys?' It's about taking a step back, recognising who you have in the room and ideally use their name. It's inclusive.

Stephen Mear: I have always aimed to show respect to all creatives and performers during my career in the industry. I choose, first and foremost, talented individuals to be in the productions that I work on. I encourage respect and diversity in order to inspire future generations to hold on to these values: it's what the arts are all about, bringing people together.

Ian Manborde: I'd also like to have discussions around class, particularly with institutions who have elite statuses, in relation to their admissions processes. How can they keep good standards as well as an inclusive admissions process that reaches out? Numerous drama schools are now getting rid of audition fees. There's also the low level of diversity in teaching staff in universities and drama schools. I'd be asking educators to [examine] how students [can be] presented with a world view that's diverse, in relation to curriculum content. How are people reflected in the curriculum and in relation to teaching staff and even teaching styles? People need to see diversity.

On directors working in drama schools and universities

Wyn Jones: There's a real skill for directors in making sure there's a feeling of a total process, but simultaneously, you're 'getting the play on'.

Lucy Kerbel: Within training there's a huge responsibility for those choosing texts and setting texts, because if a generation of students goes through an education never studying a play written by a woman, they will take the understanding into the world with them that those plays don't exist. We get stuck in presenting productions, rather than teaching, or thinking about what the learning opportunity is. The [students] have a whole lifetime ahead of them to work professionally in productions. It's about students having stories by and about women, as well as women of colour and disabled artists. If you look across reading lists that students may engage with, if repeatedly it's the same experience, then you need to question why that is.

Matt Wilde: A freelance director is trying to give them, as close as possible, a professional experience. The difference is that people are being given roles and challenges as part of their training, as opposed to that role [being] suitable or right for them. You're still there as a teacher and I call it 'teaching and directing'. And what you're expecting at level six [third year] is perhaps 80 per cent directing and 20 per cent teaching because this is about them consolidating and putting their training into practice. With level fours [first years], I've just done a scene study [from] *Boys* by Ella Hickson; I am at the other end of the scale [there]. I'm only bringing 25 per cent direction, because they're learning and acquiring skills. And thus my direct input or my guidance or my facilitation is a much bigger factor.

Lucy Kerbel: I believe drama schools and universities are able to impact what is happening in the profession, rather than just reflect the profession. We shouldn't ape the industry but shift how young people feel about the industry. There's also a greater level of responsibility for the training institutions to provide equitable opportunities regardless of race, gender or disability. That's about text choices, casting and rehearsal room strategies.

Jenny Sealey: Conversations are needed to help empower our young artists to negotiate, as well as engage them in compromise and explore coping mechanisms and strategies, as the big, bad world isn't changing quickly enough. It's about developing resilience too.

Yarit Dor: We have to empower upcoming actors of the future. For me, I want actors to know their boundaries and have courage to speak them. Their body is their right! I want companies to invite everyone to say 'no' and 'maybe' and take boundaries as a gift not as a burden. Every game has rules right? Every dance has a technique, or a fight has safety so intimacy has safety through boundaries. If actors don't know their boundaries, then that's very dangerous. Performance will never be comfortable; it will always challenge the actor however it is a slippery slope between uncomfortable, to silence, to shame, to dangerous outcomes. Actors should feel able to give counter offers to something they may not want to explore or show. A counter offer keeps true to the intention of the scene or character but is something that is more comfortable for the performer to explore. Let's invite counter offers into the space so they enable brainstorming, exploration and allow us to continue the flow after a 'no' or a 'maybe' have been said in rehearsal. 'I'm not sure about X, how about we try Y.' The days of 'yes' being the only option needs to be reconsidered. I offer you to still have the 'yes and' and add the 'no, however how about'. Test it out and see.

Matthew Xia: I question the phrase 'classic'. I think we should say: 'We're going to do a European classic.' Again, this idea that theatre started in Greece, like there was no ritualistic performance in Egypt prior to that. It is the complete history as told by the winners; as ever, as the victors write the history. So, when looking back through the lens of Roman Empire, Greek Empire, great classicism, the world of Latin, and then the British Empire, it's like sticking lenses in front of lenses, until you [arrive at] this pinpoint of white European culture, which claims that it sits at a higher level than African ritual, than Igbo culture, than Twi culture, than Zulu culture. I would love for us just to be aware of language a bit more, to investigate what I call the language of exclusion. 'We're going to do the classics.' Well, who decided that they were the classics? If they're classics because they have existed for a long time, who was archiving them? I've done so much research into trying to find classic Egyptian texts, and they don't exist in the same way. Mainly because they weren't transcribed in the same way. The theatre of politics that comes out of the South African anti-apartheid movement [for instance,] to me that's classic. And the next big [issue] is [diversifying and] decolonizing the entire curriculum, and the teaching, and the understanding of this country and its role in the world. I've just been helping to revise the lists of suggested texts. I think there were twenty-seven suggested texts at GCSE level. But only one of them was by an author of colour. So, someone external is presenting an appendix, an additional list of thirty-eight plays, almost exclusively by people of African or Asian heritage. Again, it just feels crucial: if in school you're not seeing that this world reflects you and represents you, and that you are represented within it. Diversity is the goal.

Matt Wilde: I think we've got to move beyond when some directors say the [idea] is: 'OK, let's just do colour-blind Chekhov, and we'll disregard the fact that you're not white.' If we're using certain texts for training, how can a young black actor really and truly connect to a character in Chekhov for example, if there's no relation to their cultural identity and background? How does this speak to them? We must find other material and other sources. Similarly, for more contemporary work, if you're going to spend money on getting the performance rights for . . . let's say a David Hare play, then instead commission a playwright to pen an original piece instead, and they can write specifically for your students. Personally, like many others, I prefer 'colour conscious casting', which deliberately incorporates, recognises and reflects race when casting 'non-traditionally' as opposed to seeking to ignore it. We must make diversity part of our concern when casting. This could be manifest in many ways: from recruiting and looking for actors from precise ethnic backgrounds to best enrich the story, additional time when searching and deliberating, the incorporation of race into the narrative to deliver a fresh meaning and exploring how race effects characters' lives by amending elements of the project. To be actively conscious of an actor's race can produce original and exciting qualities to well-known stories.

On learning from observing rehearsals

Gay McAuley: Ariane Mnouchkine says her role as a director is to be the unconditional spectator. The observer watches everything and tries to make sense of it. The theatre is not immune to situations of abuse and it's all to the good that people are observing it and thinking about rehearsals. There are limits and some directors overstep the mark, driven by a vision of the piece, with the actors feeling like they have to serve the director's needs and wants. I've seen that go too far. So, it's about observing the appropriate use of power. Actors explore very extreme situations in drama. An actor works their thinking into killing their own children in some plays: that is horrific. Mark Seton's work on post-dramatic stress looks at how actors need to deal with those extreme roles, and how they need to 'come down' after a performance and how actors can be affected. The nature of psychologised acting places great demands on actors. We need more insight in terms of how actors can deal with the extreme hate or violence that they are put through.

On structuring rehearsals

Michelle Terry: As a parent myself, I'm not asking for organisations to pay for my childcare: I chose to have a child. But the almost neurotic way of making work means that it is impossible to have the life that has made me the artist that I am. So, if I'm being employed to be the artist I am, which is based on my life experience, and I get into a room and my life stops, I cease to be qualified. So, it becomes about what the most creative way of working is, and championing being up until 3.00 am and celebrating working all weekend is not that. I'm not convinced that's a creative way of working. It privileges very few. So, you have to unpick the structures of power. The idea that an actor, for example, can only be creative with a director in the room is such a paternal way of thinking about their creativity. You have to think: 'What is the work being done in the rehearsal time and the enormous amount of work being done outside of the room?' This could be quantifiable, such as line learning, or something unquantifiable: what your unconscious is doing to assimilate the information, interrogate the play or prepare yourself for performance. Those aren't quantifiable. The idea that you have to be in a room to get that work done suddenly becomes a bit of a dishonest gesture.

Jenny Sealey: Money is always a fucker! I remember doing a child-friendly rehearsal period as one of the actors and I had small children, so we rehearsed from 8.30 am until 2.00 pm; not everyone liked it, but most people appreciated having more free time in the afternoon! For some people with fatigue, you just rehearse in the mornings or afternoons, but it means having a longer rehearsal period and this is where money becomes an issue, but maybe less is spent on the set as actors are the crucial asset to a play. You try to tailor the rehearsal process to manage energies. It's spinning a million plates, but then the 'show has to go on'; there's still the rigidity of a show going up at 7.30 pm on the agreed date. If you do buy into theatre, you buy into a discipline. But it really does need to be less rigorous at times, but a show needs to happen. We need to tear up the rule book!

Tamara Harvey: I'd love [a] longer [process]. More time would mean that, firstly, we could keep experimenting for longer and the more you know a piece, the braver you can be with it and the more you can chuck it around. That's when exciting things happen. Secondly, it would become possible for anyone with caring responsibilities to work, which in the end is nearly everyone. So, we could have a longer tech period and not work twelve-hour days – shorter days, but more of them. But that boils down to monetary pressures. . . . I've become braver, as I've gotten older, about spending less time in the room. I've become more aware of the work that happens outside of the room, of how thinking time and the space in between rehearsals is as important as the work that happens in the room. So, I tend to work a shorter day, knowing that thinking time in the evening and weekends is equally as important. At weekends, you need space to breathe.

A final interview: Ken Rea on the role of the actor trainer as collaborator

Ken Rea is Professor of Theatre at the Guildhall School of Music and Drama. He has trained and worked with many of the UK's leading film and stage actors, as well as undertaking corporate training with numerous business and industry bodies and corporations. Previously a theatre critic for *The Guardian* newspaper, he is also the author of the acclaimed text *The Outstanding Actor: Seven Keys to Success*.

When did you realise that it was these seven keys, or qualities,[1] on top of the core skills, that make an outstanding actor?

When I was the age of the students [I now teach], I think I got it all wrong. The turning point for me was when I left New Zealand to do a tour of study of East Asia and their forms of *kabuki*, Balinese dance and Beijing opera. I wanted to learn these codified forms of theatre. You are learning *noh* theatre that has been passed down over seven hundred years; these actors had a great

---

[1] These qualities are, for Rea, warmth, generosity, enthusiasm, danger, presence, grit and charisma.

quality of presence. My favourite quotation of all time is from an interview I did with Peter Brook, where he talked about working on *Oedipus* and doing lots of exercises. He said that one day he told his actors: 'you are just going to be chained to the balcony' and he talked about a stillness that must come from a body that can do other things, not just a body that can't do anything else. I think that quality of presence has always fascinated me, as well as how you teach presence and stillness to an actor. So, what I've looked at are the things that you can do to instil that presence; one way of doing that is to remove the things that get in the way of it.

You allude in your book to a year group that had 'something' and a certain energy about them.

Yes, that's very important: the chemistry of the room. This applies to sports and business teams, but applies particularly to theatre because actors must be the supreme example of the effectiveness of team. You have to come together; what Bruce Tuckman calls the 'Forming, Storming, Norming, Performing' model. You have to go through all those stages quickly and stay together. The director can be on the first plane out of town if it's a disaster, but the actors have to hold the production together. Therefore, they have got to find a way of coming together.

What do you look for as a director?

They say 'it's the stand-out quality that hits you in the eyes'. I've reflected on what that is, and I think it's all those people who spoke the text very, very well and made great sense of it; but some of them, a few of them, took ownership of the space in the moment that they walked into the space, in the first three seconds. Also, they let us in. The idea of 'letting us in' comes from [actor and director] Yoshi Oida, who used the phrase as a metaphor: if there's clutter in the acting process, then it stops us being 'let in'. In the actors who really stood out there, was more risk tasking: they dared to be themselves and they looked comfortable in themselves and in their skin. And that, again, is over and above the core acting skills: they have something extra. This whole idea came to me when I was on holiday on a Greek island. My wife and I were having dinner in a taverna and the TV was on, but with the sound down. You couldn't help but keep looking at the screen. There was a very early film of Gerard Depardieu's on and I was fascinated. You couldn't hear what was being said, but in every shot, your eyes were riveted to him. It's the complete focus of playing to the other actor: this fascinated me.

You often return in your book to this idea of 'radiating a presence'.

The first stage of the [training] process is about awareness. Being aware of the signals you send out. The second stage is then the degree of choice we have in controlling those signals. For example, being aware of tension, being aware you're narrowing down your choices and you can actually make bolder choices. Over the years, I've developed little tricks and techniques to help unlock some of those blocks and I can help people to develop a degree of creativity. This is not so much rehearsal work, but pre-rehearsal work; the work that the actor can bring to the drawing board because directors like an actor who can bring and offer, rather than the 'here I am, paint on me' approach.

So, your process goes back to the concept of via negativa, where you speak only in terms of what it is not, stripping away the blocks and getting back to something that isn't cluttered?

I remember working, years ago, on [the publication] *A Better Direction: A National Enquiry into the Training of Directors for Theatre, Film and Television* (1989). We asked hundreds of people: 'What is a director? What is the director's job?' My favourite definition was that you provide an environment in which people can do their best work. Your job as the director is to create an environment where everyone feels safe to be dangerous, or where they can feel comfortable with being uncomfortable. It's not lowering the stakes but taking the pressure off people, so they can afford to take risks.

So, for you training is about giving young actors a framework before they go into rehearsals and the qualities they can take in? You often say in your book that 'it's up to you' as the actor. You can't just assume the qualities will be present or the rehearsal room will be that way and therefore the actor has a responsibility for the ensemble and their place and for the creative process.

Good training will prepare actors to do that. . . . In starting to think about *The Outstanding Actor*, I wondered what the 'special' actors were doing; it comes down to particular values you can instil them. I say from day one that I want them to behave with warmth and generosity of spirit; you keep doing that and instil those values. Let me tell you about some of the key exercises or techniques I've discovered. One is related to lateral thinking. I've found that if you give somebody a different task to do, which takes their mind off the obvious question of how they can look interesting on stage, it can unlock creativity. There's a link to taking the pressure off. Keith Johnstone, with whom I've worked, his principles are very valuable. You can take the pressure off by telling the actor they don't need to do their best work.

There's a whole idea of working quite quickly on a task, which allows actors to make quick decisions, working impulsively, with less time for discussion.

Some directors may be analytical in their work, sitting around a table. Then there's the terrifying moment when you need to get up. I think it's useful not to delay that moment but to throw actors into it straight away. I think [the time element] is very important, because if you give people an hour to complete a task, they'll use fifty minutes to talk about it first. So, a lot of that hour is wasted with analytical, inefficient working and lots of 'yes, but' thinking. If you cut that out by forcing them to complete the task in an almost impossible time, there should be no negativity: there's no time for that, they must get on and do it. They have a sketch rather than a complete painting. But, in that quick sketch, there's a wonderful creative life which may lead to a brilliant idea, which I'm sure they wouldn't have got in an hour of reflective analytical thinking.

Are there different rehearsal processes for different genres, texts or groups of actors?

Yes. When William Gaskill [directed] a farce, [all he did] was just to run it. He blocked it quickly and ran it. For Gaskill, the craft of the director was important and farce depends on that, including timing, which comes from run-throughs. Joan Littlewood said she would improvise and never block. Her technique would be to leave it to the last minute and at the dress rehearsal say: 'You come on there and you come on there.' You must end up with a form. Directors sometimes complain that actors bring something new each time, which is good; but then, the next time, they'll keep bringing something new, so they are constantly reinventing the wheel, which can be gratuitous creativity. What they must learn is to build on one decision and take it further, adding something else, so you refine a choice. Otherwise, you think every rehearsal needs to be different and you may reject a good embryonic idea. And different directors work in different ways. For me, the R&D stage is very informative. With our next production, I found that the R&D stage was a very creative time. We had two R&D sessions, six months apart, with a new text.

That returns to the idea of exploring content, not form.

Exactly, because there was no pressure, the actors 'played' for a whole week.

There are also those directors who have their own companies, like Ariane Mnouchkine and Lev Dodin, who can set their stall out and say to actors: 'Come on board with me.'

They have very long rehearsal processes. Ariane Mnouchkine demands body and soul from her performers; they need to be dedicated and that's not right for everybody. The creativity aspect is the perfect match of an actor and a director: the temperament of the actor and the temperament of the director. But sometimes a director might say: 'We must have fun and do lots of improv.' Then later they think: 'We're not going anywhere, and we open in two weeks . . .' And there's no time to play as you need to work on the text.

So, any improv must be grounded and rooted in the text, moving the rehearsal forward and finding something new?

Absolutely.

I always think in rehearsal about minting afresh and what that means. For me, it's the moment in a play where the action could turn out differently, especially when we know a piece well. Hamlet may kill Claudius in that moment and the action go another way . . .

Yes, actors must play the possibilities, which creates the intensity and sense of danger: there must be the possibility of failure, or the opposite outcome. It raises the stakes. Ultimately, to prepare for this, we must cultivate an actor's imagination.

Coda: A return to the polarities and some Covid-age thinking

Polarity 1: Impulse versus technique

It is a myth that to work on impulse has nothing to do with technique. Technique concerns knowing just when to ignite impulses and when to rein them in. Knowing when to control urges, in fights and intimate scenes or when it moves outside the spirit and frame of rehearsal choices, whilst ensuring that the energy of an impulse remains is a technical skill. John Britton notes that 'for a performer to respond, in the moment, to the reality of an impulse, she must first notice that impulse. She must be attentive to the ebb and flow of impulses in her body and to the unfolding dynamic of what is happening around her' (Britton 2013: 281). Impulse must be bounded by skill and knowing when to use impulse is technique.

Polarity 2: Auteur directorial concepts versus the 'invisible' director

There are examples at both extremities: the auteur director who may be extremely visible and the 'director' who seems to do very little. I believe that the directorial frame in which the actors are working, often termed the world, sits over the centre line towards the auteur end without this being despotic. The director can become 'invisible' as the actors work confidently with freedom within predetermined frames. Leon Rubin reminds directors not to reduce a play, particularly a classic, by 'mono-focus[sing] a single theme of the play and wrap[ping] a concept or design around it ... [as] a generalised concept swamps the complexities in the play' (2021: 14).

Polarity 3: Cerebral versus somatic myth-busting

Some directors discuss cerebral techniques, others bodily ones. Yet, 'all acting and performance is psychophysical. It cannot be anything other ... "mind" and "body" are inseparable' (Whyman 2016: 166) as 'in-depth embodied knowledge is manifest in the doer as an integrated psychophysical whole. "Body" and "mind" are one' (Daboo, Loukes and Zarrilli 2013: 9). Let us finally break away from the myth that what happens in the mind does not affect the body and vice versa and experience as one.

Polarity 4: Character versus self (dual consciousness)

Lev Dodin's expectation is that the actors he trains should be able to verbally articulate their discovery: 'Actors have to learn to say it. I make my actors put their thoughts into words' (Innes and Shevtsova 2009: 44). If the actor is therefore 'simultaneously aware of self and character' (Kemp 2012: 32), choices can be consciously recognised, tested and explored in rehearsals by the actor. A third being develops, one that merges the self with the givens of the character's circumstances, creating the 'I am' state of experiencing, which ensures impulses can be checked and 'control' is in the mix.

Polarity 5: To plan versus not to plan

Planning is important. But, for van Hove, the contents of the planning backpack are not always to be explicitly displayed. Recall Wasserberg stating that 'Terry Hands gave me the best bit of advice which was: "Your job is to learn to see what you have, not what you thought you had or you wished you have but what you have". For the actor, letting go is vital. Plan consciously, whilst responding impulsively in the rehearsal room.

Some reflections on theatre-making during a pandemic

Tamara Harvey: Even with these difficulties, in each of the rehearsal rooms I've led, there have still been moments of shared discovery and of the joy of figuring out how to tell stories together.

Gareth Fry: There was much creative exploration in the early stages of lockdown, with many people finding new ways to engage audiences, rehearsing and performing on Zoom and elsewhere. Theatre will bounce back, just as it has done after every war, disaster and pandemic across the centuries. But many of the individuals and companies who once worked in theatre, won't.

Philip Dart: Rehearsing *Travels with My Aunt* during a pandemic has been a somewhat surreal experience. Everyone adjusts and new working practices emerge. Everyone becomes intensely focused, aware that rehearsals could end at any moment if someone develops symptoms. That edginess adds an interesting dynamic to the work and results in a much more tightly bonded company, as everyone is determined to get to the first night.

Tom Littler: In October at Jermyn Street Theatre I produced a series of short one-woman plays to be filmed live. This project involved over sixty people, but each one of them only met a handful of others. But in pockets, it's still magic. Once the actor is on stage and in flow, you can still forget where you are and fly into imagination. The applause that bursts from tech and camera crews at the end of run-throughs is real, and louder than normal. We feel defiant.

Adrienne Ferguson: What was interesting for me was really thinking about the need for the characters/actors to be close together or touching on stage and, whilst directing *Educating Rita* in August, search for the few moments where it was absolutely necessary for the two to come close enough to touch. Due to the nature of their relationship and the reservation and formality of behaviour, especially from the side of Frank, it was interesting to find that physical distance between the two characters within the confined space of Frank's office and [that] created a wonderful dynamic between the two. I will bring what I learned about space and distance forward into the next project.

Ken Rea: Awful as it may be, a crisis brings opportunities and I've tried to keep that mindset while teaching and directing virtually. I've noticed this goes through three stages . . . The first stage is the 'grief' phase of being constantly aware that we're not all in the same room, playing together. There's a great feeling of loss, sometimes even leading to resentment and anger, which of course is distracting. The second phase is 'acceptance': accepting that we just have to make the best of this, with the result that we start to find practical ways of making this work. But the third stage is the discovery phase: uncovering opportunities hidden in the limitations. When working with the actors online, I encouraged them to move around in the space, using wide shots, mid shots and close-ups. It was in these close-ups that we became more aware of changes of thought in the eyes. You wouldn't normally be so aware of this in an in-person rehearsal, but on-screen everything appears to be magnified. This provoked me to adjust the way I was directing and teaching, and it led me to a whole raft of new exercises to help the actors make subtext work in a way that I couldn't have done before. And I've been really excited by that. It's been marvellous for screen acting because it immediately highlights the difference between actors who look as if they are just saying the lines (their eyes don't change) and those who miraculously appear to let us into their thoughts and feelings.

Kate Wasserberg: I do believe that people are going to need theatre more than ever, to heal and to find themselves and their community again. I believe that kindness is going to be more important than ever in the rehearsal room. And justice, too. I hope we will wean ourselves away from our aspiration to be like film and television, because this time has demonstrated that there is a thirst those things cannot quench. I am determined to play my part, however small, in rebuilding a fairer and more inclusive industry. I can't wait to share space with other artists again. Actors, of course. I miss actors, those magic people. Designers. Audiences. I miss them now, so, so much. Those messy, glorious, unpredictable responses accompanied by the clink of ice in recyclable plastic glasses. I even miss queueing for the loo.

References

Alfreds, M. (2010), *Different Every Night: Freeing the Actor*, London: Nick Hern Books.

Ayckbourn, A. (2020), Personal interview, 16 March.

Baker-White, R. (1999), *The Text in Play: Representations of Rehearsal in Modern Drama*, Lewisburg, PA: Buckwell University Press.

Beadle, R., and A. J. Fletcher (2008), *The Cambridge Companion to Medieval English Theatre*, Cambridge: Cambridge University Press.

Beeman, M., and J. Kounios (2009), 'The Aha! moment: The cognitive neuroscience of insight', *Current Directions in Psychological Science*, 18 (4): 210–16.

Bennett, S., and S. Massai, eds (2018), *Ivo van Hove: From Shakespeare to David Bowie*, London: Methuen.

Bessell, J. (2001), *Research Bulletin: The 2001 Globe Season: The Rose Company, Cymbeline*. Available online https://archive.shakespearesglobe.com/CalmView/Record. aspx?src=CalmView.Catalog&id=GB+3316+SGT%2FED%2FRES%2F2%2F5%2F28 (accessed 3 April 2020).

Bessell, J. (2019), *Shakespeare in Action: 30 Makers on their Practice*, London: Bloomsbury.

Bligh, N. (2018), Personal interview, 28 November.

Boden, S. (2019), Personal interview, 15 April.

Boenisch, P. M. (2015), *Directing Scenes and Senses: The Thinking of Regie*, Manchester: Manchester University Press.

Boenisch, P. M., and T. Ostermeier (2016), *The Theatre of Thomas Ostermeier*, Abingdon: Routledge.

Bogart, A. (2001), *A Director Prepares: Seven Essays on Art and Theatre*, Abingdon: Routledge.

Booth, M. R. (1981), *Victorian Spectacular Theatre 1850–1910*, London: Routledge and Kegan Paul.

Bowen, K. (2018), *Close Quarters*, London: Nick Hern Books.

Bown-Williams, R., and R. Cooper-Brown (2019), Personal interview, 15 October.

Brandt, A., and D. Eagleman (2017), *The Runaway Species: How Human Creativity Remakes the World*, Edinburgh: Canongate Books.

Brining, J. (2018), 'Benefits of ensemble theatre extend beyond the performers', *The Stage*, 30 August. Available online: https://www.thestage.co.uk/opinion/2018/james-brining-benefits-of-ensemble-theatre-extend-beyond-the-performers/ (accessed 10 September 2019).

Britton, J., ed. (2013), *Encountering Ensemble*, London: Methuen.

Brook, P. (2008), *The Empty Space*, London: Penguin.

Brook, P. (2019), Personal e-mail correspondence, 1 August.

Bryan, C., and K. Clegg (2019), *Innovative Assessment in Higher Education: A Handbook*, Abingdon: Routledge.

Burton-Morgan, P. (2019), 'Bum notes? Why theatre needs to get better at feedback', *The Stage*, 15 August. Available online: https://www.thestage.co.uk/opinion/poppy-burton-morgan-bum-notes-why-theatre-needs-to-get-better-at-feedback (accessed 8 April 2021).

Carlson, M. (2006), *The Haunted Stage: The Theatre as Memory Machine*, Ann Arbor: University of Michigan Press.

Carnicke, S. M. (2009), *Stanislavski in Focus for the Twenty-First Century*, 2nd edn, Abingdon: Routledge.

Christie, A. (2014), *And Then There Were None*, London: Samuel French.

Christie, P. (2015), 'The what happened of experience: Reflections on the practice of the method of analysis through action', *Stanislavski Studies*, 3 (2): 153–69.

Clurman, H. (1972), *On Directing*, New York: Fireside.

Cole, S. (1992), *Directors in Rehearsal: A Hidden World*, London: Routledge.

Constable, P. (2019), Personal interview, 25 September.

Cortese, R. (2019), 'Ranters: Rehearsal and development process: How is the text enacted?', *Australasian Drama Studies*, (74): 244–338.

Coveney, M. (2017), *London Theatres*. London: Frances Lincoln.

Crawford, T. M. (2011) *Dimensions of Acting: An Australian Approach*. Redfern, NSW: Currency Press.

Crawford, T. M. (2015), 'Real Human in this Fantastical World: Political, Artistic and Fictive Concerns of Actors in Rehearsal: An Ethnography', PhD thesis, University of Sydney. Available online: https://ses.library.usyd.edu.au/handle/2123/13803 (accessed 10 September 2019).

Croall, J. (2014), *Closely Observed Theatre: From the National to the Old Vic*, Leamington Spa: Fantom Films.

Csíkszentmihályi, M. (1997), *Finding Flow: The Psychology of Engagement with Everyday Life*, New York: Basic Books.

Csíkszentmihályi, M. (2013), *Creativity: Flow and the Psychology of Discovery and Invention*, New York: Harper Perennial.

Curtis, J. (2019), Personal interview, 11 March.

Cutler, K., and J. J. Martin (2002), 'An exploratory study of flow and motivation in theatre actors', *Journal of Applied Sport Psychology*, (14): 350.

Daboo, J., R. Loukes and P. Zarrilli (2013), *Acting: Psychophysical Phenomenon and Process*, London: Palgrave Macmillan.

Dart, P. (2020), Personal interview, 5 November.

Davis, K. (2019), Personal interview, 11 March.

De Laet, T., E. Cassiers and L. van den Dries (2015) 'Creating by annotating', *Performance Research: A Journal of the Performing Arts*, 20 (6): 4–52.

Delgado, M. M., and D. Rebellato, eds (2010), *Contemporary European Theatre Directors*, Abingdon: Routledge.

Dolan, J. (2010), *Theatre and Sexuality*, London: Red Globe Press.

Dor, Y. (2019), Personal interview, 7 October.

Dromgoole, D. (2017), *Hamlet Globe to Globe: Two years, 190,000 Miles, 197 Countries, One Play*, Edinburgh: Canongate Books.

Dweck, C. (2012), *Mindset: How You Can Fulfill Your Potential*, London: Robinson.

Equity (2019a), Casting Questions Sheet. Available online: https://www.equity.org.uk/media/3286/equity_casting-questions.pdf (accessed 20 September 2020).

Equity (2019b), Inclusive Casting Policy. Available online: https://www.equity.org.uk/getting-involved/campaigns/play-fair/equity-inclusive-casting-policy/ (accessed 20 September 2020).

Equity (2019c), LGBT+ Guide. Available online: https://www.equity.org.uk/media/3465/equity_lgbt-casting-guide.pdf (accessed 20 September 2020).

Evans, M., ed. (2015), *The Actor Training Reader*, Abingdon: Routledge.

Féral, J. (1997), 'For a Genetic Approach to Performance Analysis', *Assaf*, 33: 54.

Féral, J. (2008), *Towards a Genetic Study of Performance*, Cambridge: Cambridge University Press. Available online: https://www.cambridge.org/core/journals/theatre-research-international/article/abs/introduction-towards-a-genetic-study-of-performance-take-2/AE5835137D71B0ADEAA2664ABED4E694 (accessed 5 February 2018).

Ferguson, A. (2020), Personal interview. 18 November.

Fields, C. (2011), 'From "Oh, OK" to "Ah, yes" to "Aha!": Hyper-systemizing and the rewards of insight', *Personality and Individual Differences*, 50: 115–17.

Filmer, A., and K. Rossmanith (2011), 'Space and actor formation', *Theatre Research International*, 36 (3): 228–39.

Fliotsos, A. (2012), *Interpreting the Play Script: Contemplation and Analysis*, Basingstoke: Palgrave Macmillan.

Foot, P. (2006), 'David Wood: Keeping Children Entertained with Lots of Suddenlies', *Encore*, December. Available online: https://www.davidwood.org.uk/interviews/all_about_me-suddenlies.html (accessed 12 April 2021).

Fowler, B. (2019), *The Theatre of Katie Mitchell*, Abingdon: Routledge. Available online: https://www.routledge.com/The-Theatre-of-Katie-Mitchell/Fowler/p/book/9781138600058 (accessed 15 August 2020).

French, D. S., and P. G. Bennett (2016), *Experiencing Stanislavski Today: Training and Rehearsal for the Psychophysical Actor*, Abingdon: Routledge.

Fry, G. (2019), Personal interview, 24 July.

Gardner, L. (2019), 'UK talent isn't less inventive than European – just worse off', *The Stage*, 22 April. Available at: https://www.thestage.co.uk/opinion/2019/lyn-gardner-uk-talent-isnt-less-inventive-than-european-just-worse-off/ (accessed 10 September 2019).

Gillett, J. (2014) *Acting Stanislavski: A Practical Guide to Stanislavski's Approach and Legacy*. London: Bloomsbury.

Ginters, L. (2006), ' "And there we may rehearse most obscenely and courageously': Pushing limits in rehearsal', *About Performance: Rehearsal and Performance Making Processes*, (6): 5–73.

Ginters, L., and T. Fitzpatrick (2019), 'Rehearsal before the director: Playwrights and actors taking responsibility', *European and Drama Performance Studies*, (13): 47–68.

Godwin, S. (2015), Simon Godwin on 'Man and Superman', *National Theatre Podcasts*. Available online: http://podbay.fm/show/486761654 (accessed 5 March 2015).

Godwin, S. (2018), 'Simon Godwin: As a director, you're always trying to find your niche', *The Stage*, 28 November. Available online: https://www.thestage.co.uk/features/simon-godwin-as-a-director-youre-always-trying-to-find-your-niche (accessed 28 November 2018).

Graeae Theatre (2020), Website homepage. Available online: https://graeae.org (accessed 3 January 2021).

Hagen, U. (1973), *Respect for Acting*, Hoboken, NJ: Wiley.

Hall, P., and J. Goodwin (2000), *Peter Hall's Diaries: The Story of a Dramatic Battle*, London: Oberon Books.

Hanna, G. (1992), *Notes on* A View from the Bridge, Manuscript, Held at London: Victoria and Albert Museum, Theatre and Performance Archives. THM/367/2/1/85.

Hanna, G. (1993), *Notes on* Big Maggie, Manuscript, Held at London: Victoria and Albert Museum, Theatre and Performance Archives. THM/367/2/1/85.

Hanssen J-M. (2020), *Ibsen and the Repertory System:* Peer Gynt *on the German Stage*, Cambridge: Cambridge University Press. Available online: https://www.cambridge.org/core/journals/theatre-research-international/article/abs/ibsen-and-the-repertory-system-peer-gynt-on-the-german-stage/29A0E9ABD439370FD0F3CEC73D56954E (accessed 15 August 2020).

Happé, P., ed. (1984), *English Mystery Plays: A Selection*, London: Penguin.

Harrison, S. (2019), 'Introducing the inhabiting technique: Highlighting the value of psychophysical processes originated by Konstantin Stanislavski, while showing that most aspects of Stanislavski's system of Stanislavski are inappropriate for use with Shakespeare', *Stanislavski Studies*, 6 (1): 71–85.

Harvey, T. (2019), Personal interview, 5 March.

Harvie, J., and A. Lavender (2010), *Making Contemporary Theatre: International Rehearsal Processes*, Manchester: Manchester University Press.

Harwood, R. (1984), *All the World's a Stage*, London: Secker and Warburg.

Hefferon, K., and S. Ollis (2006), 'Just clicks: An interpretive phenomenological analysis of professional dancers', *Research in Dance Education*, 7 (2): 14–59.

Heskins, T. (2019), Personal interview, 26 April.

Hodge, F. (1994), *Play Directing: Analysis, Communication and Style*, 4th edn, Needham Heights MA: Allyn and Bacon.

Hughes, G. (2011), 'Clocking on at the play factory: some thoughts on running a regional theatre', *New Theatre Quarterly*, 27 (1): 1–27.

Hume, R. D. (2007), *The Rakish Stage: Studies in English Drama 1660–1800*, Carbondale, IL: University of Southern Illinois Press.

Innes, C., and M. Shevtsova (2009), *Directors/Directing: Conversations on Theatre*, Cambridge: Cambridge University Press.

Jackson, D. (2013), 'Ribot, emotion, and the actor's creative state', *Stanislavski Studies*, 2 (1): d.

James, A. (2019), 'Safety and immersive theatre: Where should the boundaries be set?', *The Stage*, 3 September. Available online: Available online: https://www.thestage.co.uk/

features/safety-and-immersive-theatre-where-should-the-boundaries-be-set (accessed 9 April 2021).

Jays, D. (2011) 'What really goes on in the rehearsal room?', *The Guardian*, 14 January. Available online: https://www.theguardian.com/stage/theatreblog/2011/jan/14/rehearsal-room-actor-dancer-theatre (accessed 12 April 2021).

Johnston, C. (2006), *The Improvisation Game: Discovering the Secrets of Spontaneous Performance*, London: Nick Hern Books.

Jones, M. (2018), Personal interview, 25 October.

Jones, W. (2015), Personal interview, 5 June.

Kemp, R. (2012), *Embodied Acting: What Neuroscience Tells us about Performance*, Abingdon: Routledge.

Keramidas, K. (2008), *The Pay's the Thing: Intellectual Property and the Political Economy of Contemporary American Theatrical Production*, New York: City University of New York.

Kerbel, L. (2019), Personal interview, 22 July.

Knopf, R. (2017), *The Director as Collaborator*, 2nd edn, Waltham, MA: Focal Press.

Knowles, R. (2004), *Reading the Material Theatre*, Cambridge: Cambridge University Press.

Lauchlan, I. (2020), 'The arts and craft of pantomime', in L. Trott (ed.), *Actors and Performers Yearbook*, 243–5, London: Methuen.

Lesser, W. (1997), *A Director Calls: Stephen Daldry and the Theatre*, London: Faber and Faber.

Lindsay, K. and R. Norris (2019), Personal interview, 8 July.

Littler, T. (2020), Personal interview, 28 October.

Longhurst, L. (2006), 'The 'aha' Moment in co-active coaching and its effects on belief and behavioural changes', *International Journal of Evidence Based Coaching and Mentoring*, 4 (2): 61.

Luckett, S. D., and T. M. Shaffer, eds (2017) *Black Acting Methods: Critical Approaches*, Abingdon: Routledge.

Macdonald, J. (2008), Director James Macdonald on Handke, *Theatre Voice*. Available online: http://www.theatrevoice.com/audio/director-james-macdonald-on-handke/ (accessed 1 April 2020).

Marsden, R. (2018), *Close Quarters* Field Notes. 1 April to 31 May.

Malaev-Babel, A., and M. Lasinka (2016), *Nikolai Demidov: Becoming an Actor-Creator*, Abingdon: Routledge.

Manborde, I. (2019), Personal interview, 29 March.

Manfull, H. (1999), *Taking Stage: Women Directors on Directing*, London: Methuen.

Martin, C. (2020), Personal interview, 29 May.

McAuley, G. (2006), 'The emerging field of rehearsal studies', *About Performance: Rehearsal and Performance Making Processes* (6): 13.

McAuley, G. (2012), *Not Magic But Work: An Ethnographic Account of a Rehearsal Process*, Manchester: Manchester University Press.

McAuley, G. (2019), Personal interview, 11 July.

McCaw, D. (2020), *Rethinking the Actor's Body: Dialogues with Neuroscience*, London: Methuen.

McNiff, S. (2004) *Art Heals*. Boston: Shambhala Publications.

Mear, S. (2019), Personal interview, 12 December.

Merlin, B. (2010), *Acting: The Basics*, Abingdon: Routledge.

Merlin, B. (2011), *The Complete Stanislavsky Toolkit*, London: Nick Hern Books.

Merlin, B. (2013a), 'Using Stanislavski's toolkit for Shakespeare's *Richard III*,
     Part 1: Research on the text and the play', *New Theatre Quarterly*, 29 (1): 2–34.

Merlin, B. (2013b), 'Using Stanislavski's toolkit for Shakespeare's *Richard III*,
     Part 2: Research on the self in the play. *New Theatre Quarterly*, 29 (2): 15–169.

Merlin, B. (2016a), *The Complete Stanislavsky Toolkit: Revised Edition*. London: Nick
     Hern Books.

Merlin, B., and T. Packer (2020), *Shakespeare and Company: When Action is Eloquence*,
     Abingdon: Routledge.

Meyer-Dinkgräfe, D. (2001), *Approaches to Acting: Past and Present*, London: Continuum.

Miller, J.G. (2007), *Ariane Mnouchkine*, London: Routledge.

Mitchell, K. (2009), *The Director's Craft: A Handbook for the Theatre*, Abingdon: Routledge.

Mitchell, K. (2015), Personal interview, 3 November.

Morrison, H. (1984), *Directing in the Theatre*, 2nd edn, London: A & C Black.

Murray, B. (2011), *How to Direct a Play: A Masterclass in Comedy, Tragedy, Farce,
     Shakespeare, New Plays, Opera, Musicals*, London: Oberon.

Oram, D. (2018), 'Losing sight of land: Tales of dyslexia and dyspraxia in psychophysical
     actor training', *Theatre Dance and Performance Training*, 9 (1): 53–67.

Oxford English Dictionary (1989), 2nd edn, 20 vols, Oxford: Clarendon Press.

Pavis, P. (1992), *Theatre at the Crossroads of Culture*, Abingdon: Routledge.

Polanco, F., and D. B. V. Bonfiglio (2016), 'Stanislavski's objectives, given circumstances
     and magic 'if's through the lens of optimal experience', *Stanislavski Studies*, 4 (2).
     Available online: https://www.tandfonline.com/doi/abs/10.1080/20567790.2016.12340
     23?journalCode=rfst20 (accessed 12 November 2020).

Pugh, D. (2020), 'I am a theatre producer so I should produce theatre and so I am', Twitter.
     16 July. Available online: https://twitter.com/davidsoho1/status/1283874594504531970
     ?lang=en (accessed 1 February 2021).

Radosavljević, D. (ed.) (2013), *The Contemporary Ensemble: Interviews with Theatre
     Makers*, Abingdon: Routledge.

Rebellato, D. (2013), 'Booing', *Contemporary Theatre Review*, 21 (3): 11–15.

Rawlins, T. (2012), '"Disciplined improvisation" in the rehearsal and performance of
     Shakespeare: The alternative approach of Mike Alfreds', *Shakespeare Bulletin*, 30
     (4): 431–47.

Rea, K. (2014), 'Nurturing the outstanding actor: Lessons from action research in a drama
     school', *New Theatre Quarterly*, 30 (3): 231–42.

Rea, K. (2015a), Personal interview, 5 June.

Rea, K. (2015b), *The Outstanding Actor: Seven Keys to Success*, London: Bloomsbury.

Rickards, T. (1999), *Creativity and the Management of Change*, Malden MA: Blackwell.

Rossmanith, K. (2003), 'Making Theatre Making: Rehearsal Practice and Cultural
     Production', PhD thesis, University of Sydney. Available online: https://ses.library.usyd.
     edu.au/handle/2123/2007 (accessed 11 September 2019).

Rourke, J. (2005), *Correspondence on* Much Ado About Nothing, Manuscript, Held at London: Victoria and Albert Museum, Theatre and Performance Archives. THM/367/2/1/85.

Rourke, J. (2006a), *Notes on* The Long and the Short and the Tall, Manuscript, Held at London: Victoria and Albert Museum, Theatre and Performance Archives. THM/367/2/1/85.

Rourke, J. (2006b), *Notes on* King John, Manuscript, Held at London: Victoria and Albert Museum, Theatre and Performance Archives. THM/367/2/1/85.

Rourke, J. (2006c), *Notes on* Merrily We Roll Along, Manuscript, Held at London: Victoria and Albert Museum, Theatre and Performance Archives. THM/367/2/1/85

Rubin, L. (2021), *Rehearsing Shakespeare: Ways of Approaching Shakespeare in Practice for Actors, Directors and Trainers.* New York: Routledge.

Sealey, J. (2019), Personal interview, 30 October.

Selbourne, D. (2010), *The Making of 'A Midsummer Night's Dream'*, London: Faber and Faber.

Schmitz, H. (ed.) (2010), *Complicite Rehearsal Notes*, London: Complicite.

Shakespeare, W. (2008), *The Arden Shakespeare: Timon of Athens*, London: Cengage Learning.

Sher, A. (2015), *Year of the Fat Knight: The Falstaff Diaries*, London: Nick Hern Books.

Sher, A. (2018), *Year of the Mad King*, London: Nick Hern Books.

Shevtsova, M. (2020), *Rediscovering Stanislavsky*, Cambridge: Cambridge University Press.

Sidiropoulou, A. (2019), *Directions for Directing: Theatre and Method*, New York: Routledge.

Silberschatz, M. (2013), 'Creative state/flow state: Flow theory in Stanislavsky's practice', *New Theatre Quarterly*, 29 (1): 1–23.

Sloan, G. (2012) In Rehearsal. Abingdon: Routledge.

Snow, P. (2006), 'Ovid in the Torres Strait: Making a performance from 'The Metamorphoses'', *About Performance: Rehearsal and Performance Making Processes*, 6: 3–53.

Solga, K. (2015), *Theatre and Feminism*, London: Red Globe Press.

Soto-Morettini, D. (2010), *The Philosophical Actor*, Bristol: Intellect Books.

Stafford-Clark, M. (2008), *Letters to George: The Account of a Rehearsal*, Gateshead: Nick Hern Books.

Stanislavski, C. (2008), *Creating a Role*, London: Bloomsbury.

Stanislavski, C., and J. Benedetti (2010), *An Actor's Work*, Abingdon: Routledge.

Stern, T. (2000), *Rehearsal from Shakespeare to Sheridan*, New York: Oxford University Press.

Stern, T. (2018), Personal interview, 2 November.

Styan, J. (1996), *The English Stage: A History of Drama and Performance*, Cambridge: Cambridge University Press.

Supple, T. (1998a), *Notes on* Twelfth Night, Manuscript, Held at London: Victoria and Albert Museum, Theatre and Performance Archives. THM/367/2/1/85.

Supple, T. (1998b), *Notes on* As I Lay Dying, Manuscript, Held at London: Victoria and Albert Museum, Theatre and Performance Archives. THM/367/2/1/85.

Swain, R. (2011), *Directing: A Handbook for Emerging Theatre Directors*, London: Methuen.

Taylor, D. (1999), *The Greek and Roman Stage*, London: Bristol Classical Press.

Taylor, J., and A. H. Nelson (1972), *Medieval English Drama: Essays Critical and Contextual*, Chicago, IL: University of Chicago Press.

Terry, M. (2019), Personal interview, 2 June.

Thomas, B. (1998), *Charley's Aunt*, London: Samuel French.

Thomas, J. (2016), *A Director's Guide to Stanislavsky's Active Analysis*, London: Bloomsbury.

Todd, A. and J.G. Lecat (2003), *The Open Circle: Peter Brook's Theatre Environments*, New York: Faber and Faber.

Tonic Theatre (2020), Casting Toolkit. Available online: https://www.theatrecastingtoolkit.org (accessed 4 March 2021).

Toporkov, V., and J. Benedetti (2008), *Stanislavski in Rehearsal*, London: Methuen.

Tucker, P. (2002), *Secrets of Acting Shakespeare: The Original Approach*, Abingdon: Routledge.

Tuckman, B. (1965), 'Developmental sequence in small groups', *Psychological Bulletin*, 63 (6): 384–99.

Unwin, S. (2004), *So You Want to Be a Theatre Director?*, London: Nick Hern Books.

van Hove, I. (2019), Personal interview, 21 February.

Villiers, G. (2012) *The Rehearsal*, London: Forgotten Books.

Vogler, R. (2019), Personal interview, 22 July.

Walton, J. M. (2015), *The Greek Sense of Theatre: Tragedy and Comedy Reviewed*, London: Routledge.

Wasserberg, K. (2019), Personal interview, 31 August.

West, E.J., ed. (1958), *Shaw on Theatre*, Boalsburg, PA: The Colonial Press.

White, R. (2009), 'Radiation and the transmission of energy: From Stanislavski to Michael Chekhov', *Performance and Spirituality*, 1 (1): 2–46.

Whitfield, P. (2020), *Teaching Strategies for Neurodiversity and Dyslexia in Actor Training*, Abingdon: Routledge.

Whyman, R. (2011), *The Stanislavski System of Acting: Legacy and Influence in Modern Performance*, Cambridge: Cambridge University Press.

Whyman, R. (2016), 'Explanations and implications of 'psychophysical' acting', *New Theatre Quarterly*, 32 (2): 157–68.

Wickham, Glynne (1974), *The Medieval Theatre*, London: Weidenfeld and Nicolson.

Wilde, M. (2020), Personal interview, 17 August.

Wright, D.L. (2001) 'It's Not as Thick as It Looks: Unpacking the Rehearsal Practices of Theatre Professionals and the Significance for the Teaching of Reading and Writing', PhD thesis, University of New Hampshire, Durham. Available online: https://www.semanticscholar.org/paper/It%27s-not-as-thick-as-it-looks%3A-Unpacking-the-of-and-Wright/cbfc85e9cadcf7776dfc00f3646b7326a2724201 (accessed 11 September 2019).

Xia, M. (2020), Personal interview, 30 June.

Zybutz, T., and C. Farquharson (2016), 'Psychophysical performance and the dyspraxic actor', *Journal of Neurodiversity in Higher Education*, 2: 76–87.

Index

Gardner, Lyn 54n. 1, 55
Garrick, David 36
Gaskill, William 11, 210
The Genetics of Performance 5
'genetic studies' 5–6
genres 2, 4, 19–20, 36, 44, 46, 55–7,
    78–81, 103–4, 118–19, 131–2, 143–4,
    153, 183
  Harvey on 110
gestural language 26, 30, 35–7, 40
'ghosting' 17, 44, 53
Ghosts 40
Gilbert, Theo 95
Gillett, J. 132
Ginters, Laura 31
Globe 59, 195
Godwin, Simon 132
Gogol 38
Graeae Theatre 4, 69, 204
Grosseteste, Robert xiii
Guildhall School of Music and
    Drama 4, 207

Hagen, Uta 9, 130
Hall, Edward 111
Hamlet 13, 30, 197
Hands, Terry 181, 215
Hanna, Gillian 11–12, 166
Hanssen, Jens-Morten 41, 184–5
Hare, David 205
Harris, Augustus 41
Harry Potter 4, 83
Harvey, Tamara 4, 21, 66, 73, 78, 93, 96,
    108, 110, 158, 184, 195, 200, 207, 215
Harvie, Jen 9
Harwood, Ronald 23, 27
Hebden, Malcolm 119
Hedda Gabler 134
Hefferon, K. 126
Henley, Darren 170
Henry VIII, by Shakespeare 39
Her Majesty's Theatre 39
Heskins, Theresa 4, 20, 45, 62–3, 71, 78–9,
    96, 100–2, 117, 162, 193–5
Hill-Gibbins, Joe 178
Hinds, Ciaran 107
Hodge, Francis 103
Home, I'm Darling 66
hotseating 129

The House of Bernarda Alba 69–70, 137
How to Direct a Play, by Murray 112
Hughes, Gwenda 54, 166
Hume, Robert D. 35
humours 33, 159
  Galen using 34
Hunter, Kathryn 70, 138

Ibsen, Henrik 40
identities 68, 135, 145, 148, 195
imposter syndrome 179
The Improvisation Game 156
improvisatory techniques 160
Impulse versus technique 17, 158, 213
indoor tennis courts 34; as public
    theatres xiv
inner thoughts/inner lives 134, 153, 158,
    166. *See also* experiencing; lived
    experiences
An Inspector Calls, by Priestly 13
inspiration 9, 111, 130
Institutio Oratoria ('The Institutes of
    Oratory'), by Quintilian 26
Intendant system 38
internal plausibility, Thomas on 56
interpretation 36, 48, 53–4, 60, 187, 190
Interregnum xiv
interviews 3, 13, 41, 46, 72, 81, 107, 119–
    20, 144, 171, 174, 181, 186, 207–8
In the Name of Identity, by Maalouf 135
intimacy 2, 70–1, 105–6, 154, 173, 191,
    203
Into the Woods 74–5
invisible director 17–18, 61, 154, 213
Irving, Henry 39
Ivanov 188

Jackson, Anthony 36, 41
Jacobean period 29–31
Japanese *noh* theatre 46
Jays, David 1
Jermyn Street Theatre 4, 215
Johnson, Daniel 57
Johnston, Chris 156
Johnstone, Keith 209
jokes 139, 168
Jones, Max 4, 58–9, 64–5, 91, 107, 136,
    179, 181
Jones, Wyn 4, 17, 91, 106, 202